The Lighthearted Cookbook

RECIPES FOR HEALTHY HEART COOKING

The Lighthearted Cookbook

ANNE LINDSAY

CANADIAN
HEART
FOUNDATION

KEY PORTER·BOOKS

Canadian Cataloguing in Publication Data

Lindsay, Anne, date.
  The lighthearted cookbook

Includes index.
ISBN 1-55013-068-4

1. Heart—Diseases—Diet therapy—Recipes.
I. Title.

RC684.D5L55 1988   641.5'6311   C87-095279-X

Key Porter Books Limited
70 The Esplanade
Toronto, Ontario
Canada M5E 1R2

Photography: Fred Bird
Illustrations: Bo-Kim Louie
Design: Marie Bartholomew
Typesetting: Compeer Typographic Services Ltd.
Printing and Binding: Tri-Graphic Printing (Ottawa) Limited
Printed and Bound in Canada

90 91 92 93 94 95   15 14 13 12 11 10 9

Front Cover: Barbecued Skewered Halibut with Red Peppers and Snow Peas, Brochette of Pork with Lemon and Herb Marinade

Back Cover: Strawberry Meringue Tart

Contents

Acknowledgements

I'm very grateful to the Heart and Stroke Foundation of Ontario for asking me to write this book and for all the help and enthusiastic encouragement they have given me, in particular:

*Dr. Anthony Graham, president of the Heart and Stroke Foundation of Ontario and Chief, Cardiology Division, Wellesley Hospital, who has volunteered many hours and been enthusiastically involved in all stages of the book from its initial concept to review, approval and promotion.

*Dr. Bruce Holub, chairman, nutrition task force, Heart and Stroke Foundation of Ontario, Professor, Department of Nutritional Sciences, University of Guelph, for providing very current information and reviewing the manuscript.

*Kelly Sheard, and Nancy Fisher of the Heart and Stroke Foundation of Ontario for coordinating the project.

*Carol Dombrow, nutritionist, Heart and Stroke Foundation of Ontario, for her many readings of the manuscript and help with the diabetic food choices.

My largest thanks goes to my good friend dietitian Shannon Graham for her many hours of work, help with testing recipes and general support.

My appreciation to the advisory committee: Denise Beatty, public health nutritionist for the City of Etobicoke and columnist for the *Toronto Star* and *Canadian Living's Food* magazine; Dr. Elizabeth Bright-See, nutritional scientist, Ludwig Institute; Carmen Connolly, public health nutritionist, City of Toronto; Carol Ferguson, Editor, *Canadian Living's Food* magazine; Dr. Carol Greenwood, associate professor, Department of Nutritional Sciences, Faculty of Medicine, University of Toronto; Marg Metzger, health educator, North York Public Health Department; Heather Nielsen, Chief of Nutrition Programs Unit, Health and Welfare Canada.

Thanks to the Canadian Diabetes Association's Sub-Committee of the National Nutrition Committee for reviewing all the recipes' food choice values for diabetics as assigned by Donna Hennyey, R.P. Dt.

I'm extremely thankful to my friends who have shared their recipes, and for help and advice from Elizabeth Baird, Marg Fraser and Bev Renahan from *Canadian Living* magazine and Caroll Allen, editor, *Recipes Only* magazine. Some recipes first appeared in these magazines and in *Verve* magazine and have been adapted for this book.

Thanks to Olga Truchan for her wonderful food styling for the photographs, to photographer Fred Bird and to Grant's Fine China Store for supplying the props for the photographs.

Thanks to Sharyn Joliat at Info Access for the nutrient analysis and to my brother, Jim Elliott, and KEA Systems in Vancouver for the programming and setting up of my computer.

Maggie MacDonald, Key Porter Books, deserves special thanks for her expert editorial skill.

And thanks most of all to my best and most critical tasters and supporters, my husband, Bob, and my children, Jeff, John and Susie, for their understanding and patience while I was totally consumed with writing this book.

Anne Lindsay

Dear Reader:

The Lighthearted Cookbook has been written especially for you.

You will find it contains recipes for meals which are appealing to the eye, sumptuous to the taste, and healthy for the heart. In fact everything in the book is directly related to improving the cardiovascular health of you, your family, and your dining guests.

Anne Lindsay is to be commended for her effort. She has done a splendid job by providing readable and useful information which will help reduce the incidence of cardiovascular disease.

The Canadian Heart Foundation acknowledges the professional dedication and expertise, of the Heart and Stroke Foundation of Ontario, which was required to produce this book.

Cliff Sinclair
President
Canadian Heart Foundation

The Canadian Heart Foundation gratefully acknowledges the generous support of Thomas J. Lipton Inc. in helping to make this cookbook possible.

Thomas J. Lipton Inc. is committed to providing the general public and health professionals with accurate, up-to-date information regarding the relationship between diet and coronary heart disease; identifying ways to reduce an individual's risk of developing heart disease; and encouraging all Canadians to adopt a healthy heart lifestyle that includes exercise, a diet low in cholesterol, saturated fats and sodium, and high dietary fiber. *The Lighthearted Cookbook* is an example of Thomas J. Lipton Inc.'s commitment to helping Canadians "eat heart smart".

Preface

The prime stimulus for *The Lighthearted Cookbook* comes from the continuing scientific information that clearly links the importance of diet with the development of atherosclerosis, or hardening of the arteries, which is the most common cause of heart disease and stroke. This research shows that:
— The level of blood fats, i.e., cholesterol, is too high in the majority of Canadian adults.
— The Lipid Research Clinic's Study (1984) showed that every 1% reduction in cholesterol levels results in a 2% reduction in the incidence of coronary artery disease.
— The Helsinki Heart Study (1987) showed that an 8% reduction in total cholesterol levels reduced all coronary artery disease complications by 34%.
— Dietary treatment is the cornerstone of therapy to reduce blood cholesterol levels.

The Canadian Heart Foundation as part of its commitment to providing Canadians with the most up-to-date information on heart health has developed a revised set of nutritional recommendations. The aim of these recommendations, which were developed by a group of nutritional experts, is to translate current scientific information into practical dietary recommendations for all Canadians. The view that diet modification is impractical or doomed to failure is not justified. Many people have successfully modified their diets and substantially reduced their blood cholesterol levels.

The Lighthearted Cookbook shows that a heart-healthy eating pattern can be not only easy, tasty and satisfying but also consistent with good nutrition. The prime aim of this book is to encourage the reader to substitute a number of current recipes with new heart-healthy ones which can be used on a regular basis. It is hoped that this book will also stimulate the reader to take more control over his or her own health by implementing a heart-healthy diet pattern.

Anthony F. Graham, M.D., F.R.C.P. (C)
President, Heart and Stroke Foundation of Ontario
Chief, Cardiology Division, The Wellesley Hospital,
University of Toronto

FOR THE TIME OF YOUR LIFE

Most people want to live as well as possible, as long as possible. This cookbook has been designed to help you do just that.

Recent research into the cause of cardiovascular disease (heart-related ailments and stroke) shows that the health of your heart may be more in your control than you've realized. There appears to be a direct connection between what you eat and your chances of developing a heart condition or stroke.

The dietary changes recommended to give your heart its best chance are not drastic. If you follow the Canadian Heart Foundation's recommendations, you'll be enjoying a wide variety of delicious foods, perhaps an even greater variety than you've enjoyed before.

The Lighthearted Cookbook contains everything you need to know to put your healthy heart plan into action—menus, recipes, lifestyle tips for various age groups and some basic heart and nutrition information.

But before you start cooking, let's look at the scientific backdrop to this cookbook and the background for the Canadian Heart Foundation's recommendations.

YOUR HEART AND YOU

Cardiovascular Disease—Canada's Number 1 Killer

This year alone, roughly 80,000 Canadians will die of heart- and blood vessel-related ailments. Many more will suffer non-fatal heart attacks or strokes. Currently, three million Canadians suffer from some form of heart or blood vessel disease, many of them middle-aged or younger.

While these statistics are frightening, the picture is not as bad as it once was. In the past 25 years, there has been a 34 percent reduction in the heart-related death rate of people under 65. Increased public education, lifestyle changes and breakthroughs resulting from medical research have all contributed to the decline. But more and more, the role of the individual to change those habits that lead to cardiovascular disease is becoming increasingly important.

Defining a Complex Disease

The term "cardiovascular disease" includes all diseases of the heart and of the blood vessels that lead to various parts of the body. Two of the most common conditions, heart attack and stroke, are usually caused by narrowed blood vessels.

A heart attack occurs when there is an inadequate flow of blood to the heart muscle, while a stroke is usually caused by a lack of blood flow to the brain. The narrowing of the blood vessels leading to both the heart and brain, commonly referred to as hardening of the arteries, is caused by atherosclerosis.

How the arteries become narrowed over the years is that cholesterol, fat and calcium in the blood are deposited in the artery walls. It's like the accumulation of plaque on teeth, only the results are more serious. The arterial build-up makes it harder for the blood to pass through, and should a blockage occur, as a result of a blood clot or of fatty deposits breaking off from the arterial wall, a heart attack or stroke results.

Controlling the Risk

Over the years, scientists have identified a number of factors that increase your chances of developing heart disease. Some, like heredity, you can do nothing about. But many of the major risk factors can be controlled, as you can see from these lists:

Uncontrollable Risk Factors	*Potentially Controllable Factors*
Family history of heart disease	Smoking
	High blood pressure
Sex	Elevated blood cholesterol
Increasing age	Poor eating habits
	Excess weight or obesity
	Diabetes
	Excess alcohol
	Stress
	Lack of exercise

As you can see, the factors that are within your control far outnumber the ones that aren't. In this book, the focus is on those you can change, with particular emphasis on those factors that involve diet. But to start with, here's a short list of changes you should consider.

Eight Ways to a Healthier Heart
1) Avoid smoking.
2) Have your blood pressure checked regularly and have it treated if it is elevated.
3) Have your blood fats, especially cholesterol, medically checked regularly.
4) Exercise at least three times a week, for a half hour each time.
5) Keep your stress level at a minimum.
6) Maintain a healthy body weight.
7) Limit your alcohol intake to one drink or less a day.
8) Eat a healthy diet based on Canada's Food Guide (page 213).

THE FOOD FACTORS

Food plays a large part in the enjoyment of life, and as the previous list indicates, a large part in minimizing your risk of heart disease. Blood pressure, weight control, healthy arteries and blood cholesterol levels are all tied to diet.

If you've paid little attention to what you ate in the past, now is the time to take a hard look at your eating habits and make those changes that will help your heart. What are they? Here's the Canadian Heart Foundation's list of recommendations.

The Canadian Heart Foundation's Guide to Better Eating for Healthy Adults
1) Eat a wide variety of foods and maintain a healthy body weight.
2) Limit your fat intake to 30 percent or less of total calories.
3) Limit saturated fats to no more than 10 percent of total calories.
4) Moderate your intake of high cholesterol foods.
5) Protein intake should be about 15 percent of calorie intake.
6) Include more complex carbohydrates, such as fruits, vegetables and cereal grains for their fiber and nutrient content.
7) Reduce excess sodium intake.
8) Consume only one alcoholic drink or less per day.

Figuring Out the Numbers
Recommendations are all very well, but what does this mean? Am I now eating more than 30 percent of my calories from fat? In the following pages, each of the recommendations is explored in more depth. *The Lighthearted Cookbook* gives you examples of the amounts of fat, sodium, cholesterol, and so on, found in food. The recipes include that kind of information, too, and follow the Canadian Heart Foundation's recommendations. Basically, what you should remember is:

– *LESS* **total fat, less saturated fat and salt**
– *MORE* **fruit, vegetables, fish, and whole grain breads and cereals.**

If you're a typical Canadian, here's what you're currently consuming compared to what you should be eating.

	Current typical consumption	Recommended consumption
Carbohydrates	45% of calories	55% of calories
Fats	40% of calories	30% of calories
Proteins	15% of calories	15% of calories
Sodium	4700 mg	reduce intake
Cholesterol	450 mg	reduce intake

The following sections go through the dietary recommendations to explain why they are necessary and what you can do to bring your eating habits in line with healthy living.

Fat—the Major Factor
In a typical day, Canadians consume 40 percent or more of their calories in the form of fats. That's one-third above the level considered to minimize the risk of cardiovascular disease.

Of course, a certain amount of fat in the diet is needed. An extremely low-fat diet is considered dangerous since fat performs many important functions in the body, like the transportation of some vitamins and the provision of essential fatty acids and energy. But most people go overboard. Here's where fat is found in the average Canadian diet:

Common Sources of Fat

Fats and oils (half from prepared products)	43%
Meat, fish and poultry	39%
Dairy products (excluding butter)	12%
Fruits and vegetables	6%

The Three Faces of Fat
All fats are not equal in their effect on blood cholesterol. Foods containing fats are made up of a variety of different kinds of fat. They are listed here under the kind of fat they are highest in.

Fat type	Form	Sources
Saturated	Usually solid at room temperature	Butter, lard, vegetable shortening, coconut oil, palm oil, highly hydrogenated margarines, meat, poultry, cheese, dairy products, egg yolks, chocolate, coconut
Monounsaturated	Liquid at room temperature	Canola oil, olive oil, peanut oil, peanuts, peanut butter, cashews, avocado
Polyunsaturated	Liquid at room temperature	Safflower oil, sunflower oil, corn oil, soybean oil, cottonseed oil, some margarines, mayonnaise (depending on oil used in making it), fish, almonds, hazelnuts, pecans

Separating the "Good" from the "Bad" Cholesterol
All fats, including cholesterol, are transported through the body in the form of lipoproteins, which are a combination of fat and protein and can be considered "good" or "bad".

High-Density Lipoproteins—The "Good"
HDL's are relatively durable fat-carrying protein compounds that actually carry excess cholesterol to the liver for processing and elimination from the body.

Low-Density Lipoproteins — The "Bad"
LDL's are less stable and more likely to break apart and to deposit cholesterol in the blood vessels, which can lead to atherosclerosis. Most people with high blood cholesterol levels also have elevated LDL levels.

Accentuate the Positive
A simple blood test will determine your HDL to LDL ratio. The higher the HDL, the better your chances of arterial health. There are a number of steps you can take to raise your level of HDL's.
— Increase your exercise.
— Keep your weight at a healthy level (overweight people are more likely to have higher levels of LDL's and are at an increased risk of developing diabetes).
— Don't smoke.
— Reduce your intake of saturated fat.
  The most effective dietary measure in reducing blood cholesterol is to reduce saturated fat. In everyday living the best way to do this is to reduce your total fat intake.

The Canadian Heart Foundation recommends that you divide your daily fat intake evenly among the three types of fat. This means 10 percent of your caloric intake from each of the fats — saturated, polyunsaturated and monounsaturated — to make up not more than 30 percent of daily calories

Good News about Polyunsaturated Fats
Polyunsaturated fats, such as safflower oil, help to decrease blood-cholesterol levels, and some recent research indicates that some monounsaturated fats, such as canola oil, may do the same thing.

Recent developments in heart research show that one type of polyunsaturated fat, the omega 3 fatty acid from fish oils may help to prevent atherosclerosis. Omega 3 fatty acids are found in fish such as salmon, sardines, mackerel and herring. These omega 3 fatty acids are also believed to lower blood pressure and blood fat in the form of triglycerides. This makes the blood less sticky, thereby less susceptible to the risk of blood clots.

The Canadian Heart Foundation doesn't recommend that you take fish oil supplements. But eating fish two or three times a week is considered a healthy investment in the future.

Cutting Out Cholesterol
An issue related to fat is cholesterol, a fatty substance the body needs in small amounts. The problem with cholesterol is that your liver will produce it, even if you eat no cholesterol in your food. A high level of blood cholesterol has been identified as a major risk factor in heart disease. You can do very little about the amount of cholesterol your body produces, but most people

can lower blood cholesterol by limiting the amount of fat, particularly saturated fat, in their diet.

As well the Canadian Heart Foundation suggests you moderate your cholesterol intake. Cutting down on foods high in cholesterol, such as egg yolks, organ meats, and shrimp will have the effect of lowering blood cholesterol in many people. A complete list of high cholesterol foods is on page 214.

Just as it's important to have your blood pressure checked, you could ask your doctor about a blood cholesterol check, especially if you have any of the risk factors.

Butter Versus Margarine
Both butter and margarine are fats, but butter is high in saturated fat and cholesterol, and should be avoided. Instead use a margarine from the recommended list on page 216. For cooking, try an oil that is low in saturated fat.

Hydrogenation is a process used to turn a liquid oil into a solid fat. It is used in the production of most margarines so that the oil-based product can be spread at room temperature. But as a result of the hydrogenation process, a polyunsaturated vegetable oil becomes more saturated.

Not all margarines have the same degree of hydrogenation. In most cases, the harder the margarine, the more hydrogenated and more saturated it will be. The Canadian Heart Foundation recommends that you use those margarines subjected to the least degree of hydrogenation, so that they are lower in saturated fat and higher in polyunsaturated or monounsaturated fat.

To sort out margarines for yourself, read the labels. Avoid those that don't give the amount of polyunsaturates on the label and look for those that have at least 40 percent polyunsaturates. Some margarines declare as much as 55 percent polyunsaturates. (See page 216 for Recommended Margarines.)

Compare:	mg cholesterol per 1 tbsp/15 ml	g saturated fat per 1 tbsp/15 ml
Butter	30	7
Hard or soft margarine	0	1.5 – 3

Estimating Fat
The suggested menus and recipes in this book are all relatively low in fat and give the grams of fat per serving.

For this to be meaningful look at the chart that follows to see how many grams of fat you need in a day to follow the 30 percent of calories guideline. (See page 218 for a height, weight and corresponding calorie recommended intake table.)

Calorie intake/day	Grams fat/day to equal 30% of calories
1200	40
1800	60
2200	73
2500	83
3000	100
3200	107

If you follow Canada's Food Guide, choosing the low-fat foods within each food group, and limiting the fat used in preparing these foods, you'll probably meet that goal.

Safety Switch — to Reduce Fats

Choose	Instead of	Grams of fat saved
1 glass skim milk	1 glass whole milk	9
¼ cup/50 mL grated part-skim mozzarella	¼ cup/50 mL grated Cheddar	5
¼ cup/50 mL creamed cottage cheese	¼ cup/50 mL cream cheese	17
4 oz/120 g chicken, no skin	4 oz/120 g chicken, with skin	6
Bread with 1 tsp/5 mL margarine	Bread with 1 tbsp/15 mL margarine	7
Salad, 1 tbsp/15 mL light mayonnaise	Salad, 2 tbsp/30 mL regular mayonnaise	15
1 pear or tomato	1 avocado	30
½ cup/125 mL unbuttered popcorn	½ cup/125 mL peanuts	38
Apple crisp	Apple pie	13
Bran Muffin	Croissant	8

Trimming the Fat
- Use as little butter, margarine and oil as possible (where possible use a high polyunsaturated or low-fat variety) on toast, sandwiches, vegetables and, especially, in cooking. Use lemon juice or herbs on vegetables instead of butter.
- Instead of frying, try the low-fat cooking methods — broiling, baking, steaming, poaching and boiling.
- Roast meats on a rack and sauté in a nonstick skillet. Sauté vegetables in 1 tsp/5 mL oil and ¼ cup/50 mL water.
- After browning meat, spoon off all the fat.
- Trim the visible fat from meat and remove the skin from poultry. Choose lean cuts and watch serving sizes of meat, too. Three or four ounces, about the size of a pack of cards, is a good portion.
- Keep salad dressings to a minimum and switch to low-fat dressings, and light mayonnaise.
- Serve low-fat relishes and sauces, like cranberry or mint sauce, with meat, rather than rich sauces or gravies.

– Substitute skim milk or 2% for whole milk and opt for other low-fat dairy products—part-skim cheese, light sour cream, skim-milk yogurt.
– Snack on fresh fruits, vegetables and unbuttered popcorn; avoid chips, peanuts, french fries, rich desserts, whipped cream.

Salt—Licking the Habit

Everyone thinks it makes peanuts taste better, but people may not be aware that salt may lead to a stroke, hypertension or kidney failure. Canadians consume 4000 to 5000 mg of sodium per day, much more than needed for the average person to stay healthy. Most of it is in the form of salt (sodium chloride).

The problem with sodium is that there's a lot around you don't see. It's in processed foods, sauces, snack foods and many other surprising items. In fact, here's where your sodium intake comes from:

Sources of Sodium in the Average Diet

Processed foods	50%
Salt shaker	25%
Naturally occurring in foods and water	24%
Non-food items (e.g., medications)	1%

The Canadian Heart Foundation recommends that excess sodium intake should be reduced. Here's how you might try cutting down.

Salt Shakers
– The taste for salt is acquired and can be un-acquired. Think about the salt you use and always taste *before* you add salt, gradually decreasing the amount.
– Don't automatically add salt to cooking water. Add it, if necessary, after tasting, just before serving.
– Take the salt shaker off the table or use a pepper shaker for the salt (smaller holes) instead.
– Season foods with lemon juice, vinegar, a pinch of sugar, mustard, herbs, spices, peppers, ginger, garlic, onion or wine instead of salt.
– Watch out for such high salt foods as processed luncheon meats, bacon, sausages, smoked meats or fish, potato chips, pretzels, salted crackers, pickles, soya sauce, MSG, canned or dried soups and processed cheese.
– Read labels and avoid sodium compounds as well as salt, if you can. For example, MSG, which stands for monosodium glutamate, is very high in sodium.

Safety Switch — to Reduce Sodium

Choose	Instead of
Tomato paste	Tomato sauce
Canned whole tomatoes	Stewed tomatoes
Garlic	Garlic salt
Onion	Onion salt
Homemade Chicken Stock (page 46)	Bouillon cubes
Homemade soups	Dehydrated soups
Unsalted crackers	Salted crackers
Shredded wheat	Rice Krispies
Regular or quick-cooking oatmeal	Ready-to-serve oatmeal
Fresh, frozen or low-sodium canned vegetables	Canned vegetables
Unsalted nuts	Salted nuts
Old Fashioned Pickled Beets (page 142)	Olives and dill pickles
Tortilla Chips (page 21)	Potato chips, corn chips
Low-salt Bagel Thins (page 22)	Pretzels
Unsalted popcorn	Salted popcorn
Homemade Ketchup (page 145)	Ketchup

Generally speaking, foods made from scratch are better for you than processed or convenience foods, because *you* can control the amount of fat, salt and other ingredients.

Sugar — Sweet Surrender
The average Canadian consumes about 1½ pounds of sugar a week, enough to make your fillings ache. As with salt, the problem is not only the sugar you eat directly in desserts or tea and coffee, but the hidden sugar in prepared foods, from cereal to ketchup. Sugar is a simple carbohydrate that supplies energy to the body but little else in the way of nutrition. The high calorie count can lead to weight gain, one of the risk factors in heart disease. Also, if you are consuming a lot of sugar, you may be missing out on more nutritious foods, especially good snack foods like fruit, raw vegetables and whole grains.

To kick the sugar habit, see the tips in the shopping section on page 205 and the recipe modification section on page 147.

Fiber — Naturally Right
Fiber is a substance in food that is not digested or is partially digested. Your grandparents called it roughage and knew it helped keep them regular. Now there is growing evidence that certain types of fiber, such as in oat bran, may help lower blood cholesterol, as well. Fiber may also help protect the body against certain types of cancer, particularly colorectal cancer.

To increase your fiber intake, look to Canada's Food Guide and eat more fruits, vegetables and whole grain breads and cereals. Be sure to include a variety, since different types of fiber perform different functions in the body. As a bonus, fiber-rich foods are nutritious and are usually low in calories and fat too. A complete list of fiber-rich foods is on page 215.

How much is enough? The Report of the Expert Committee on Dietary Fiber to Health and Welfare Canada recommends that healthy Canadians at least double their current intake of dietary fiber from a variety of foods. Fiber supplements are not recommended. Too much fiber isn't healthy either, as food then passes through the intestines too quickly and some vitamins and minerals will not be absorbed. It's important to increase fiber levels slowly, so that you don't suffer any discomfort. The recipe section of this book also includes suggestions for fiber.

Tips for Increasing the Fiber in Your Diet:
– Have four to five servings of fruits and vegetables a day.
– Eat the edible skins of fruits and vegetables and choose whole fruits over juices.
– Use whole wheat flour. In most recipes you can substitute half of the all-purpose flour with whole wheat flour.
– Choose whole wheat foods when buying bread, pasta, English muffins, spaghetti, pita bread, hamburger buns, crackers
– Add chick peas or kidney beans to soups, salads, casseroles.
– Add bran or wheat germ to muffins, cereals, casserole toppings, meat loaf, cookies. Oat bran is particularly good for lowering blood cholesterol.
– Add dried fruits (prunes, raisins) and nuts to your cereals; use them to top fruit or ice cream desserts.
– Have fruits and vegetables for snacks as well as in meals.
– Choose breakfast cereals with at least 2 grams fiber per serving.

Safety Switch — to Increase Fiber

Choose	Instead of
Fresh orange	Orange juice
Whole wheat bread	White bread
Cereals with 2 grams or more fiber/serving	Cereals with less than 2 grams fiber/serving
Bran muffin	White bun
Chili	Hot dog
Lentil or bean soup	Noodle soup
Canned baked beans	Canned pasta
Spinach salad	Iceberg lettuce salad
Potato with skin	Potato without skin
Raw vegetables and dip	Chips and dip
Fruit desserts	Puddings, pastries

Potassium — a Cautionary Note
Potassium, a mineral found in fruits, juices, milk and most vegetables, helps the body get rid of sodium, and may be involved in controlling blood pressure. Some medication for high blood pressure, and other medications, may cause a loss of potassium. Check with your doctor if you are on medication. The list on page 215 gives food sources of potassium.

THE LIFESTYLE FACTORS

Good food alone will not keep your heart healthy. There are a few other adjustments you may need to make in your life.

Smoking — Butt Out
To put it bluntly, don't smoke. Twenty-six thousand people in Canada will die of smoke-related cardiovascular ailments this year. Most will die of a heart attack, and if you smoke a pack of cigarettes a day, your risk of a heart attack doubles. Smoke even more and your risk rises higher. Smoking is probably the single most preventable cause of heart disease.

Exercise — Work Out
Modern conveniences make it easy to lead a fairly sedentary existence. Unless you plan for exercise, you might not get it. Yet moderate exercise can greatly reduce your risk of heart disease — by halving your risk of hypertension, by lowering your blood cholesterol level, by controlling your weight and your stress level.

Aerobic exercise, such as running, walking, swimming, cycling and basketball, increases the body's ability to use oxygen and strengthens the heart muscle. Try for at least three 30-minute periods of aerobic exercise per week.

Alcohol — Hold Out
Excess alcohol consumption can damage your body in many ways, including increasing your risk of heart disease. Alcohol can prevent your body from absorbing important nutrients. If you drink, try to limit your consumption to no more than one drink a day.

IN GOOD COMPANY

Many of the recommendations of the Canadian Heart Foundation are shared by the recent Canadian Cholesterol Consensus Conference and health organizations, like the Canadian Cancer Society, which also suggests limiting total fat, increasing your fiber intake and reducing salt. Because diabetes is also a risk factor in heart disease, it is an added reason for diabetics to follow the Canadian Heart Foundation's guidelines. See page 219ff for the diabetic food choices for each recipe.

What this means to you is that the good food practices given here are recommended by a wide variety of health professionals. Eating for a healthy heart means eating for a better chance of overall health. And that means eating for a better, and perhaps longer, life for you and your family.

SAMPLE DAILY MENU PLANS

The following menus do not exceed 2000 calories per day and follow the Canadian Heart Foundation's recommendations to limit your food intake to 30 percent or less of total calories and to moderate your intake of high cholesterol foods and to reduce excess sodium intake. Persons who need to eat more than 2000 calories should follow these menus, simply increasing the portions by the appropriate amount to meet their energy needs.

Recipes for dishes noted with asterisks appear in this book and can be found by using the index.

Menu 1	Sample Daily Menu with a Restaurant Lunch			
% of Calories from Fat = 28%	g fat	mg cholesterol	mg sodium	calories
Breakfast				
Cantaloupe (½)	Trace	0	12	93
Buttermilk, Bran and Blueberry Muffin*	8	31	111	189
Fruit-flavored 2% yogurt (½ cup/125 mL)	2	7	88	131
Restaurant lunch				
Apple juice (½ cup/125 mL)	Trace	0	4	62
Sliced chicken sandwich (sliced chicken from ½ breast, lettuce, 2 slices bread, and 1 tsp mayonnaise)	5	74	384	313
Tossed green salad with oil and vinegar dressing (1 tsp oil and 3 tsp/5 mL vinegar)	5	0	5	56
2% milk (1 cup/250 mL)	5	19	129	128
Dinner				
Mexican Rice and Bean Casserole*	5	12	371	275
Broccoli spears (1 cup/250 mL)	Trace	0	9	48
Spinach Salad with Sesame Seed Dressing*	9	0	48	116
Slice toast (1)	Trace	Trace	142	76
Margarine (2 tsp/10 mL—for broccoli and toast)	8	0	66	66
2% milk (1 cup/250 mL)	5	19	129	128
Applesauce-Raisin Squares*	3	11	6	73
Totals	55	173	1504	1754

*Recipes included.

Menu 2	Sample Daily Menu with a Brown-Bag Lunch			
% of Calories from Fat = 26%	g fat	mg cholesterol	mg sodium	calories
Breakfast				
Orange juice (½ cup/125 ml)	Trace	0	2	59
Whole-wheat cereal — Shreddies (200 mL)	Trace	0	–	169
Sliced banana (1)	Trace	0	1	105
Slice toast (1)	Trace	Trace	142	76
Margarine (1 tsp/5 mL)	4	0	33	33
2% milk (1 cup/250 mL)	5	19	129	128
Brown-bag lunch				
Gouda cheese (1½ oz/45 g)	13	52	376	164
Bagel (1)	2	0	245	200
Margarine (1 tsp/5 mL)	4	0	33	33
Carrot and celery sticks	Trace	0	0	37
Easy Oat Bran and Date Cookie* (1)	4	8	64	97
Apple juice (½ cup/125 mL)	Trace	0	4	62
Dinner				
Linguine with Salmon and Chives*	12	23	149	400
Tossed Seasonal Greens*	2	0	13	30
Roll (1)	2	2	313	156
Margarine (1 tsp/5 mL)	4	0	33	33
Pineapple-Orange Sorbet*	Trace	0	1	93
2% milk (1 cup/250 mL)	5	19	129	128
Totals	57	123	1667	2003

*Recipes included.

Menu 3	Sample Daily Menu with an At-Home Lunch			
% of Calories from Fat = 27%	g fat	mg cholesterol	mg sodium	calories
Breakfast				
Grapefruit (½)	Trace	0	0	39
Bran flakes	Trace	0	291	139
Slice whole-wheat toast (1)	Trace	Trace	132	61
Peanut butter (1 tbsp/15 mL)	8	0	3	95
2% milk (1 cup/250 mL)	5	19	129	128
At-home lunch				
Pasta and Fresh Vegetable Salad*	6	0	77	165
Tuna fish (½ cup/125 mL) (canned in water)	1	48	468	135
Roll (1)	2	2	313	156
Margarine (1 tsp/5 mL)	4	0	33	33
2% milk (1 cup/250 mL)	5	19	129	128
Dinner				
Pork Chops with Rosemary and Orange*	9	67	70	201
Garlic-Parsley Potatoes*	2	0	22	119
Stir-Fry Ratatouille*	7	0	12	107
Grated Carrot and Green Pea Salad*	1	2	79	71
Sliced Peaches (1 cup/250 mL)	Trace	0	10	115
Plain biscuits (2)	2	Trace	48	57
Totals	52	157	1816	1749

*Recipes included.

Menu 4	Sample Daily Menu with a Brown-Bag Lunch			
% of Calories from Fat = 25%	g fat	mg cholesterol	mg sodium	calories
Breakfast				
Orange slices (1 orange)	Trace	0	0	62
Slices toast (2)	Trace	Trace	284	152
Partly skimmed mozzarella cheese (2 oz/60 g)	9	35	282	154
Brown-bag lunch				
Classic Tuna Salad with Fresh Dill sandwich*	5	21	559	238
Cucumber slices (½ cup/250 mL)	Trace	0	1	7
Pear	Trace	0	0	100
2% milk (1 cup/250 mL)	5	19	129	128
Buttermilk Apple Cake*	5	1	152	174
Dinner				
6 oz Grilled Tandoori Chicken* with rice (1 cup/250 mL)	14	88	127	440
Green beans (1 cup/250 mL)	Trace	0	4	46
Winter Fruit Compote with Figs and Apricots (one serving)*	1	0	6	148
2% milk (1 cup/250 mL)	5	19	129	128
Totals	44	183	1673	1777

*Recipes included.

GUIDELINES FOR NUTRIENT RATINGS OF RECIPES

Our rating system is based on the guidelines in Canada's Food and Drug Regulations (D.01.005 and D.02.004), the most current available figures at time of printing. Each serving of food must provide the following amount of each nutrient to qualify as either a good or excellent source. Fiber ratings based on Canadian Cancer Society rating. Percent of Recommended Daily Intake based on the highest recommended intake for each nutrient. Nutrient analysis was done by Info Access using CBORD software system with the Canadian Nutrient File.

Nutrient	Good Source	% of Recommended Daily Intake	Excellent Source	% of Recommended Daily Intake
Vitamin A (IU)	600	14	1200	28
Thiamine (mg)	0.25	19	0.45	35
Riboflavin (mg)	0.40	25	0.75	47
Niacin (mg)	2.50	34	4.50	63
Vitamin C (mg)	7.5	13	15.0	25
Calcium (mg)	150.0	14	300.0	27
Phosphorus (mg)	150.0	14	300.0	27
Iron (mg)	2.0	14	4.0	28
Dietary fiber (g)	2.0		4.0	

Unless otherwise stated, all recipes in this book were tested and analyzed using 2% milk, 2% yogurt, 2% cottage cheese and a soft margarine. Because everyone's taste for salt varies and we hope you will gradually reduce your taste for salt, most of the recipes in this book call for no salt or salt to taste, and have been analyzed without any or using a minimum of salt.

Microwave Note: Recipes have been tested in a 700-watt full-size microwave oven with a turntable. If your oven is different, cooking times may have to be adjusted slightly. If you don't have a turntable you may have to rotate dishes once or twice during cooking.

DAILY TOTAL PROTEIN, FAT AND CARBOHYDRATE INTAKE ACCORDING TO PERCENTAGE OF
TOTAL CALORIES ACCORDING TO THE CANADIAN HEART FOUNDATION'S DIETARY
RECOMMENDATIONS

Calorie Intake	% calories from protein	grams protein per day	% calories from fat	grams fat per day	% calories from carbohydrate	grams carbohydrate per day
1200	15	45	30	40	55	165
1500	15	56	30	50	55	206
1800	15	68	30	60	55	248
2100	15	79	30	70	55	289
2300	15	86	30	77	55	316
2600	15	98	30	87	55	357
2900	15	109	30	97	55	399
3200	15	120	30	107	55	440

APPETIZERS AND SNACKS

An appetizer or small first course makes a meal more special. Appetizers are my favorite part of restaurant meals; I will often pass on dessert in favor of an interesting salad or soup and will sometimes order two appetizers rather than a main course.

Some appetizers or hors d'oeuvres, such as meat or chicken liver pâtés and creamy cheeses, can be terribly high in fat, cholesterol, sodium and calories and can quickly add to our daily calories. On the other hand, there are many terrific-tasting appetizers that aren't too heavy in calories or other elements we should keep to a minimum. Try the Shrimp Mousse with Dill or Spiced Meatballs with Coriander Dipping Sauce or others in this section, or any of the soup or salad recipes for starters, which your family and guests will ask for again and again.

Salmon Spread with Capers

I keep a can of salmon on the shelf and a bottle of capers in the refrigerator in case someone drops in unexpectedly. Then I can make this in a few seconds to serve as a spread with crackers or pita bread, or use to stuff vegetables, such as cherry tomatoes or snow peas. Green onions, chives, sweet peppers or fresh dill can be used instead of celery. Choose sockeye salmon for its bright red color.

1	can (7.75 oz/220 g) salmon	1
⅓ cup	capers, drained	75 mL
⅓ cup	finely chopped celery	75 mL
2 tbsp	low-fat plain yogurt or light sour cream	25 mL
1 tsp	lemon juice	5 ml
	Hot pepper sauce	
2 tbsp	chopped fresh parsley	25 mL

In small bowl, flake salmon along with juices and well-mashed bones. Add capers, celery, yogurt or sour cream, and lemon juice; mix well. Add hot pepper sauce to taste. Spoon into serving bowl and sprinkle with parsley. Makes about 1¼ cups/300 mL.

PER 1-tbsp/15 mL SERVING	
calories	17
g fat	1
mg cholesterol	3
mg sodium	50
g protein	2
g carbohydrate	0

Nutrition Note
Be sure to crush salmon bones and include them as they are an excellent source of calcium; also include the juices because they contain omega 3 fatty acids, which may help in reducing the risk of heart disease.

PER 1-tbsp/15 mL SERVING (made with low-fat plain yogurt)	
calories	10
fat	0
mg cholesterol	1
mg sodium	96
g protein	1
g carbohydrate	1

Variations

Parsley-Onion Dip:
Instead of spinach, substitute 1 cup/250 mL coarsely chopped fresh parsley.

Fresh Basil-Onion Dip:
Instead of spinach, substitute ½ cup/125 mL coarsely chopped fresh basil leaves.

Artichoke-Onion Dip:
Instead of spinach, substitute 1 cup/250 mL drained, coarsely chopped canned artichokes.

Dill Dip:
Instead of spinach, substitute ¼ cup/50 mL coarsely chopped fresh parsley and ⅓ cup/75 mL chopped fresh dill (or 1 tbsp/15 mL dried dillweed).

Shrimp, Crab or Clam Dip:
Instead of spinach, add 1 cup/250 mL (or 5 oz/142 g can) drained rinsed crab, small shrimp or clams.

Curry Dip:
Instead of spinach, add 1 tsp/5 mL each curry powder and ground cumin; mix well then season with more to taste.

*Instead of low-fat cottage cheese, dip is made with 1 cup/250 mL of ingredients listed.

**Although cream cheese is lower in total fat than mayonnaise, it is not recommended because it is higher in cholesterol and saturated fat.

Spinach-Onion Dip

This is a good creamy yet low-fat base for many dips. Instead of spinach, you can add other vegetables, herbs or seasonings (see Variations). Serve this dip surrounded with fresh, crisp vegetables, such as carrots, celery, sweet peppers, blanched snow peas, asparagus, broccoli or cauliflower. It's best to make it at least four hours in advance so that flavors can develop.

1	pkg (10 oz/284 g) fresh spinach (or frozen chopped, thawed)	1
1 cup	low-fat cottage cheese	250 mL
1 tbsp	lemon juice	15 mL
½ cup	light sour cream or low-fat plain yogurt	125 mL
½ cup	chopped fresh parsley	125 mL
¼ cup	chopped green onion	50 mL
1 tsp	salt	5 mL
	Freshly ground pepper	

Trim stems and coarse leaves from spinach. Wash spinach, cook, covered, over medium heat for 3 minutes or until wilted. (If using frozen, no need to cook.)

Thoroughly drain, squeezing out excess moisture; coarsely chop and set aside.

In blender or food processor, process cottage cheese with lemon juice until blended. Add spinach, sour cream, parsley, onion, salt, and pepper to taste; process just until mixed.

Cover and refrigerate for at least 4 hours or overnight to blend flavors. Makes 2¼ cups/550 mL.

Compare: Many dips are made with mayonnaise or cream cheese as a base; these are much higher in fat and calories. Just as good-tasting, if not better, dips can be made using cottage cheese and/or yogurt.

Spinach-Onion Dip* per cup/250 mL	g fat	calories
Low-fat yogurt	4	158
2% cottage cheese	5	214
Light sour cream	13	220
Sour cream	46	475
Light mayonnaise	80	928
Mayonnaise	176	1632
Cream cheese**	80	832

Broccoli and Mushroom Dip

Chopped broccoli adds color, flavor and fiber to this low-cal dip.

2 cups	chopped broccoli (include stalks)	500 mL
1 tbsp	vegetable oil	15 mL
1	clove garlic, minced	1
½	onion, chopped	½
¼ lb	mushrooms, coarsely chopped	125 g
¾ cup	low-fat cottage cheese	175 mL
¼ cup	low-fat plain yogurt or light sour cream	50 mL
	Salt and freshly ground pepper	

In pot of boiling water, cook broccoli just until tender-crisp (3 minutes). Drain and refresh under cold water; drain again and set aside.

In nonstick skillet, heat oil over medium heat; add garlic, onion and mushrooms and cook, shaking pan to prevent sticking, for 5 minutes or until onion is tender. Set aside.

In food processor, combine cottage cheese and yogurt; process until smooth. Add mushroom mixture and broccoli; season with salt and pepper to taste. Process with on/off motion just until mixed. Cover and refrigerate for up to 2 days. Makes 2¼ cups/550 mL.

PER 1-tbsp/15 mL SERVING (made with low-fat plain yogurt)	
calories	12
g fat	0.5
mg cholesterol	0
mg sodium	22
g protein	1
g carbohydrate	1

Crackers
When buying crackers it pays to spend a few minutes reading the labels. Many crackers are high in salt and contain hydrogenated vegetable oil (palm or coconut), which means they have saturated fat.

Melba toast and crispbreads are two kinds of crackers without hydrogenated vegetable oil.

For dips and spreads, instead of crackers use raw vegetables, whole-wheat pita bread rounds (tear into smaller pieces) or Low-Salt Bagel Thins (page 22) and Quick Homemade Melba Toast (page 21).

Raw Veggies for Snacks
If you keep a supply of cut-up celery and carrots, broccoli or cauliflower in the refrigerator they will often be chosen for snacks over cookies and chips.

However, if you store them in a bowl of water, they will lose most of their vitamin C; instead, store them in a plastic bag with a few drops of water.

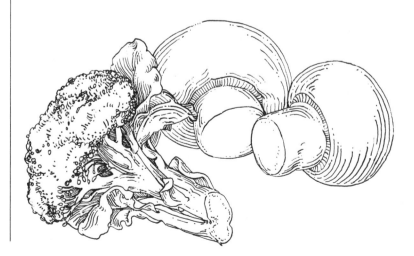

PER 1-tbsp/15 mL SERVING	
calories	12
g fat	0.5
mg cholesterol	9
mg sodium	28
g protein	1.5
g carbohydrate	0.5

To Unmold Shrimp Mousse with Dill

Run a knife around mousse to loosen from mold. Invert onto serving platter. Cover with hot, damp tea towel for 1 minute. Hold mold and platter securely and give a strong shake to release mousse. Remove mold.

Shrimp Mousse with Dill

Serve as part of a light salad plate, or surround with crackers, Melba toast or fresh vegetables for a delicious appetizer spread. (Recipe pictured opposite page 22.)

1	envelope unflavored gelatin	1
½ cup	cold water	125 mL
⅓ cup	minced green onions or chives	75 mL
½ cup	chopped fresh dill (not packed)	125mL
1 tbsp	lemon juice	15 mL
½ tsp	salt	2 mL
½ tsp	granulated sugar	2 mL
Dash	hot pepper sauce	Dash
2 tbsp	tomato paste	25 mL
¾ cup	low-fat plain yogurt	175 mL
½ cup	light sour cream	125 mL
½ cup	finely chopped celery	125 mL
1¾ cups	small cooked salad shrimp (12 oz/ 375 g), coarsely chopped	425 mL
	Dill sprigs	

In microwave-safe bowl or small saucepan, sprinkle gelatin over cold water; let stand until softened, about 5 minutes. Microwave at high (100%) power for 40 seconds or warm over medium heat until gelatin is dissolved; let cool slightly.

In bowl combine onions, dill, lemon juice, salt, sugar, hot pepper sauce, tomato paste, yogurt, sour cream, celery and gelatin; mix well. Stir in shrimp and refrigerate until mixture begins to set. Spoon into lightly oiled 4 cup/1 L mold or, alternatively, spoon into serving bowl. Cover and refrigerate until firm, at least 3 hours.

Unmold onto serving plate or serve in bowl and garnish with sprigs of fresh dill. Makes about 4 cups/1 L.

Appetizer or First Course
When planning menus try to make sure each course has different foods and that the whole meal is a pleasing combination of colors, textures, seasonings, flavors and temperature. If you have a filling first course such as Fettuccine and Mussel Salad, plan a light main course of perhaps a fish and a green vegetable. If you have a main course that is high in fat and calories choose a light first course such as a soup without cream.

As well as the recipes in this section consider a soup, salad, pasta or fish for a first course.

Tortilla Chips These are a healthy alternative to store-bought tortilla chips, which are high in calories, fat and sodium. Use fresh, frozen or canned tortillas (whole wheat if you can find them) for these crisp easy-to-make chips.

Dip each tortilla in water; drain off excess. Cut into 6 wedges and place on baking sheet. Bake in 500°F (260°C) oven for 5 minutes. Let cool and store in airtight container for up to 2 weeks. (1 oz/28 g of chips has about 1 g fat, 62 calories.)

Compare: This type of spread is often made with mayonnaise and whipping cream. I prefer a lighter version made with yogurt and sour cream.

Shrimp Mousse with Dill

per ¼ cup/50 mL	g fat	mg cholesterol	calories
Made with: yogurt and sour cream	2	36	48
or with: mayonnaise (½ cup/125 mL) and whipping cream (¾ cup/175 mL)	8	48	108

Quick Homemade Melba Toast
Choose fine-grained bread such as whole wheat, pumpernickel or sandwich bread. Cut in very thin slices (remove crusts if you want) and arrange in a single layer on a cookie sheet. Bake in 250°F/120°C oven for 20 to 30 minutes or until crisp. Time will vary depending on how old the bread and how thick the slices.

Snacks and Nibbles
These can quickly add up to a great deal of fat and calories. For example, if you consume about 2000 calories a day you should have no more than 66 grams of fat.

High-Fat Snacks	g fat
Peanuts (½ cup/125 mL)	35
Potato chips (1 small bag/40g)	14
Chicken liver pâté (¼ cup/50 mL)	26
Cheddar cheese (1½ oz/45 g, a 2 inch/5 cm cube)	15

Lower-Fat Alternative Snacks	g fat
Popcorn (unbuttered) (1 cup/250mL)	0
Shrimp Mousse with Dill (¼ cup/50 mL) (page 20)	2
Skim-milk cheese (1½ oz/45 g)	3
Fresh Vegetables with Spinach-Onion Dip (page 18)	trace

Low-Salt Bagel Thins

If you love crisp, salty snacks such as potato chips, here is a healthy alternative. How good they are depends on how thin you can slice the bagel.

1	bagel	1
2 tsp	soft margarine, melted	10 mL
1 tsp	dried oregano	5 mL

Using very sharp serrated knife, slice bagel into very thin rounds. Arrange in single layer on baking sheet; brush with margarine. Sprinkle with oregano. Bake in 350°F/180°C oven for 12 minutes. Let cool and store in airtight container for up to 1 week. Makes 20 pieces.

PER 1-piece SERVING	
calories	14
g fat	0.5
mg cholesterol	0
mg sodium	15
g protein	0
g carbohydrate	2

Italian Tomato Bruschetta

Traditionally, this Italian-style garlic bread is made by toasting thick slices of Italian bread, then rubbing them with a cut clove of garlic and drizzling with a top-quality (first-pressed, dense and green-colored) olive oil. Sometimes the toast is topped with diced tomato or cheese. Here's a low-calorie, low-fat version that is equally delicious. Serve for a first course or as a snack after bridge or tennis, as an hors d'oeuvre on tiny toasted bread rounds or as part of a soup-and-salad meal. (Recipe pictured opposite page 23.)

To prepare Italian Tomato Bruschetta for a group, use the round Italian bread. Cut in half horizontally; prepare, and then cut into wedges to serve.

After Bridge Snack

Italian Tomato Bruschetta (page 22)
Blueberry Cream Flan (page 161)

8	slices French or Italian bread, ½-inch/1 cm thick	8
2	cloves garlic, halved	2
1 tsp	olive oil	5 mL
2 tbsp	minced onion	25 mL
1	large tomato, diced	1
Pinch	dried oregano	Pinch
Pinch	freshly ground pepper	Pinch
2 tsp	freshly grated Parmesan cheese (optional)	10 mL

PER SERVING (including Parmesan)	
calories	105
g fat	2
mg cholesterol	1
mg sodium	190
g protein	3
g carbohydrate	19

Photo:
Shrimp Mousse with Dill (page 20)

Under broiler or in toaster oven, toast bread on both sides until brown. Rub one side of hot toast with cut side of garlic. While bread is toasting, heat oil in nonstick skillet over

Mussels aren't nearly as high
in cholesterol as previously
thought; about 3½ oz (approx.
100 g) of mussels (meat only)
has 50 mg cholesterol.

Photo:
Mussels on the Half Shell
(page 23), Italian Tomato
Bruschetta (page 22),
Marinated Mushrooms (page
26), Marinated Spiced Carrots
(page 27), Mushroom-Stuffed
Zucchini Cups (page 26)

medium-high heat; add onion and cook, stirring, until tender.
Add tomato, oregano and pepper; stir to mix.

Spoon tomato mixture over garlic side of hot toast and serve
immediately. Alternatively, sprinkle with Parmesan and (if using)
broil for 1 minute. Makes 4 servings (2 slices each).

Mussels on the Half Shell

These mussels look great on an hors d'oeuvre platter, aren't
difficult to make and are inexpensive compared to crab or
shrimp. (Recipe pictured opposite page 23.)

3 lb	mussels	1.5 kg
¼ cup	white wine or water	50 mL
2 tbsp	vegetable oil	25 mL
2 tbsp	lemon juice	25 mL
3	cloves garlic, minced	3
½ cup	chopped fresh parsley	125 mL
2	medium tomatoes, diced	2

Scrub mussels and discard any that do not close when tapped;
cut off any hairy beards. In large heavy saucepan, bring wine or
water to boil. Add mussels, cover and cook over medium high
heat for 5 to 7 minutes or until mussels open. Discard any that
do not open.

Remove from heat; reserve 2 tbsp/25 mL of cooking liquid.
When mussels are cool enough to handle, using small knife,
separate mussels from shell and set aside; reserve half the shells.

In bowl, combine reserved cooking liquid, oil, lemon juice,
garlic, parsley and tomatoes; add mussels and stir gently. Cover
and refrigerate for 3 hours.

To serve, place a mussel in each half shell; spoon tomato
mixture over. Arrange on a platter and pass with drinks, or
arrange on individual plates and serve as first course.

Makes about 6 first-course servings or 50 to 60 pieces.

PER SERVING (9 mussels)		PER PIECE	
calories	114	calories	12
g fat	6	g fat	0.5
mg cholesterol	33	mg cholesterol	4
mg sodium	197	mg sodium	21
g protein	10	g protein	1
g carbohydrate	5	g carbohydrate	0.5
GOOD: vitamin C, iron, niacin			

Green Bean Appetizer Salad with Fresh Tomato-Chive Dressing   Serve this as a light first course in the summer and fall when green beans and tomatoes are at their sweetest and best flavor. It's also a great way to use up any leftover cooked beans.

Line salad plates with leaf lettuce. Arrange crisp-cooked and chilled beans and sliced raw mushrooms over lettuce. Spoon Fresh Tomato Chive Dressing (page 63) over beans (sprinkle feta cheese on top if not already added to dressing). Garnish with lemon wedges or chopped fresh herbs such as cilantro (coriander), dill or basil.

PER SERVING (1 meatball)	
calories	28
g fat	1
mg cholesterol	7
mg sodium	9
g protein	2
g carbohydrate	2

Bake rather than fry meatballs; not only is there less fat as a result, it's also much easier.

Spiced Meatballs with Coriander Dipping Sauce

Middle Eastern seasonings of cinnamon, allspice and garlic, plus crunchy water chestnuts and juicy raisins, make these meatballs the best I've tasted; salt will never be missed. Fresh coriander, also called cilantro, is available at some supermarkets and most Oriental grocery stores. Don't substitute the dried coriander; instead add curry powder to taste. (Recipe pictured opposite page 23.)

Meatballs:

¼ cup	raisins	50 mL
½ lb	lean ground lamb	250 g
⅓ cup	minced water chestnuts	75 mL
2 tbsp	minced green onions	25 mL
1	clove garlic, minced	1
½ tsp	ground allspice	2 mL
½ tsp	cinnamon	2 mL
	Freshly ground pepper	

Coriander Dipping Sauce:

¾ cup	plain 2% yogurt	175 mL
¼ cup	minced fresh coriander leaves, lightly packed	50 mL
	Freshly ground pepper	

Meatballs: Soak raisins in hot water for 15 minutes; drain and chop. In bowl, combine raisins, lamb, water chestnuts, onions, garlic, allspice, cinnamon and pepper to taste; mix well.

Shape into 25 bite-size balls. Arrange in single layer in ungreased baking dish. Bake, uncovered, in 400°F/200°C oven for 20 minutes.

Coriander Dipping Sauce: Meanwhile, in small bowl combine yogurt, coriander, and pepper to taste; cover and refrigerate for at least 30 minutes for flavors to develop. Serve hot meatballs with toothpicks for dipping into sauce. Makes 1 cup/250 mL sauce, 25 meatballs.

Seafood Lettuce Rolls

These surprise packages are an intriguing and delicious first course. Serve with Coriander Dipping Sauce (page 24) or Nuoc Cham Dipping Sauce.

1	head Boston or leaf lettuce	1
1	can (7½ oz/213 g) salmon	1
1	dried red chili pepper or 1 fresh hot pepper	1
½ cup	low-fat plain yogurt	125 mL
1 cup	small shrimp	250 mL
2 cups	alfalfa sprouts	500 mL
	Fresh cilantro (coriander) leaves (optional)	

Cut large lettuce leaves in half down center vein. In bowl, flake salmon along with juices and well-mashed bones. Split chili pepper in half lengthwise, discard seeds and vein; finely chop and mix into yogurt.

On narrow end of each lettuce piece, place 1 tbsp/15 mL flaked salmon, top with 1 or 2 shrimp, then approximately 2 tbsp/25 mL alfalfa sprouts, dollop of yogurt, and 1 or 2 cilantro leaves (if using). Roll into cylinder shape. Makes 5 servings of 3 rolls each.

PER SERVING	
calories	138
g fat	6
mg cholesterol	54
mg sodium	85
g protein	17
g carbohydrate	3
GOOD: calcium	
EXCELLENT: niacin	

If you enjoy Vietnamese cooking, serve the lettuce rolls with a nuoc cham dipping sauce and include rice vermicelli noodles in rolls. Thin strips of cooked pork can be used instead of salmon.

Nuoc Cham Dipping Sauce
Split 2 dried chili peppers in half and discard seeds and membranes; chop finely. In small dish combine peppers, 1 clove minced garlic, 1 tbsp/15 mL granulated sugar, 1 tbsp/15 mL lime juice, 3 tbsp/45 mL water and 2 tbsp/25 mL bottled fish sauce (available in Oriental food stores).

Marinated Mushrooms and Artichokes
Drain one can (14 oz/398 mL) artichokes. Cut in half and add to mushroom mixture before marinating.

Marinated Mushrooms

Pass these zippy mushrooms with drinks or serve as part of a relish tray or salad plate. (Recipe pictured opposite page 23.)

⅔ cup	tarragon vinegar	150 mL
⅓ cup	vegetable oil	75 mL
2 tbsp	granulated sugar	25 mL
1 tsp	each dried basil and thyme	5 mL
½ tsp	salt	2mL
2 tbsp	water	25 mL
Dash	hot pepper sauce	Dash
¼ tsp	dried hot pepper flakes (optional)	1 mL
1	clove garlic, minced	1
	Freshly ground pepper	
1	onion, sliced	1
1½ lb	medium mushrooms	750 g

In large bowl, combine vinegar, oil, sugar, basil, thyme, salt, water, hot pepper sauce, dried hot pepper flakes if using, garlic, and pepper to taste; stir until well mixed.

Separate onion into rings. Wash mushrooms and trim bases. Add onions and mushrooms to vinegar mixture; mix lightly. Cover and refrigerate for at least 8 hours, stirring occasionally. Drain before serving. Makes 10 appetizer servings.

PER SERVING	
calories	39
g fat	2
mg cholesterol	0
mg sodium	29
g protein	2
g carbohydrate	5
GOOD: niacin, fiber	

Mushroom-Stuffed Zucchini Cups (Recipe pictured opposite page 23.)
For a light, refreshing, hot hors d'oeuvre follow recipe on page 128 using very thin zucchini cut into bite-size pieces. Serve on platter along with Spiced Meatballs with Coriander Dipping Sauce (page 24) and cherry tomatoes.

PER SERVING	
calories	27
g fat	0
mg cholesterol	0
mg sodium	13
g protein	0.5
g carbohydrate	6
EXCELLENT: vitamin A	

Marinated Spiced Carrots

These are a favorite with the bridge club I used to play with when I lived in Ottawa. The members have been serving these along with the Marinated Mushrooms (page 26) at their year-end party for the last 20 years. A few cherry tomatoes on the platter look nice and add extra color. (Recipe pictured opposite page 23.)

1 lb	small carrots, scraped	500 g
½ cup	granulated sugar	125 mL
½ cup	white vinegar	125 mL
½ cup	water	125 mL
1 tbsp	mustard seeds	15 mL
3	whole cloves	3
1	3-inch (8 cm) stick cinnamon, broken	1

Cut carrots into 3-inch-long (8 cm), very thin sticks. Blanch in boiling water for 3 minutes; drain and cool under cold water. Drain again and place in bowl.

In saucepan, combine sugar, vinegar, water, mustard seeds, cloves and cinnamon; bring to boil. Reduce heat and simmer for 10 minutes; pour over carrots. Let cool, then cover and refrigerate for at least 8 hours or overnight. Drain well; discard cloves and cinnamon. Makes about 10 appetizer servings.

PER SERVING	
calories	100
g fat	8
mg cholesterol	0
mg sodium	40
g protein	3
g carbohydrate	7

EXCELLENT: vitamin A, vitamin C, fiber

September Dinner Party

Warm Vegetable Salad (page 28)
Brochette of Pork with Lemon and Herb Marinade (page 80)
Barley and Mushroom Pilaf (page 137)

Tomatoes Broiled with Goat's Cheese and Basil (page 133)
Lemon Roll with Fresh Fruit (page 162)

Warm Vegetable Salad with Tomato-Shallot Dressing

Warm vegetables over cool greens is a very pleasing combination. You can prepare the vegetables and dressing in advance, then just before serving quickly blanch vegetables and add dressing. It's a lovely dinner-party first course or a light lunch. (Recipe pictured opposite page 55.)

½ lb	spinach*	250 g
1	small Belgian endive	1
1 cup	green beans, cut 2 in/5 cm long and sliced lengthwise	250 mL
1 cup	julienne carrots	250 mL
1 cup	small cauliflower florets	250 mL
1 cup	small broccoli florets	250 mL
3 tbsp	sunflower seeds	45 mL

Tomato-Shallot Dressing:

¼ cup	vegetable oil	50 mL
¼ cup	water	50 mL
¼ cup	lemon juice	50 mL
2	shallots, minced	2
1 tbsp	chopped fresh basil (or ½ tsp/2 mL dried)	15 mL
½ tsp	Dijon mustard	2 mL
	Salt and freshly ground pepper	
3	medium tomatoes, peeled and diced	3

   Trim, wash and dry spinach; tear into large pieces. Separate endive leaves. On 6 salad plates, arrange spinach and endive leaves.
   Tomato-Shallot Dressing: In food processor or mixing bowl, combine oil, water, lemon juice, shallots, basil and mustard; mix well. Season with salt and pepper to taste.
   Five minutes before serving: In large pot of boiling salted water, blanch green beans, carrots, cauliflower and broccoli for 2 minutes; drain. Spoon warm vegetables onto greens; stir

Leftover Chicken or Turkey

Thanksgiving or Christmas turkey or Sunday night chicken leftovers can be used for a lovely lunch or dinner in the following recipes:
Curried Chicken Croustades (page 29)
Turkey Noodle Soup (page 33)
Tarragon Chicken Salad (page 47)
Curried Chicken Crepes (page 85)
Chicken and Shrimp Creole (page 89)
Old-Fashioned Chicken Pot Pie (page 85)
Pizza topping

PER CROUSTADE	
calories	30
g fat	1
mg cholesterol	6
mg sodium	56
g protein	3
g carbohydrate	3

Use leftover bread trimmings to make bread crumbs. Use in Herb-Breaded Chicken (page 195) or Fish Fillets with Herbed Crumbs (page 96).

tomatoes into dressing and spoon dressing over vegetables. Sprinkle with sunflower seeds. Serve immediately before vegetables cool. Makes 8 servings.

*This salad is best made with fresh leaf spinach (usually bought by the bunch) available in the summer and fall. One 10 oz/284 g package of fresh spinach can also be used.

Curried Chicken Croustades

Serve these savory tidbits at a cocktail party or make larger croustades and serve for a luncheon dish. In this recipe tiny shells of bread are toasted and filled with curried chicken. Both parts can be made in advance, then reheated before serving. The croustades are perfect low-calorie, low-fat containers for savory fillings.

40	thin slices bread (about 2 loaves)	40
	Curried Chicken filling for crêpes (page 85)	

Using 2-inch (5 cm) cookie cutter or glass, cut out 40 rounds of bread. Press bread rounds into very small tart tins (about 1½ inches/4 cm in diameter). Bake in 300°F/150°C oven for 20 minutes or until toasted. Remove from oven and let cool. (Croustades can be prepared in advance and stored in covered container for up to 1 week or frozen for up to 2 months.)
Fill croustades with Curried Chicken mixture and place on baking sheet. Heat in 400°F/200°C oven for 15 minutes or until hot. Makes 40 appetizers.

Quick, Low-Calorie, Low-Fat Hors d'Oeuvres

Cucumber Canapes:
Use round cucumber slices as the base for canapes. If you wish, scoop out a tiny portion of cucumber from center to form a hollow; top with a spoonful of:

   –Shrimp Mousse with Dill (page 20);

   –Salmon Spread with Capers (page 17);

   –Classic Tuna Salad with Fresh Dill (page 50);

   –or Curried Chicken (page 85).

Mini-Pitas:
Cut small (1½-inch/4 cm) pita bread rounds in half so that you have 2 pockets. Line pocket with a soft leaf lettuce and fill with any of the fillings listed above with Cucumber Canapes.

Fill hollowed-out cherry tomatoes, zucchini rounds, snow peas or mushroom caps with any of the above spreads, or with the dip recipes in this book.

Use Belgian endive spears instead of crackers or chips for dipping.

SOUPS

Homemade soup is such a treat and so easy to make that I wish I always had some on hand. In this section there are elegant soups to serve as first courses at a dinner party—such as Cream of Parsnip Soup with Ginger or Fresh Beet Soup with Yogurt— or there's a Hearty Vegetable Bean Soup, which is a wonderfully warming main-course dish. Main-course soups are easy to prepare, make good use of leftovers and can be made ahead of time.

Canned and Packaged Soups

Canned and packaged soups are very high in sodium. If you use only canned or packaged soups, your family will acquire a taste for heavily salted soups. To increase the nutrients and decrease the sodium of packaged or canned soup you can use them as a base, and add more vegetables, such as grated carrot, grated zucchini, chopped green beans, broccoli, cubed potatoes and/ or chopped onion.

Whenever possible, add skim or 2% milk instead of water to canned soups; this way you increase the soup's protein and calcium content.

I often add leftover cooked rice or noodles, chicken or meats, an extra mushroom or green onion to soups.

Soup Tips

*The most effective way to reduce fat in soups is to cut down the amount of butter, margarine or oil you put in them. Many recipes call for more of these than is necessary. Another way is to substitute light cream or milk for whipping cream. If you do need more fat for flavor, add it at the end of cooking—just before serving. This will give the maximum flavor for the least amount of fat.

*Traditional high-fat and high-cholesterol soup thickeners are whole milk, cream, egg yolks and high-fat cheese. Instead, thicken soups with rice, noodles, potato, legumes, puréed vegetables, low-fat cheese, 2% milk, low-fat plain yogurt.

NOTE: If you add ¼ tsp/1 mL salt to 1 cup/250 mL homemade soup, you add 581 mg sodium.

Compare Homemade and Canned Soups

per cup/250 mL	g fat	mg sodium
Asparagus and Potato Bisque (page 32)	1	52
Canned cream of asparagus (with water added)	3	996
Mushroom Bisque with Tarragon (page 37)	5	257
Canned cream of mushroom (with water added)	9	1091

Compare	mg sodium per 1 cup/250 mL
Chicken stock diluted from can	
Chicken stock from a cube	740 +
Chicken stock from powder	
Basic chicken stock (unsalted) (page 46)	56

To get the maximum flavor with the least amount of fat: When making a vegetable soup, if you cook the vegetables first in margarine (¼ cup/50 mL margarine has 56 g fat), the margarine becomes absorbed into the vegetables. Instead cook vegetables in only 1 tsp/5 mL margarine and some chicken stock, or better still in only chicken stock. To add richness of flavor add ¼ cup/50 mL cream or milk (light cream will add 8 g fat; whipping cream 20 g fat) just before serving. You will achieve the same effect with much less fat. (The same principle applies to salt; add it at the end of cooking or just before serving.)

PER SERVING (made with yogurt and unsalted chicken stock)	
calories	103
g fat	1
mg cholesterol	4
mg sodium	39
g protein	5
g carbohydrate	19

GOOD: fiber, niacin
EXCELLENT: vitamin C

Asparagus and Potato Bisque

Potato helps to thicken this soup without adding the extra calories or preparation time of a butter/flour-thickened soup. Its delicious served hot or cold, but when serving hot, substitute either light cream or milk for the yogurt, since yogurt tends to curdle easily when heated. (Recipe pictured opposite half-title page.)

1	large potato, peeled and diced	1
1	small onion, chopped	1
1½ cups	water or chicken stock	375 mL
1 lb	fresh asparagus	500 g
2 tsp	lemon juice	10 mL
1 cup	2% milk	250 mL
½ cup	low-fat plain yogurt, or light cream or milk	125 mL
	Salt and freshly ground pepper	
Pinch	nutmeg	Pinch

In saucepan, combine potato, onion, and water or chicken stock; cover and simmer until potato is nearly tender, 5 to 10 minutes.

Meanwhile, cut asparagus into about 1½-inch lengths (4 cm). Add to potato mixture; cover and simmer for 5 minutes or until asparagus is tender.

Using slotted spoon, remove asparagus tips and let cool in cold water to prevent further cooking. Drain and reserve for garnish.

In food processor or blender, purée asparagus-potato mixture; add lemon juice. Pour into bowl; cover and refrigerate until chilled. Stir in milk and yogurt; season with salt, pepper and nutmeg to taste. Serve cold or reheat. Garnish each serving with reserved asparagus tips. Makes 6 servings, ¾ cup/175 mL each.

*Instead of using salt to add flavor to soups, use onion or celery, herbs (thyme, rosemary, oregano, chives, parsley, to name just a few), lemon juice, a pinch of sugar, pepper, nutmeg or garlic. Also use more of the vegetable itself, i.e., if you are making carrot soup, add extra carrots.

Turkey Noodle Soup

Whenever you roast a turkey or chicken, make this comforting soup from the leftovers. Don't be put off by the long list of ingredients; it's really quite easy to prepare. I usually start the stock simmering while I'm making dinner one night, let it simmer for a few hours that evening then finish it the next night. If you prefer, add rice instead of noodles.

Stock*:

1	carcass from roast chicken or turkey	1
7 cups	water	1.75 L
1	bay leaf	1
1	stalk celery, chopped	1
1	onion, quartered	1

Soup:

¼ cup	broken noodles (½-inch/1 cm pieces)	50 mL
1	stalk celery (including leaves), chopped	1
1	carrot, chopped	1
3	green onions, sliced	3
⅓ cup	grated zucchini	75 mL
1 tsp	dried basil	5 mL
1 tsp	dried thyme	5 mL
Dash	hot pepper sauce	Dash
	Salt and freshly ground pepper	

PER SERVING	
calories	91
g fat	3
mg cholesterol	32
mg sodium	137
g protein	11
g carbohydrate	5
GOOD: vitamin C	
EXCELLENT: vitamin A, niacin	

*If you don't have a leftover turkey or chicken carcass, use 6 cups/1.5 L chicken stock instead of the stock here. For a main course soup and to increase fiber add 1 can (19 oz/540 mL) chickpeas or kidney beans, drained. Other additions: green peas, chopped fresh spinach, asparagus, chopped broccoli, diced potato, squash or turnip.

Stock: In stockpot or large saucepan, combine carcass, water, bay leaf, celery and onion. Simmer, covered, for 4 hours. Strain, reserving stock. Let bones cool, then pick out any meat and add to stock.

Soup: In stockpot or saucepan, bring stock to boil; add noodles and simmer for 5 minutes. Add celery, carrot, green onions, zucchini, basil and thyme; simmer for 10 minutes. Stir in hot pepper sauce; season with salt and pepper to taste. Makes 6 servings (¾ cup/175 mL each).

Mussel, Clam and Fish Chowder

Serve this wonderfully warming seafood stew for lunch, dinner or as late-night party fare. If fresh mussels and clams aren't available, use canned or bottled ones. Shrimp can be added, but that will raise the cholesterol level. Some fish markets sell fresh fish pieces, often called chowder bits or pieces. These are usually inexpensive and ideal for this recipe; remove any skin or bones.

2 tsp	vegetable oil	10 mL
1	onion, chopped	1
1	stalk celery, chopped	1
1	carrot, chopped	1
2	cloves garlic, minced	2
1	bay leaf	1
1 tsp	dried thyme	5 mL
1 tsp	dried basil	5 mL
1	can (19 oz/540 mL) tomatoes (undrained)	1
2 cups	water	500 mL
2	potatoes, diced	2
1 lb	mussels	500 g
1 lb	small clams (or one 5-oz/142 g can)	500 g
1 lb	fresh white flesh fish (cod, haddock, monkfish)	500 g
½ cup	white wine	125 mL
	Salt and freshly ground pepper	
1 cup	chopped fresh parsley	250 mL

PER SERVING

calories	185
g fat	3
mg cholesterol	65
mg sodium	467
g protein	21
g carbohydrate	19

GOOD: fiber, niacin, iron
EXCELLENT: vitamin A, vitamin C

In large saucepan, heat oil over medium heat; cook onion, celery and carrot, stirring, for 5 minutes. Add garlic, bay leaf, thyme, basil, tomatoes, water and potatoes; bring to simmer. Cover and cook over low heat for 25 minutes or until vegetables are tender. Remove bay leaf.

Meanwhile, scrub mussels and clams under cold running water; cut off any hairy beards from mussels. Discard any clams

*Jiffy Gazpacho
Don't throw away leftover tossed green salads made with an oil-and-vinegar dressing. Instead, purée in a blender or food processor and add tomato juice to taste. Refrigerate until cold then serve in soup bowls, topped with finely chopped tomato, green pepper and garlic croutons.

or mussels that do not close when tapped. Add clams to saucepan; simmer for 5 minutes. Add mussels, fish (if using monkfish cut into chunks) and wine. Simmer for 5 minutes or until clams and mussels open; discard any that don't open. Season with salt and pepper to taste. Just before serving sprinkle with parsley. (Chowder can be prepared up to 1 day in advance, refrigerated and reheated.) Makes 6 servings (1¾ cups/425 mL each).

Chilled Cucumber-Chive Soup

Quick to prepare, this wonderful summer soup is perfect for lunch or picnic or a first course for an alfresco dinner. For packed lunches it's easy to transport in a Thermos.

½ cup	low-fat cottage cheese	125 mL
½ cup	sour cream	125 mL
2 cups	buttermilk	500 mL
½	unpeeled English cucumber diced	½
¼ cup	chopped fresh parsley	125 mL
⅓ cup	diced red radishes	75 mL
¼ cup	chopped fresh chives or green onions	50 mL
	Salt and freshly ground pepper	

In blender or food processor, process cottage cheese and sour cream until smooth; add buttermilk and process to mix.

Transfer to bowl; stir in cucumber, parsley, radishes and chives. Season with salt and pepper to taste. Refrigerate until chilled. Makes 6 servings, ¾ cup/175 mL each.

PER SERVING	
calories	85
g fat	4
mg cholesterol	12
mg sodium	168
g protein	6
g carbohydrate	7
GOOD: vitamin C, calcium	

Chicken Stock
The main nutritional
advantage to homemade
chicken stock (besides its
better flavor) is that it is low in
sodium. However, if you add
salt, the sodium level will be
close to that of commercial
soups. Anyone on a low-
sodium diet should use
homemade stock without
adding salt. If you use stocks
from a can or cube, remember
that they are high in salt, so
don't add any more. Doubling
the ratio of water to stock
powder, a stock cube or
canned stock will halve the
sodium content.

New wide-mouth unbreakable
Thermos containers make
soups easy to pack for lunch.

PER SERVING	
calories	151
g fat	2
mg cholesterol	2
mg sodium	444
g protein	9
g carbohydrate	25

GOOD: vitamin C, iron
EXCELLENT: fiber, vitamin A,
niacin

Chunky Vegetable-Bean Soup

Onion and potato are the basis for this soup—the potato helps
to thicken it, the onions add flavor. You can add any seasonal
fresh vegetables—broccoli, mushrooms, zucchini, carrots,
tomatoes—that you have on hand. Instead of canned kidney
beans, you can add ¼ cup/50 mL uncooked noodles, or rice or
barley, along with the potato. (Recipe pictured opposite inside
front cover.)

1	large onion, chopped	1
1	large potato, peeled and cubed	1
4 cups	chicken stock	1 L
2	stalks celery, diced	2
¼ lb	green beans, cut in 1-inch/2.5 cm pieces	125 g
¼	small cabbage, thinly sliced, and/ or ½ pkg spinach, coarsely sliced	¼
1	carrot, grated or chopped	1
¼ cup	chopped sweet red pepper	50 mL
1 tsp	dried dillweed (or ¼ cup/50 mL chopped fresh)	5 mL
1	can (19 oz/540 mL) kidney beans, drained	1
	Salt, cayenne and freshly ground pepper	
¼ cup	grated Parmesan cheese (optional)	50 mL

In large heavy saucepan, combine onion, potato and chicken
stock; bring to a boil. Reduce heat and simmer for 10 minutes.
Add celery, green beans, cabbage and/or spinach, carrot,
sweet pepper, dillweed and kidney beans; cover and simmer for
10 minutes or until vegetables are tender.
Season with salt, cayenne and pepper to taste. Sprinkle each
serving with Parmesan (if using). Makes 8 servings, ¾ cup/175
mL each.

PER SERVING	
calories	107
g fat	5
mg cholesterol	7
mg sodium	257
g protein	6
g carbohydrate	10
GOOD: vitamin C, niacin	

Mushroom Bisque with Tarragon

Easy to make, this creamy soup tastes so much better than anything out of a can.

½ lb	mushrooms	250 g
1 tbsp	margarine	15 mL
2 tbsp	minced onion	25 mL
2 tbsp	all-purpose flour	25 mL
1 cup	hot chicken stock	250 mL
1½ cups	2% milk	375 mL
1 tsp	dried tarragon	5 mL
⅓ cup	minced fresh parsley	75 mL
	Salt and freshly ground pepper	

Thinly slice 4 mushroom caps and set aside; coarsely chop remaining mushrooms (if using food processor, use on-off turns).

In saucepan, melt margarine over medium heat; add onion and cook for 2 minutes, stirring occasionally. Add chopped mushrooms and cook for 4 minutes, stirring often; sprinkle with flour and stir until mixed. Whisk in hot chicken stock and bring to boil, whisking constantly. Reduce heat to low and add milk, tarragon, parsley and reserved sliced mushrooms; simmer, uncovered, for 4 minutes.

Season to taste with salt and pepper. Makes 4 servings, ¾ cup/ 175 mL each.

Compare

per 1 cup/250 mL	calories	g fat	mg sodium*	g protein	g fiber
Canned Chunky Vegetable Soup	104	3	837	3	3
Canned Vegetable Soup	80	2	770	2	1
Homemade Chunky Vegetable-Bean Soup	151	2	444*	9	7

*Sodium values based on using canned chicken stock, or stock made from a cube. If homemade, sodium is greatly reduced.

Fresh Corn Bisque with Green Onions

In fresh corn season, as markets overflow with locally grown corn on the cob, try this fresh-tasting, economical soup. The recipe can easily be halved, or you can freeze any extra in container sizes to suit your household.

PER SERVING	
calories	91
g fat	4
mg cholesterol	0
mg sodium	150
g protein	2
g carbohydrate	14
GOOD: fiber, vitamin A	

2 tbsp	vegetable oil	25 mL
1	onion, chopped	1
1	carrot, chopped	1
1	stalk celery, chopped	1
2	cloves garlic, minced	2
½ tsp	turmeric	2 mL
1	bay leaf	1
4 cups	water	1 L
5	ears of corn, husked*	5
½ tsp	salt	2 mL
	Cayenne pepper	
¼ cup	chopped green onions or fresh coriander**	50 mL

*To make Corn Bisque using kernel corn: After adding bay leaf and water, simmer for 10 minutes. Add 4 cups (1 L) kernel corn, simmer 5 minutes; discard bay leaf. In blender or food processor purée in batches. Return to saucepan and add 1 cup (250 mL) corn kernels. Simmer 5 minutes. Season and garnish as in above recipe.

In large saucepan or soup kettle, heat oil over medium heat. Add onion, carrot, celery and garlic; cook, stirring, for 2 minutes. Stir in turmeric and cook for 1 minute. Add bay leaf and water; bring to simmer.

Cut corn kernels from cobs and set aside. Add cobs to saucepan; cover and simmer for 10 minutes. Add corn kernels and simmer for 10 minutes longer. Discard corn cobs and bay leaf. Reserve about 1 cup/250 mL corn kernels.

In blender or food processor, purée mixture in batches. Return to saucepan and add reserved corn kernels, salt, and cayenne to taste. Serve hot or cold and garnish with green onions or coriander. Makes 8 servings, ⅔ cup/150 mL each.

**Fresh coriander is also called cilantro, or Chinese parsley. It is an excellent addition to this soup.

Cream of Parsnip Soup with Ginger

This splendid soup is the creation of Doug Andison, my friend and good cook. He microwaves parsnips and leeks separately in large amounts then freezes them in smaller portions so he can prepare this soup easily at the last minute. He also likes to press the gingerroot through a garlic press instead of grating or chopping and might use cream instead of 2% milk.

1	onion (or 2 whites of leeks), chopped	1
4	medium parsnips, peeled and cubed (about 10 oz/280 g)	4
1 cup	water	250 mL
1 tbsp	soft margarine	15 mL
2 tbsp	all-purpose flour	25 mL
1 cup	chicken stock	250 mL
1½ tsp	grated fresh gingerroot	7 mL
¾ cup	2% milk	175 mL
	Salt and white pepper	

In saucepan, combine onion, parsnips and water; simmer, covered, for 8 to 10 minutes or until parsnips are tender. Purée in blender or food processor and set aside.

In saucepan, melt soft margarine over medium heat; stir in flour and cook for 1 minute. Stir in chicken stock and cook, stirring, until mixture comes to boil and thickens.

Add puréed parsnip mixture, gingerroot, milk, and salt and pepper to taste. Stir to mix well and heat through. Serve hot or cold. (If too thick, thin with more milk or chicken stock.) Makes 5 servings, ⅔ cup/150 mL each.

PER SERVING	
calories	111
g fat	3
mg cholesterol	3
mg sodium	194
g protein	3
g carbohydrate	17
GOOD: fiber, vitamin C	

PER SERVING	
calories	99
g fat	4
mg cholesterol	2
mg sodium	202
g protein	3
g carbohydrate	13
GOOD: vitamin C, niacin	

Harvest Pumpkin and Zucchini Soup

This is a delightful fall soup. If you don't peel the zucchini, the soup will be green in color; if peeled it will be pumpkin-colored. You can use nearly any kind of squash instead of pumpkin. I've even made it using spaghetti squash — it always tastes terrific.

3 cups	peeled, cubed pumpkin or squash	750 mL
3 cups	cubed zucchini	750 mL
2	medium potatoes, peeled and cubed	2
1	large onion, sliced	1
2 cups	chicken stock	500 mL
2 tbsp	vegetable oil	25 mL
2 tbsp	chopped fresh parsley	25 mL
2	cloves garlic, chopped	2
¾ cup	2% milk	175 mL
1 tsp	dried basil (or 2 tbsp/25 mL chopped fresh)	5 mL
	Fresh mint leaves or chopped fresh parsley	

In large saucepan, combine pumpkin, zucchini, potatoes, onion, chicken stock, oil, parsley and garlic. Cover and simmer, stirring occasionally, for 45 minutes or until vegetables are tender. If stock simmers down, add water to reach original level.

In food processor or blender, purée mixture in batches; return to saucepan. Add milk and basil; heat until hot. Garnish each serving with mint leaves. Makes 8 servings, ¾ cup/175 mL each.

Zucchini and Watercress Vichyssoise

This light, elegant, quick-to-prepare soup is perfect for the first course of a dinner party. Serve it hot in the spring when the first crop of watercress appears, or chilled in the summer for a refreshing starter.

1 lb	zucchini (about 4 small), sliced	500 g
1	large potato, peeled and diced	1
1	medium onion, chopped	1
2 cups	chicken stock	500 mL
1 tbsp	lemon juice	15 mL
½ cup	lightly packed watercress leaves	125 mL
1½ cups	2% milk	375 mL
	Salt and freshly ground pepper	

In saucepan, combine zucchini, potato, onion and chicken stock; cover and simmer until vegetables are tender, 15 to 20 minutes.

In food processor or blender, purée hot mixture with lemon juice and watercress until smooth. Stir in milk, salt and pepper to taste; reheat if necessary and serve hot. Alternatively, cover and refrigerate until cold. To serve, thin with additional milk if too thick and garnish with watercress leaves. Makes 8 servings, ¾ cup/175 mL each.

Microwave Method:
In microwave-safe dish, combine zucchini, potato and onion with 2 tbsp/25 mL of the chicken stock. Cover and microwave at high (100% power) until vegetables are tender, 10 to 13 minutes, rotating every few minutes and stirring after 6 minutes.

In food processor or blender, purée mixture until smooth, adding some of the remaining chicken stock if too thick to process. Return to dish and stir in remaining chicken stock, lemon juice, watercress and milk. Add salt and pepper to taste and reheat or serve cold.

Fresh Beet Soup with Yogurt

This beautiful red soup has a wonderful fresh beet taste when made with small, tender beets. I once made the mistake of making it in the winter using large, old beets and it was not as good. (Recipe pictured opposite half-title page.)

2 lb	small beets	1 kg
1 tbsp	soft margarine	15 mL
1	large onion, chopped	1
¼ cup	lemon juice	50 mL
2 tbsp	drained horseradish	25 mL
1	large carrot, grated	1
1 cup	chicken stock	250 mL
⅔ cup	low-fat plain yogurt	150 mL
	Salt and freshly ground pepper	
Garnish:	Yogurt and thin strips or slices lemon or orange rind	

   Wash beets and trim, leaving 1 inch/2.5 cm of the ends attached.

   In large saucepan, cover beets with water and bring to boil; reduce heat and simmer, covered, for 20 to 30 minutes or until tender. Remove beets from saucepan; reserve cooking liquid. When beets are cool enough to handle (or under cold running water), slip off skins and stems. Cut beets in half.

   In large saucepan, melt margarine over medium heat; add onion and cook until tender. Add 3 cups/750 mL reserved cooking liquid, beets, lemon juice, horseradish, carrot and chicken stock; simmer for 5 minutes.

   In blender or food processor, purée mixture in batches and return to saucepan; stir in yogurt. Season with salt and pepper to taste. Reheat over medium-low heat being careful not to boil. Garnish each serving with spoonful of yogurt and strips of orange or lemon rind. Makes 8 servings, ¾ cup/175 mL each.

PER SERVING	
calories	75
g fat	2
mg cholesterol	1
mg sodium	185
g protein	3
g carbohydrate	12

GOOD: fiber, vitamin C
EXCELLENT: vitamin A

Harvest-Dinner Party

Fresh Beet Soup with Yogurt (page 42)
Roasted Red Pepper, Chèvre and Arugula Salad (page 51)
Lamb Tenderloins with Rosemary and Peppercorns (page 78)
Mushroom-Stuffed Zucchini Cups (page 128)
Spaghetti Squash with Parsley and Garlic (page 119)
Peach Crêpes with Easy Grand Marnier Sauce (page 167)

Fresh Tomato Soup Provençal

Fresh herbs add a delightful flavor to this soup. If the herbs called for here aren't available, use other fresh herbs, such as dill instead of basil and oregano instead of thyme. For a lighter soup, omit milk and add a little more chicken stock.

3	large tomatoes, quartered (about 1¼ lb/625 g)	3
1	medium onion, sliced	1
1	clove garlic, chopped	1
1¼ cups	chicken stock	300 mL
2 tbsp	tomato paste	25 mL
¼ cup	chopped fresh parsley	50 mL
¼ cup	chopped fresh basil (or 1 tsp/5 mL dried*)	50 mL
1 tbsp	chopped fresh thyme (or ½ tsp/ 2 mL dried)	15 mL
⅔ cup	2% milk	150 mL
	Salt and freshly ground pepper	
Garnish:	Fresh thyme sprigs or basil leaves	

PER SERVING

calories	50
g fat	1
mg cholesterol	2
mg sodium	182
g protein	3
g carbohydrate	8

GOOD: fiber, vitamin A
EXCELLENT: vitamin C

In saucepan, combine tomatoes, onion, garlic, chicken stock; cover and simmer for 15 minutes.

Transfer to blender or food processor; add tomato paste and process until smooth. Stir in parsley, basil, thyme and milk; season with salt and pepper to taste.

Cover and refrigerate to serve chilled, or reheat over medium heat and serve hot. Garnish each serving with thyme sprigs or basil leaves. Makes 6 servings, ¾ cup/175 mL each.

*A general rule for substituting fresh for dried herbs is to use 3 times the amount of fresh. However, with Tomato Soup Provençal I like a lot more fresh herbs than usual. The amount will also vary depending upon how hard you pack the fresh herbs when measuring.

Split Pea, Bean and Barley Soup

When you want something that is a light yet warming meal, this soup is just right. Serve it with toast or hot French bread and a green salad.

1 tbsp	vegetable oil	15 mL
2	onions, chopped	2
½ cup	dried green split peas	125 mL
¼ cup	dried lima beans	50 mL
¼ cup	barley	50 mL
5 cups	water	1.25 L
1	bay leaf	1
1 tsp	celery seeds	5 mL
1	potato, diced	1
1	carrot, chopped	1
1	stalk celery (including leaves), chopped	1
1 tsp	dried basil	5 mL
1 tsp	salt	5 mL
½ tsp	dried thyme	2 mL
¼ tsp	freshly ground pepper	1 mL

   In large heavy saucepan, heat oil over medium heat; add onions and cook, stirring, until tender.
   Rinse split peas and lima beans, discarding any shrivelled or discolored ones. Add to saucepan along with barley, water, bay leaf and celery seeds. Bring to boil; reduce heat and simmer, covered, for 1½ hours.
   Add potato, carrot, celery, basil, salt, thyme and pepper; simmer for 30 minutes or until vegetables are tender. Remove bay leaf. If too thick, add water to reach desired thickness. Makes 6 servings, 1 cup/250 mL each.

PER SERVING	
calories	154
g fat	3
mg cholesterol	0
mg sodium	401
g protein	6
g carbohydrate	27

GOOD: niacin, iron
EXCELLENT: fiber, vitamin A

Chilled Carrot and Coriander Soup

Be sure to use tender young carrots when making this sweet, flavorful soup. Fresh coriander, also called cilantro, adds a special extra flavor; it's available at most Chinese food stores and many fruit and vegetable stores that sell fresh herbs. Coriander seeds can easily be ground in a coffee or spice grinder. (Recipe pictured opposite half-title page.)

1	onion, chopped	1
1 lb	young carrots, scraped and sliced	500 g
1 tsp	ground coriander	5 mL
3½ cups	chicken stock	875 mL
¼ cup	chopped fresh coriander leaves or parsley	50 mL
	Salt and freshly ground pepper	
Garnish:	Yogurt or sour cream, sunflower seeds, coriander leaves or parsley	

PER SERVING

calories	58
g fat	1
mg cholesterol	0
mg sodium	482
g protein	4
g carbohydrate	9

GOOD: fiber, niacin
EXCELLENT; vitamin A

In saucepan, combine onion, carrots, ground coriander and chicken stock; cover and simmer until vegetables are tender, 15 to 20 minutes.

In food processor or blender, purée mixture until smooth. Stir in fresh coriander. Add salt and pepper to taste. Serve hot, or cover and refrigerate until cold.

Garnish each serving with spoonful of yogurt or sour cream, sprinkling of sunflower seeds and chopped fresh coriander leaves or parsley. Makes 6 servings, ¾ cup/175 mL each.

Microwave Method:
In microwave-safe dish, combine onion, carrots, ground coriander and 2 tbsp/25 mL chicken stock. Cover and microwave at high (100%) power for 8 to 12 minutes or until carrots are tender. (Time will vary depending on thickness of slices and age of carrots.)

In food processor or blender, purée mixture until smooth. Stir in fresh coriander and remaining chicken stock; season with salt and pepper to taste. Reheat or refrigerate until cold.

PER 1 cup/250 mL SERVING	
calories	3
g fat	0
mg cholesterol	3
mg sodium	4
g protein	0
g carbohydrate	0

Basic Chicken Stock

As well as its much better flavor, the main reason for recommending homemade chicken stock is its low salt content. If you're not in the habit of making chicken stock, it can seem very time-consuming. Once you start making it you'll realize how easy it is. Any pieces of chicken can be used, even a whole chicken (giblets removed). Backs and necks are least expensive.

4 lb	chicken, whole or pieces	2 kg
12 cups	cold water	3 L
2	carrots, chopped	2
2	onions, chopped	2
2	stalks celery, chopped	2
2	bay leaves	2
6	black peppercorns	6
2	sprigs fresh thyme (or pinch each dried thyme, basil and marjoram)	2

In stockpot, combine chicken and water; bring to boil. Skim off any scum. Add carrots, onions, celery, bay leaves, peppercorns and thyme; simmer, uncovered, for 4 hours.

Remove from heat and strain; cover and refrigerate stock until any fat congeals on surface. Remove fat layer. Refrigerate for up to 2 days or freeze for longer storage. Makes about 8 cups/2 L.

Compare	mg sodium* per 1 cup/250 mL
This recipe	4
Canned chicken broth	746
Chicken broth from cube	762

When Making Stock

After chicken is cooked, remove meat from bones and use in salads (see Tarragon Chicken Salad, page 47), Curried Chicken Crêpes (page 85), Curried Chicken Croustades (page 29), sandwiches or add to soups.

Freeze homemade chicken stock in ice-cube trays or ½-cup/125 mL containers and use in cooking whenever you want extra flavor without added salt. Use in soups, salad dressings, sauces, stir-frys.

Variations
Turkey Stock:
Use turkey bones or carcass instead of chicken.
Beef, Veal or Lamb Stock:
Use beef, veal or lamb bones instead of chicken. For added flavor, roast bones before simmering in water. Spread bones in roasting pan and bake in 400°F/200°C oven for 1 hour or until browned; transfer to stock-pot and continue as in Basic Chicken Stock recipe.

*Sodium values are based on using stock made from a cube or powder or canned. If using homemade chicken stock, sodium falls to 47 mg per serving.

SALADS AND DRESSINGS

My favorite salads are so simple that they hardly qualify as recipes. I love thick slices of juicy tomatoes sprinkled with fresh basil, coarsely ground pepper and a tiny drizzle of olive oil. Another favorite is fresh, tender spinach leaves, sliced mushroom and balsamic vinegar, or Boston lettuce and Walnut Oil Vinaigrette.

Salad dressings are easy to make. Homemade dressings taste much better, and are less expensive and often healthier than store-bought. Commercial salad dressings tend to be high in calories and sodium, while low-calorie dressings still have a significant amount of sodium. Both are generally made of poorer-quality fats and oils.

For salad dressings I usually use safflower oil or olive oil or a combination of both. For a special green salad I love to add some walnut oil. See page 217 for more information on oils.

Tarragon Chicken Salad

This light and easy-to-make salad is lovely for a special lunch or dinner on a hot summer day. Serve on lettuce or with a green salad and chilled cooked asparagus or sliced tomatoes. Cook chicken in microwave or simmer in water and use liquid for stock (see Basic Chicken Stock recipe page 46).

3 cups	cooked cubed chicken	750 mL
1½ cups	sliced celery	375 mL
¼ cup	chopped chives or green onions	50 mL
½ cup	low-fat plain yogurt	125 mL
¼ cup	light sour cream or light mayonnaise	50 mL
1½ tsp	dried tarragon	7 mL
2 tbsp	toasted* slivered almonds	25 mL
	Salt and freshly ground pepper	

In large bowl, combine chicken, celery, chives or onions, yogurt, sour cream or mayonnaise and tarragon; mix lightly. Cover and refrigerate for 1 hour or up to 24 hours. Just before serving, add almonds; season with salt and pepper to taste. Makes 6 servings.

Chicken Salad Sandwich Deluxe
Spread Tarragon Chicken Salad on pumpernickel, a bagel, or toasted Italian bread. Add any combination of alfalfa sprouts or watercress or leaf lettuce and sliced tomato. Serve open-faced or top with bread.

PER SERVING	
calories	170
g fat	8
mg cholesterol	61
mg sodium	91
g protein	21
g carbohydrate	4
EXCELLENT: niacin	

*To toast almonds, roast on pie plate in 350°F/180°C oven for 5 minutes or until golden.

When Making Salads or Choosing from a Salad Bar

High-fat foods to avoid or choose less of:
–most important is salad dressing—don't use any more than absolutely necessary
–avocado
–bacon bits
–olives
–high-fat cheese* (cheddar, blue cheese)
–nuts

High-sodium foods to avoid or choose less of:
–anchovies
–olives
–salted or prepared croutons
–bacon bits

High-cholesterol foods to avoid or choose less of:
–egg yolks*
*If salad is the main course, a certain amount of protein foods, such as cheese and egg, is acceptable.

PER SERVING	
calories	107
g fat	4
mg cholesterol	0
mg sodium	10
g protein	5
g carbohydrate	15

GOOD: vitamin C, iron
EXCELLENT: fiber

Red kidney beans or chickpeas can be used instead of white kidney beans. All are an excellent source of fiber.

   Remember this salad when you are making packed lunches. It will be a welcome change from sandwiches.

White Bean, Radish and Red Onion Salad

This looks attractive on red leaf lettuce. It goes well on a summer salad plate, a buffet dinner, or with barbecued hamburgers and lamb chops.

1	can (19 oz/540 mL) white kidney beans, drained	1
½ cup	red onion, chopped	125 mL
1 cup	thinly sliced or diced cucumber	250 mL
¾ cup	sliced radishes	175 mL
1	clove garlic, minced	1
½ cup	chopped fresh parsley	125 mL
3 tbsp	lemon juice or sherry vinegar	45 mL
2 tbsp	vegetable oil	25 mL
	Salt and freshly ground pepper	
	Red leaf lettuce	

   In sieve or colander, rinse beans under cold water; drain and place in salad bowl. Add onion, cucumber, radishes, garlic and parsley; toss to mix. Add lemon juice and oil, salt and pepper to taste; toss. Salad can be prepared to this point, covered and refrigerated for up to 2 days.

   At serving time, arrange salad on bed of red lettuce. Makes 8 servings, ½ cup/125 mL each.

Compare	per serving		
Tarragon Chicken Salad made with:	g fat	mg sodium	calories
Yogurt (½ cup/125 mL) plus sour cream (¼ cup/50 mL)	8	91	170
Sour cream (¾ cup/ 175 mL)	10	85	186
Mayonnaise (¾ cup/ 175 mL)	27	207	331

Snow Pea and Red Pepper Buffet Salad

This colorful dish is perfect for buffet meals any time of year. The salad can be prepared in advance; however to keep the snow peas' bright green color, add the dressing just before serving. To make a larger amount double salad ingredients but use same amount of dressing. (Recipe pictured opposite page 54.)

¾ lb	snow peas	375 g
2 tbsp	sesame seeds	25 mL
½ lb	mushrooms, sliced	250 g
1	small sweet red pepper, cut in thin strips	1

Walnut Orange Dressing:

1	clove garlic, minced	1
½ cup	orange juice	125 mL
3 tbsp	cider or white wine vinegar	45 mL
1 tsp	granulated sugar	5 mL
¼ tsp	salt	1 mL
2 tbsp	vegetable or walnut oil	25 mL
	Freshly ground pepper	

Top and string peas; blanch in boiling water for 2 minutes or until bright green and slightly pliable. Drain and rinse under cold water; dry thoroughly and set aside.

In ungreased skillet over medium heat, cook sesame seeds, shaking pan often, for 2 minutes or until lightly browned. Set aside.

Dressing: In food processor or bowl, combine garlic, orange juice, vinegar, sugar and salt. With machine running or while mixing, gradually add oil.

In salad bowl, combine snow peas, mushrooms and red pepper. Just before serving, add dressing and sesame seeds; toss to mix. Makes 8 servings.

PER SERVING

calories	80
g fat	5
mg cholesterol	0
mg sodium	70
g protein	3
g carbohydrate	8

GOOD: fiber, niacin
EXCELLENT: vitamin C

Nut oils, such as walnut oil, add a delicious flavor to salads. Use with tossed green salads or as suggested in the Snow Pea and Red Pepper Buffet Salad. Store walnut oil in refrigerator and use within a few months, as it can become rancid.

PER SERVING	
calories	86
g fat	5
mg cholesterol	21
mg sodium	275
g protein	10
g carbohydrate	1
EXCELLENT: niacin	

*If you only have tuna packed in oil, drain thoroughly and add more yogurt to taste.

Tuna Fish
When buying canned tuna fish, choose tuna packed in water rather than tuna packed in oil because it is lower in fat. Both kinds have the same amount of omega 3 fatty acids from fish oils. (The oil tuna is packed in is not usually from fish oils.)

Hidden Fat in Salad Dressings
The fat content in salads comes mainly from the oil in the dressing and can be very deceptive. The amount of oil in the Tomato, Broccoli and Pasta Salad (page 110) is at least half the amount that you would find in most salad recipes of this type. And, even with a reduced amount of oil and a small amount of low-fat cheese the fat content is higher than some of the meat, chicken and fish recipes in this book. A tossed green salad with 2 tbsp/25 mL of a standard oil-and-vinegar dressing per serving has 20 g of fat. This is ⅓ of the fat most women require in a day.

Classic Tuna Salad with Fresh Dill

Use this easy-to-make tuna salad as part of a summer salad plate — served, perhaps, in a hollowed-out tomato or papaya half — for sandwich fillings, or as an hors d'oeuvre when stuffed in cherry tomatoes, mushrooms or hollowed-out cucumber rounds.

1	can (6.5 oz/184 g) tuna, packed in water	1
¼ cup	diced celery	50 mL
¼ cup	chopped fresh dill	50 mL
2 tbsp	chopped fresh parsley	25 mL
2 tbsp	chopped chives or green onions	25 mL
2 tbsp	light mayonnaise	25 mL
2 tbsp	low-fat plain yogurt	25 mL
½ tsp	Dijon mustard	2 mL

In bowl, mash tuna with juices.* Add celery, dill, parsley, chives, mayonnaise, yogurt and mustard; mix well. Makes 5 servings, ¼ cup/50 mL each.

Alfresco Summer Supper (22% of calories are from fat)

per serving	g fat	calories
Chilled Cucumber-Chive Soup (page 35)	4	85
Pasta and Fresh Vegetable Salad (page 61)	6	165
Sliced cold chicken breast (no skin) (4 oz/125 g)	4	187
Whole-wheat rolls	2	156
(1 tsp/5 mL margarine	4	33
Sliced peaches and blueberries	0	90
Milk (skim, 8 oz/250 mL)	0	90
Totals	20	806
Calories from fat = 22%		

Roasted Red Pepper, Chèvre and Arugula Salad

In the summer and early fall, look for locally grown arugula (out of season it is very expensive). This oak-leaf-shaped salad green, with its nutty, peppery taste, is a delicious addition to any tossed salad. If not available, use red or green leaf lettuce and/or radicchio. Buy a soft chèvre or goat cheese, or substitute feta cheese.

1	sweet red pepper	1
4 cups	arugula leaves, not packed	1 L
1	small head Boston lettuce, torn	1
1½ oz	chèvre, crumbled	40 g
¼ cup	Ranch-Style Buttermilk Dressing (page 65) or Mustard-Garlic Vinaigrette (page 64)	50 mL
	Freshly ground pepper	

On baking sheet, bake red pepper in 400°F/200°C oven for 20 to 30 minutes, turning once or twice, or until pepper is soft and skin is blackened and blistered (or barbecue until skin is blistered). Place in plastic bag; seal and let pepper steam for 10 minutes. Scrape skin from peppers; discard seeds and cut pepper into about 1-in/2.5 cm-long, thin strips.

In salad bowl, toss together red pepper, arugula, Boston lettuce, chèvre, and dressing; season with pepper to taste. Makes 5 servings.

(Made with Ranch-Style Buttermilk Dressing)		(Made with Mustard-Garlic Vinaigrette)	
PER SERVING		PER SERVING	
calories	52	calories	76
g fat	3	g fat	6
mg cholesterol	10	mg cholesterol	10
mg sodium	142	mg sodium	117
g protein	3	g protein	3
g carbohydrate	4	g carbohydrate	4
GOOD: vitamin A EXCELLENT: vitamin C			

Sliced Cucumbers with Chives, Yogurt and Basil

Serve this cooling salad with curries, paella, seafood or as part of a salad plate or buffet any time of year. If chives aren't available, substitute green onions, and fresh chopped dill can be used instead of basil.

1	English cucumber	1
¼ tsp	salt	1 mL
¼ cup	light sour cream	50 mL
¼ cup	plain low-fat yogurt	50 mL
2 tbsp	chopped chives	25 mL
2 tsp	lemon juice	10 mL
1 tbsp	chopped fresh basil (or ¼ tsp/1 mL dried)	15 mL
¼ tsp	granulated sugar	1 mL
	Freshly ground pepper	

PER SERVING	
calories	33
g fat	2
mg cholesterol	4
mg sodium	101
g protein	1
g carbohydrate	4

Peel cucumbers only if skin is tough or waxy. In food processor or by hand, thinly slice cucumbers. Place in colander and sprinkle with salt. Toss then let stand for 30 to 40 minutes. Rinse under cold water, then pat dry.

In bowl, combine sour cream, yogurt, chives, lemon juice, basil and sugar; mix well. Stir in cucumber; season with pepper to taste.

Serve in shallow bowl or on plate. Makes 6 servings, ½ cup/ 125 mL each.

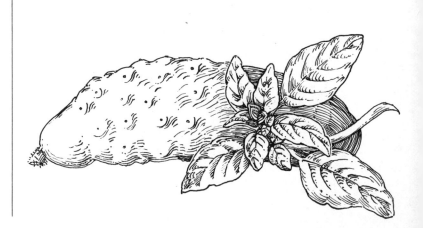

Curried Rice Salad
Prepare Italian Rice Salad but substitute 1 tsp (5 mL) each curry powder and cumin for thyme, basil and oregano. Add more curry to taste.

Picnic at the Beach or on the Boat

Sliced roast beef
Italian Rice and Mozzarella Salad with Vegetables (page 53)
Old-Fashioned Pickled Beets (page 142)
Whole-wheat buns
Nectarines
Easy Oat Bran and Date Cookies (page 154)

PER SERVING	
calories	187
g fat	7
mg cholesterol	8
mg sodium	97
g protein	5
g carbohydrate	25
GOOD: vitamin A, vitamin C, niacin	

Italian Rice and Mozzarella Salad with Vegetables

This is a handy salad to have on hand for quick summer meals and is a great way to use up leftover cooked rice; use brown rice if you have it. It's not necessary to follow this recipe exactly; rather, use it as a guide and add whatever vegetables or cooked meats you have on hand. Chopped zucchini, cauliflower or artichokes are nice additions. (Recipe pictured opposite page 54.)

3 cups	cooked rice	750 mL
¼ cup	diced carrots	50 mL
¼ cup	diced celery	50 mL
¼ cup	diced sweet red or green pepper	50 mL
½ cup	frozen green peas	125 mL
¼ cup	chopped red onion	50 mL
¼ cup	chopped fresh parsley	50 mL
¼ cup	diced low-fat cheese (e.g., mozzarella)	50 mL
3 tbsp	cider vinegar	45 mL
2 tbsp	olive or vegetable oil	25 mL
2 tbsp	orange juice	25 mL
1 tbsp	light mayonnaise	15 mL
¼ tsp	dried thyme (or 1 tsp/5 mL fresh)	1 mL
¼ tsp	dried basil (or 1 tsp/5 mL fresh)	1 mL
¼ tsp	dried oregano (or 1 tsp/5 mL fresh)	1 mL
	Freshly ground pepper	

In salad bowl, combine rice, carrots, celery, sweet pepper, peas, onion, parsley and cheese; set aside. In small bowl, combine vinegar, oil, orange juice, mayonnaise, thyme, basil and oregano; mix well. Pour over salad and toss to mix. Season with pepper to taste. Makes 4 cups/1 L, about 6 servings.

PER SERVING	
calories	30
g fat	2
mg cholesterol	0
mg sodium	13
g protein	1
g carbohydrate	3
GOOD: vitamin C	

Seasonal Salad Additions
Winter:
Cherry tomatoes, sections of
orange or grapefruit, sliced
green apples, alfalfa or radish
sprouts, sunflower seeds
Spring:
Blanched and drained
fiddleheads, blanched
asparagus, chives, watercress
Summer:
Radish, cucumber, tomato,
green onions, fresh basil —
parsley, rose or geranium
petals
Fall:
Red, green or yellow sweet
peppers, cauliflower, broccoli,
radicchio
Nutrition Note
The darker the green in
lettuce, the higher the vitamins
A and C content.
Choose spinach more often
than lettuce for salads; it is
higher in nutrients, particularly
vitamins A and C, iron and
fiber.

Photo:
Snow Pea and Red Pepper
Buffet Salad (page 49), Carrot
and Cracked-Wheat Salad with
Yogurt-Herb Dressing (page
56), Italian Rice and
Mozzarella Salad with
Vegetables (page 53), Shell
Pasta Salad with Salmon and
Green Beans (page 59)

Tossed Seasonal Greens

The best green salads are made up of an interesting and colorful variety of lettuces combined with a delicious dressing. Choose whatever lettuces are freshest in the market — leaf lettuce (red or green), Boston or butter or Bibb, mâche, endive, radicchio, or spinach and Belgian endive. Add watercress or a seasonal fruit or vegetable, such as the suggestions on the side of this page.

1	small head red leaf lettuce	1
1	small butter lettuce or romaine	1
1	red onion, thinly sliced	1

Herb Vinaigrette:

1	clove garlic, minced	1
2 tbsp	tarragon or white wine vinegar	25 mL
1 tsp	Dijon mustard	5 mL
1 tbsp	olive or walnut oil	15 mL
¼ cup	water, orange juice, unsweetened pineapple juice or chicken stock	50 mL
1	green onion, minced	1
¼ cup	chopped fresh parsley	50 mL

Wash lettuce leaves; spin dry or dry in paper or tea towels. Wrap in paper towels and refrigerate until needed.

Herb Vinaigrette: In food processor, blender or bowl, combine garlic, vinegar, mustard, oil and water; mix well. Stir in onion and parsley.

Just before serving, tear lettuce into pieces and place in salad bowl. Separate red onion into rings; add to bowl. (Add any other seasonal salad ingredients if using.) Drizzle with dressing and toss to mix. Makes 8 servings.

Compare: One way to reduce the fat in a salad dressing is to substitute another liquid for part of the oil. For example, in the Tossed Seasonal Greens with Herb Vinaigrette there is only 1 tbsp oil (15/mL) and ¼ cup/50 mL water or stock or fruit juice.

per serving	g fat	calories
This recipe	2	30
Seasonal greens using dressing made with ⅓ cup/75 mL oil	9	93

Spinach Salad with Sesame Seed Dressing

Bright red strawberries are beautiful in this entertaining salad. In winter, use mandarin oranges, grapefruit sections or sliced green apple instead of strawberries.

1 lb	spinach	500 g
⅓ cup	sliced almonds	75 mL
2 cups	firm strawberries, sliced	500 mL

Sesame Seed Dressing:

1 tbsp	sesame seeds	15 mL
¼ cup	cider vinegar	50 mL
3 tbsp	vegetable or walnut oil	45 mL
3 tbsp	water	45 mL
1 tbsp	granulated sugar	15 mL
1 tsp	poppy seeds	5 mL
¼ tsp	paprika	1 mL
¼ tsp	Worcestershire sauce	1 mL
1	green onion, minced	1

Trim, wash and dry spinach; tear into bite-size pieces (you should have about 10 cups 2.5 L, lightly packed). Place in salad bowl and set aside.

Sprinkle almonds on baking sheet and roast in 350°F/180°C oven for 5 minutes or until golden brown; set aside.

Sesame Seed Dressing: Place sesame seeds in ungreased skillet, stir over medium-high heat until lightly browned. In bowl or jar, combine sesame seeds, vinegar, oil, water, sugar, poppy seeds, paprika, Worcestershire and green onion; mix well.

Just before serving, pour dressing over spinach and toss well to coat. Add strawberries and almonds; toss lightly. Makes 10 servings.

PER SERVING	
calories	93
g fat	7
mg cholesterol	0
mg sodium	39
g protein	3
g carbohydrate	6

GOOD: fiber, iron
EXCELLENT: vitamin A, vitamin C

Photo:
Warm Vegetable Salad with Tomato-Shallot Dressing (page 28)

For a Main-Course Salad
Add to the platter slices of chicken, either Classic Tuna Salad with Fresh Dill (page 50), or strips of low-fat cheese. To complete it, choose from what you have on hand—such as florets of broccoli or cauliflower.

To Cook Bulgur or Cracked Wheat
In saucepan combine with twice as much water and simmer for 15 to 20 minutes or until tender but not mushy.

To serve as a vegetable add seasonings such as salt, pepper, lemon juice, herbs or vegetables.

To use in salads drain well, cool and combine with dressing and chopped vegetables.

To use in stuffings combine with onion and herbs, such as sage and thyme.

PER SERVING	
calories	152
g fat	5
mg cholesterol	13
mg sodium	69
g protein	6
g carbohydrate	22
GOOD: fiber, vitamin C EXCELLENT: vitamin A	

Carrot and Cracked-Wheat Salad with Yogurt-Herb Dressing

Bulgur or cracked wheat, available at some supermarkets and most health food stores, is a nutty-tasting grain that is delicious in salads or as a vegetable. It's a good source of fiber. Save any leftover dressing and use as a dip with vegetables or as a sauce with fish. (Recipe pictured opposite page 54.)

½ cup	bulgur or cracked wheat	125 mL
½ cup	chopped green onions	125 mL
½ cup	chopped celery	125 mL
½ cup	grated carrot	125 mL
	Salt and freshly ground pepper	
½	head Boston or romaine lettuce	½
Garnish:	Sliced tomatoes, cucumber, mushrooms and radishes, chopped fresh parsley	

Yogurt-Herb Dressing:

½ cup	low-fat plain yogurt	125 mL
½ cup	light sour cream	125 mL
1 tsp	Dijon mustard	5 mL
1 tsp	each dried oregano and basil (or 2 tbsp/25 mL chopped fresh)	5 mL
	Salt and freshly ground pepper	

In bowl, cover bulgur with very hot water. Let stand for 1 hour; drain well. Add green onions, celery, and carrot.

Yogurt-Herb Dressing: Combine yogurt, sour cream, mustard, oregano, basil, salt and pepper to taste; mix well. Pour just enough dressing over bulgur mixture to moisten, reserving remaining dressing; toss to mix. Cover and refrigerate for at least 1 hour or up to 2 days.

Just before serving, toss salad again; add salt and pepper to taste. On large platter, arrange lettuce leaves. Mound bulgur salad in center.

Garnish: Surround salad with slices of tomato, cucumber, mushrooms and radishes; sprinkle with parsley. Pass extra dressing separately. Makes 4 large servings.

Danish Potato Salad with Dill

Dijon mustard and fresh dill add extra flavor to this summer salad. If fresh dill isn't available, use 1 tsp/5 mL dried dillweed and ½ cup/125 mL chopped fresh parsley.

2 lb	potatoes	1 kg
1 cup	low-fat plain yogurt	250 mL
3 tbsp	light mayonnaise	45 mL
¼ cup	minced green onion	50 mL
1 tsp	curry powder	5 mL
1 tsp	Dijon mustard	5 mL
½ tsp	salt	2 mL
⅓ cup	chopped fresh dill	75 mL
	Freshly ground pepper	
Garnish:	Watercress (optional)	

Wash potatoes and cook in large pot of boiling water until tender. Drain and let cool slightly; peel only if skins are tough and cut into thin slices.

In bowl, mix together yogurt, mayonnaise, onion, curry powder, mustard and salt. Add potatoes, dill, and pepper to taste; stir gently. Garnish each serving with watercress (if using). Makes 6 servings, ¾ cup/175 mL each.

PER SERVING

calories	169
g fat	4
mg cholesterol	6
mg sodium	225
g protein	5
g carbohydrate	31

GOOD: fiber, niacin
EXCELLENT: vitamin C

Potatoes, including skin, are a good source of fiber. Without the skin the amount of fiber is reduced by half.

Compare	per ¾ cup/175 mL serving			
Salad made with:	g fat	mg cholesterol	mg sodium	calories
Low-fat plain yogurt (plus 3 tbsp/ 45 mL light mayonnaise)	4	6	291	169
Light mayonnaise	16	25	631	269
Mayonnaise	33	24	407	420

Curried Vermicelli Noodle Salad

Pastel restaurants in Vancouver are known for their top-quality, healthy food, and this is one of their most popular salads. It's easy to prepare, especially in large quantities, and is perfect for buffets or hot-weather dining.

½ lb	vermicelli noodles*	250 g
½ cup	pine nuts	125 mL
1 cup	coarsely chopped fresh parsley	250 mL

Curry Dressing:

1 cup	pearl onions	250 mL
¼ cup	olive oil	50 mL
2 tsp	curry powder	10 mL
1½ tsp	ground coriander	7 mL
½ tsp	ground cardamom	2 mL
¼ tsp	turmeric	1 mL
½ tsp	minced garlic	2 mL
1½ cups	beef or chicken stock	375 mL
½ cup	golden raisins	125 mL

PER SERVING	
calories	200
g fat	10
mg cholesterol	0
mg sodium	117
g protein	6
g carbohydrate	25
GOOD: fiber, vitamin C, niacin, iron	

*Vermicelli, very thin noodles, are available in the pasta section of most supermarkets. I prefer rice vermicelli, sometimes called rice sticks, which are clear, very thin noodles often sold in the Chinese food section of the supermarket. If unavailable, use 4 cups/1 L cooked thin noodles.

In large pot of boiling water, cook vermicelli according to package directions or for 3 to 5 minutes, just until al dente (tender but firm). Don't overcook, because noodles become mushy. Rinse under cold water; drain well and set aside.

On a pie plate, bake pine nuts in 350°F/180°C oven for 5 minutes or until golden. Set aside.

Curry dressing: In saucepan of boiling water, blanch pearl onions for 3 minutes; drain. Let cool slightly, then peel.

In saucepan, heat oil over medium heat. Add curry powder, coriander, cardamom and turmeric; cook for 3 minutes, stirring occasionally. Add garlic, pearl onions, stock and raisins. Simmer for 5 minutes or until onions are tender. Remove from heat and let cool.

Toss noodles with dressing. (Salad can be covered and refrigerated for up to 1 day.) Just before serving, add pine nuts and parsley; toss well. Makes 10 servings.

Salmon is an excellent source
of omega 3 polyunsaturated
fatty acids, which some studies
have found help to lower
blood pressure and to reduce
the risk of heart disease.

PER SERVING	
calories	230
g fat	7
mg cholesterol	21
mg sodium	75
g protein	17
g carbohydrate	23
GOOD: iron	
EXCELLENT: niacin	

Shell Pasta Salad with Salmon and Green Beans

This is one of my favorite pasta salads. Fresh dill adds a
wonderful flavor, but if not available, use fresh basil to taste. In
a pinch, use 1 tsp/5 mL dried basil or dill plus ½ cup/125 mL
finely chopped fresh parsley. (Recipe opposite page 54.)

½ lb	small pasta shells or macaroni	250 g
¼ lb	green beans	125 g
¼ cup	low-fat cottage cheese	50 mL
¼ cup	low-fat plain yogurt	50 mL
1 tbsp	fresh lemon juice	15 mL
½ cup	coarsely chopped fresh dill	125 mL
2	cans (7.75 oz/220 g) salmon, drained	2
	Freshly ground pepper	
	Boston or red leaf lettuce	

In large pot of boiling water, cook pasta until al dente (tender
but firm). Drain and rinse under cold water; drain again and set
aside.

Cut green beans into 1½-in/4 cm lengths and blanch in
boiling water for 2 minutes. Drain and rinse under cold water;
drain thoroughly and set aside.

In food processor or through sieve, purée cottage cheese.
Combine with yogurt and lemon juice; mix well.

In bowl, combine pasta, green beans, yogurt mixture and dill;
stir to mix. Discard skin from salmon and break into chunks;
add to salad and stir gently to mix. Add pepper to taste. Line
serving plates with lettuce leaves and mound salad on top.
Makes 8 servings.

Tortellini with Tuna Salad

Pasta salads are great for lunch, picnics, buffets and light suppers. You don't really need a recipe; just add any of the usual salad ingredients, such as cooked or raw vegetables, (except for lettuces) to cooked noodles or any type of pasta and toss with a dressing.

¾ lb	tortellini	375 g
1 cup	frozen peas	250 mL
½	sweet red pepper, diced	½
½ cup	chopped red onion	125 mL
1	can (6.5 oz/184 g) tuna, packed in water, drained	1
1	can (14 oz/398 mL) artichokes, drained and quartered (optional)	1
½ cup	chopped fresh parsley	125 mL
¼ cup	chopped fresh basil (or 2 tsp/ 10 mL dried)	50 mL

Dressing:

1	clove garlic, minced	1
1 tsp	Dijon mustard	5 mL
3 tbsp	lemon juice or white wine vinegar	45 mL
¼ cup	orange juice	50 mL
3 tbsp	olive oil	45 mL
¼ cup	low-fat plain yogurt	50 mL
¼ cup	finely chopped fresh basil	50 mL
	Salt and freshly ground pepper	

In large pot of boiling water, cook tortellini until al dente (tender but firm); drain and rinse under cold water. Drain thoroughly. Thaw peas under cold water.

In salad bowl, combine pasta, peas, sweet pepper, onion, tuna, artichokes (if using), parsley and basil; toss lightly to mix.

Dressing: In blender, food processor or bowl, combine garlic, mustard, lemon and orange juice; mix well. With machine running or while mixing, gradually add oil. Add yogurt, basil, and salt and pepper to taste; mix. Pour over salad and toss to mix. Cover and refrigerate for up to 2 days. Makes 8 servings, ¾ cup/175 mL each.

PER SERVING

calories	278
g fat	6
mg cholesterol	13
mg sodium	172
g protein	16
g carbohydrate	40

GOOD: fiber, iron
EXCELLENT: vitamin C, niacin

Grated Carrot and Green Pea Salad   For a quick, easy high-fiber salad combine cooked frozen green peas, grated carrot, diced celery, chopped green onion and fresh parsley. Mix equal parts of light sour cream and yogurt, add ½ tsp/ 2 mL or more Dijon mustard, and freshly ground pepper to taste; mix lightly with carrot mixture.

Sliced water chestnuts or artichoke hearts are good additions.

Green peas—fresh, frozen or canned are an excellent source of dietary fiber. Add them to soups, salads, stir-frys and pasta dishes.

Pasta and Fresh Vegetable Salad

This is the kind of salad I often make during the summer using whatever vegetables I have on hand. It's great with cold meats, salmon or tuna salad, poached fish, or chicken and sliced tomatoes. It keeps well for a few days in the refrigerator and is fine for lunches or picnics.

½ lb	macaroni or rotini or any pasta (about 3 cups/750 mL)	250 g
1	sweet green pepper, chopped	1
4	small carrots, thinly sliced	4
4	green onions, chopped	4
6	radishes, sliced	6
½	head cauliflower, cut in small florets	½
1 cup	chopped fresh parsley	250 mL

Italian Vinaigrette Dressing:

¼ cup	cider or tarragon vinegar	50 mL
¼ cup	vegetable oil	50 mL
¼ cup	orange juice	50 mL
2 tsp	Dijon mustard	10 mL
1 tbsp	grated Parmesan cheese	15 mL
1	clove garlic, minced	1
1 tsp	each dried basil and oregano	5 mL
¼ tsp	salt	1 mL
¼ tsp	freshly ground pepper	1 mL

PER SERVING	
calories	165
g fat	6
mg cholesterol	0
mg sodium	77
g protein	5
g carbohydrate	24

EXCELLENT: vitamin A, vitamin C, fiber

In large pot of boiling water, cook pasta until al dente (tender but firm). Drain and rinse under cold water; drain thoroughly.

In large bowl, combine cooked pasta, green pepper, carrots, onions, radishes, cauliflower and parsley.

Italian Vinaigrette Dressing: In bowl or food processor, combine vinegar, oil, orange juice, mustard, cheese, garlic, basil, oregano, salt and pepper; mix well. Pour over salad and toss to mix. Cover and refrigerate for up to 2 days. Makes 10 servings.

When cooking pasta for dinner, cook extra to use another day in a salad. Rinse cooked pasta under cold water to prevent it sticking together. About 12 oz/375 g uncooked fettuccine is five cups/1.25 L cooked.

Before the Concert Light Supper

Fettuccine and Mussel Salad (page 62)

Sliced tomatoes with fresh basil
Flatbread Crackers (page 159)
Fresh strawberries

PER SERVING	
calories	308
g fat	8
mg cholesterol	25
mg sodium	178
g protein	15
g carbohydrate	43

GOOD: iron
EXCELLENT: fiber, vitamin C, niacin

For other salad recipes see

Beets Vinaigrette, Old-Fashioned Pickled Beets (page 142)
Tomato, Broccoli and Pasta Salad (page 110)
Warm Vegetable Salad with Tomato-Shallot Dressing (page 28)

Fettuccine and Mussel Salad

This easy-to-make salad is delicious with any kind of cooked pasta, from linguine to spaghetti noodles to shells. Serve as a first course or with soup for a light dinner or as part of a buffet supper.

¾ lb	fettuccine	375 g
3 lb	mussels	1.5 kg
¼ cup	water	50 mL
1½ cups	frozen peas, thawed	375 mL
1	sweet red or green pepper, chopped	1
4	green onions, chopped	4
1 cup	chopped fresh parsley	250 mL
¼ cup	lemon juice	50 mL
¼ cup	vegetable or olive oil	50 mL
2	cloves garlic, minced	2
	Salt and freshly ground pepper	

In large pot of boiling water, cook fettuccine until al dente (tender but firm). Drain and rinse under cold water; drain thoroughly and set aside. You should have about 5 cups/1.25 L.

Scrub mussels under cold running water and remove any hairy beards. Discard any that do not close when tapped. In large heavy saucepan, combine water and mussels. Cover and bring to boil over high heat; reduce heat and simmer for 5 to 8 minutes or until mussels open. Discard any that do not open. Let cool; reserve ½ cup/125 mL cooking liquid and remove meat from shells.

In large salad bowl, combine fettuccine, mussels, peas, sweet pepper, green onions and parsley.

In small bowl or food processor, combine reserved mussel cooking liquid, lemon juice, oil and garlic; mix well. Pour over pasta mixture and toss to mix. Season with salt and pepper to taste. Cover and refrigerate until chilled. Makes 8 servings.

Ways to Reduce Fat in Salad Dressings
Oil-based dressing:
Replace half of the oil you usually use with water, fruit juice or chicken stock.
Mayonnaise-based dressing:
Use light mayonnaise and replace half of the mayonnaise with low-fat plain yogurt, or light sour cream.

Fresh Tomato-Chive Dressing

This light dressing is particularly good on appetizer salads or spooned over cold cooked vegetables. In order to get the most fiber, don't peel or seed tomatoes. If you prepare the dressing in advance, add cheese just before serving.

2	medium tomatoes, diced	2
2 tbsp	cider or white wine vinegar	25 mL
2 tbsp	vegetable oil	25 mL
2 tsp	Dijon mustard	10 mL
1	clove garlic, minced (optional)	1
3 tbsp	chopped chives or green onion	50 mL
	Freshly ground pepper	
¼ cup	crumbled feta cheese	50 mL

In small bowl, combine tomatoes, vinegar, oil, mustard, garlic (if using), chives, and pepper to taste; mix well. Cover and refrigerate for up to 3 days. Just before serving, stir in cheese. Makes 2 cups/500 mL.

PER 1-tbsp/15 mL	
calories	12
g fat	1
mg cholesterol	1
mg sodium	17
g protein	0
g carbohydrate	0

Mustard-Garlic Vinaigrette

By adding water to reduce the fat and mustard and garlic to increase the flavor we have a lower-calorie, yet flavorful, dressing.

1	clove garlic, minced	1
2 tsp	Dijon mustard	10 mL
2 tbsp	lemon juice	25 mL
¼ cup	water	50 mL
½ tsp	granulated sugar	2 mL
¼ cup	vegetable oil	50 mL
1 tsp	grated Parmesan cheese	5 mL
	Freshly ground pepper	

In blender, food processor or mixing bowl, combine garlic, mustard, lemon juice, water and sugar; mix well. With machine running or while mixing, gradually add oil. Add Parmesan; season with pepper to taste. Makes about ⅔ cup/150 mL.

Compare

per tbsp/15 mL	g fat	calories
This recipe	5	50
Standard vinaigrette recipe (4 parts oil; 1 part vinegar)	10	95

PER 1-tbsp/15 mL SERVING

calories	50
g fat	5
mg cholesterol	0
mg sodium	17
g protein	0
g carbohydrate	0.5

Walnut Oil Vinaigrette
Prepare Mustard-Garlic Vinaigrette but substitute walnut oil for vegetable oil and omit Parmesan cheese.

PER 1-tbsp/15 mL SERVING	
calories	17
g fat	1
mg cholesterol	2
mg sodium	47
g protein	0.5
g carbohydrate	1

Variations
Blue-Cheese Dressing:
Add 2 tbsp/25 mL crumbled blue cheese.
Fresh Herb:
Add 2 tbsp/25 mL chopped fresh dill, or 1 tbsp/15 mL chopped fresh basil, or 2 tsp/ 10 mL chopped fresh tarragon.
Watercress:
Add ¼ cup/50 mL chopped watercress leaves.
Onion or Chive:
Add 2 tbsp/25 mL chopped green onions or chives (or to taste).
Celery:
Add 1 tsp/5 mL celery seed and 2 tbsp/25 mL chopped celery leaves. (Use on coleslaw.)
Cumin:
Add ½ tsp/2 mL dried ground cumin.
Curry:
Add 1 tsp/5 mL curry powder.
Tomato:
Add 2 tbsp/25 mL tomato paste.

Ranch-Style Buttermilk Dressing

Even though this dressing contains mayonnaise, it is much lower in fat and calories than most creamy dressings. Use it with tossed green salads, coleslaw or chilled cooked vegetables.

1 cup	buttermilk	250 mL
⅓ cup	light mayonnaise	75 mL
1	small clove garlic, minced	1
½ tsp	granulated sugar	2 mL
½ tsp	dried dillweed	2 mL
¼ tsp	dry mustard	1 mL
Pinch	freshly ground pepper	Pinch
2 tbsp	chopped fresh parsley	25 mL

In small bowl or jar, combine buttermilk, mayonnaise, garlic, sugar, dillweed, mustard, pepper and parsley; mix well. Cover and refrigerate for up to 4 days. Makes 1⅓ cups/325 mL.

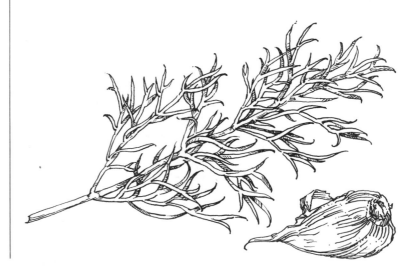

PER 2-tbsp/30 mL SERVING	
calories	55
g fat	4
mg cholesterol	1
mg sodium	14
g protein	1
g carbohydrate	5

Yogurt-Orange Dressing

This quick and easy dressing is delicious with a fruit salad.

⅔ cup	low-fat plain yogurt	150 mL
2 tbsp	vegetable oil	25 mL
2 tbsp	frozen orange-juice concentrate	25 mL
1 tbsp	packed brown sugar	15 mL
1 tsp	grated orange rind	5 mL

In small bowl, combine yogurt, oil, orange juice, sugar and orange rind; mix thoroughly. Cover and refrigerate for up to 2 days. Makes about 1 cup/250 mL.

Creamy Herb Dressing

Use this light yet creamy dressing on pasta salads, vegetable salads and lettuce salads. Because the flavors develop upon standing, if you want to use the dressing immediately increase the mustard, oregano and basil to ½ tsp/2 mL each or more to taste.

PER 2-tbsp/25 mL SERVING (made with cottage cheese)	
calories	22
g fat	0.5
mg cholesterol	2
mg sodium	10
g protein	3
g carbohydrate	2

Light sour cream has half the fat of regular sour cream. If you use a small amount of dressing, it isn't going to make a great deal of difference in this recipe whether you use cottage cheese or light sour cream—either is much lower in fat than oil. One-quarter cup (50 mL) dressing made with sour cream has 4 g fat; light sour cream has 2 g fat; cottage cheese has 1 g fat.

¼ cup	low-fat cottage cheese or light sour cream	50 mL
¼ cup	low-fat plain yogurt	50 mL
¼ tsp	Dijon mustard	1 mL
¼ tsp	each dried oregano and basil (or 1 tbsp/15 mL chopped fresh)	1 mL
	Salt and freshly ground pepper	

In blender or food processor, process cottage cheese until smooth. Add yogurt, mustard, oregano and basil. Add salt and pepper to taste; process to mix. Cover and refrigerate for 4 hours or up to 3 days. Makes ½ cup/125 mL.

Salads aren't always a light meal when it comes to considering the fat content. Lunch of a roll and salad can add up to more than half the amount of fat you need in a day.

The amount of dressing (2 tbsp/25 mL) used in this chart is a conservative amount of salad dressing. If you like a lot of dressing, you could easily be using double this amount. If this is the case you could be eating 30 g of fat just in a salad, which is about half the daily fat requirement for someone consuming 1800 calories a day.

If you spread your bread or roll with 1 tbsp/15 mL butter or margarine you are adding another 14 g of fat.

For other salad dressing recipes see:

Herb Vinaigrette (Tossed Seasonal Greens, page 54)
Tomato-Shallot Dressing (Warm Vegetable Salad with Tomato-Shallot Dressing, page 28)
Sesame Seed Dressing (Spinach Salad with Sesame Seed Dressing, page 55)
Yogurt-Herb Dressing (Carrot and Cracked-Wheat Salad with Yogurt-Herb Dressing, page 56)
Curry Dressing (Curried Vermicelli Noodle Salad, page 58)
Mustard Vinaigrette (Tomato, Broccoli and Pasta Salad page 110)
Italian Vinaigrette Dressing (Pasta and Fresh Vegetable Salad, page 61)
Walnut Orange Dressing (Snow Pea and Red Pepper Buffet Salad, page 49)

Hidden Fat

Next time you make a salad at home or at a salad bar estimate how much dressing you use and compare to this:

per 2 tbsp/25 mL*	g fat	mg sodium	calories
Mustard-Garlic Vinaigrette (page 64)	10	34	100
Standard home vinaigrette	20	125**	190
Italian (store-bought)	16	570	160
Italian Reduced Calorie (store-bought)	1	420	12
Ranch-Style Buttermilk Dressing (page 65)	2	94	34
Ranch Style (store-bought)	14	250	140
Blue Cheese (page 65)	4	132	44
Blue cheese (store-bought)	14	306	142
Light Blue Cheese (store-bought)	6	390	80
Creamy Herb Dressing (page 66)	1	10	22
Mayonnaise-type dressing (store-bought)	12	164	120

*A portion in a small ladle or a heaping dessert spoonful
**based on ½ tsp/2 mL salt per 1 cup/250 mL dressing.

Choosing an Oil for Salad Dressings

Oils are made up of a combination of different fats; some are much more saturated than others. The flavor should also be considered when choosing an oil.

Choose:
safflower   walnut   olive
sunflower   soybean   corn
canola (has the least amount of saturated fat)
sesame (strong flavor, so use in small amounts)

Sesame oil has a distinct, strong nutty flavor and is used sparingly, usually combined with another oil as a flavoring to a stir-fry or salad dressing.

Because walnut and olive oils are heavier you can use a smaller amount and often combine them with another oil (such as safflower); these oils are nice for salads. I find corn oil not appealing for salads; it is better for cooking.

Avoid:
palm oil (high in saturated fat)
coconut oil (high in saturated fat)
vegetable oil (when the kind of oil isn't stated on a container, it is likely to be palm or coconut or cottonseed oil)

MEAT AND POULTRY

People often tell me about how healthily they are eating and how their diet has changed over the years. One of the first things they say is that they don't eat red meat anymore.

Red meat has been given bad press; there is no reason to eliminate it from your diet completely. Meat is an important source of complete protein, useable iron, B vitamins (thiamin, niacin and B12) and minerals, but it also contains a high proportion of saturated fats. For this reason, the selection of meats, the size of the servings and the method of cooking become very important.

For years Canadian food tables used American information. Recent Canadian studies show that Canadian beef and pork are much leaner than previously believed.

Compare		g fat*
12-oz/352 g serving rib roast, including fat: (244 mg cholesterol)		72
6-oz/176 g serving roast beef, including fat		36
1 tbsp/15 mL butter or margarine (for a roll)		11
2 tbsp/25 mL mayonnaise (for a salad)		22
	Total	69
3-oz/88 g serving top round steak (lean only)		5
1 tsp/5 mL butter or margarine (for a roll)		4
1 tbsp/15 mL light mayonnaise (for a salad)		5
	Total	14

*The average woman's daily fat requirement is about 70 grams a day; a rough estimate for an average man is about 100 g of fat a day.

Recommended Cuts

Beef: round, flank, sirloin-tip roast, sirloin steak (if well trimmed), tenderloin and rump
Pork: choose lean cuts or those easy to trim, sirloin roast, tenderloin and loin chops, pork steaks (choose ham and bacon less often because of their high salt and fat content)
Lamb: cuts from leg and loin section
Veal: lower in fat than beef and other red meats but slightly higher in cholesterol; all cuts are lean except those from the breast, i.e., stewing veal

If you do buy cuts higher in fat, then choose a cooking method with which you can pour off the fat. For example, if you buy regular ground beef, use it in spaghetti sauce so that you can brown the meat first then pour off the fat before adding other ingredients. If you use stewing veal, make the dish a day ahead and refrigerate. The next day you can easily remove the fat that will have hardened on top of the dish.

When possible, choose lean or medium ground beef. Ground pork varies in fat content and often isn't very different from regular ground beef. When compared with beef, pork looks fattier because the meat is only ground once; beef is ground twice so it is more uniform in color.

Selecting Poultry

Turkey, chicken, Cornish game hens, quail or partridge are good choices. Avoid self-basting turkeys because they are injected with saturated fats. Duck and goose are very high in fat. Removing the skin from poultry significantly reduces fat content.

Which meat has the most fat: beef, pork, lamb or chicken? Whether or not beef has more fat than pork is not really the issue. *What is most important is the kind of cut you buy, the way you cook it and the amount you eat.* A lean cut of pork has less fat than a prime rib roast. Pork spareribs have more fat than top round steak. Try to choose a lean cut, remove all visible fat and cook it without adding any fat.

PER SERVING	
calories	324
g fat	12
mg cholesterol	60
mg sodium	95
g protein	20
g carbohydrate	35

GOOD: fiber, iron
EXCELLENT: vitamin A, vitamin C, thiamin, niacin

This dish is equally good made with 1 can (7½ oz/213 mL) tomato sauce instead of tomato paste and water, but it is higher in sodium.

Family Favorite Shepherd's Pie

My mother always made shepherd's pie from leftover Sunday roast beef, gravy, and mashed potatoes. However, since we seldom have roasts, I make shepherd's pie using ground meat—either beef or pork or lamb. If you don't have leftover mashed potatoes, boil 5 medium potatoes; drain and mash with milk.

1 lb	lean ground beef or pork or lamb, or a combination of these	500 g
2	onions, chopped	2
2	cloves garlic, minced	2
1	carrot, minced (optional)	1
⅓ cup	tomato paste	75 mL
⅔ cup	water	150 mL
1 tsp	dried thyme	5 mL
2 tsp	Worcestershire sauce	10 mL
	Freshly ground pepper	
	Paprika	
2 cups	mashed potatoes	500 mL

In skillet over medium heat, cook beef, stirring to break up meat, until brown; pour off fat. Add onions, garlic, and carrot (if using); cook until tender. Add tomato paste, water, thyme, Worcestershire sauce, and pepper to taste. Simmer for 5 minutes, stirring up any brown bits on bottom of pan.

Spoon meat mixture into 8-cup/2 L baking or microwave-safe dish; spread mashed potatoes evenly on top. Sprinkle with paprika to taste. Bake in 375°F/190°C oven for 35 minutes or until heated through, or microwave at high (100%) power for 9 minutes. Makes 5 servings.

Compare Shepherd's Pie	mg sodium per serving
Made with tomato paste plus water	95
Made with tomato sauce	342

Beef and Tomato Stir-Fry

Make this easy, tasty dish in the summer and fall when garden-fresh tomatoes are plentiful. Serve over rice or noodles. In winter substitute green peppers, broccoli or snow peas instead of tomatoes and cook until crisp-tender, adding water if necessary to prevent burning.

PER SERVING	
calories	206
g fat	9
mg cholesterol	39
mg sodium	288
g protein	20
g carbohydrate	12

GOOD: fiber, vitamin A, iron
EXCELLENT: niacin, vitamin C

¾ lb	top round or flank steak	375 g
2 tbsp	cornstarch	25 mL
2 tbsp	sherry	25 mL
1 tbsp	soy sauce	15 mL
2 tbsp	vegetable oil	25 mL
1	onion, thinly sliced	1
2	cloves garlic, minced	2
4	tomatoes, cut in wedges	4
4	green onions, cut in thin 2-in/5 cm-long strips	4

Cut beef across the grain into thin strips; cut strips into 2-in (5 cm) lengths. In bowl, combine cornstarch, sherry and soy sauce; mix until smooth. Add beef and toss to coat.

In wok or nonstick skillet, heat oil over high heat. Add beef and stir-fry for 2 minutes; add onion and stir-fry for 1 minute or until beef is browned. Add garlic and tomatoes; stir-fry until tomatoes are heated through, 1 to 2 minutes. Stir in green onions and serve immediately. Makes 4 servings.

If you're cooking for one, buy a flank steak and cut it into three portions. Use one portion for the Ginger-Garlic Marinated Flank Steak, one for the Beef and Tomato Stir-Fry (page 71, cut recipe in half) and one for the Stir-Fry for One (page 204).

PER SERVING	
calories	134
g fat	4
mg cholesterol	49
mg sodium	38
g protein	23
g carbohydrate	1
GOOD: iron	
EXCELLENT: niacin	

Grey Cup Buffet

Ginger-Garlic Marinated Flank Steak (cold) (page 72)
Tossed Seasonal Greens (page 54)
Whole-Wheat Oatmeal Bread (page 156)
Streusel Plum Cake (page 166)
Apricot Yogurt Parfaits (page 168)

Most marinade recipes call for more oil than necessary. Even though the marinade is poured off before cooking, I recommend keeping the oil at a minimum.

Ginger-Garlic Marinated Flank Steak

This is a favorite in our household. If I'm organized, I try to marinate it early in the day. The steak can marinate for two days and, once cooked, it is good hot or cold. (In other words, if no one arrives home for dinner—your kids get invited out and your husband has to work late—you can cook it the next day. Or, if only one person shows up, you can cook it and serve the rest the next day.) If you're cooking for two, have it hot the first night and cold the second.

1	flank steak, about 1 lb/500 g	1
	Italian Herb Marinade or Ginger-Garlic Marinade (recipes follow)	

Lightly score (cut) beef about ⅛-in/3 mm deep in diagonal slashes. Place in shallow dish. Pour marinade over; cover and refrigerate for at least 2, or up to 48 hours, turning meat once or twice.

Remove meat from marinade and broil or grill for 4 to 5 minutes on each side or until desired doneness. Cut diagonally across the grain into thin slices. Serve hot or cold. Makes 4 servings.

Ginger-Garlic Marinade

Use with fish, shrimp, chicken, turkey, beef, pork or lamb.

2 tbsp	rice or cider vinegar	25 mL
2 tbsp	water	25 mL
1 tbsp	vegetable oil	15 mL
1 tbsp	grated fresh gingerroot (or 1 tsp/5 mL ground ginger)	15 mL
1 tsp	granulated sugar	5 mL
1	clove garlic, minced	1

Combine vinegar, water, oil, ginger, sugar and garlic; mix well. Makes about ⅓ cup/75 mL, enough for one 1-lb/500 g steak.

Italian Herb Marinade

Use with beef, pork, lamb, chicken or turkey.

¼ cup	red wine vinegar	50 mL
1 tbsp	vegetable oil	15 mL
2 tbsp	chopped fresh parsley	25 mL
1 tsp	dried marjoram or oregano (or 1 tbsp/15 mL chopped fresh)	5 mL
1 tsp	dried thyme (or 1 tbsp/15 mL chopped fresh)	5 ml
1	bay leaf, crumbled	1
1	small onion, minced	1
2	cloves garlic, minced	2
	Freshly ground pepper	

In small bowl mix together vinegar, oil, parsley, marjoram, thyme, bay leaf, onion, garlic and pepper to taste. Makes about ⅓ cup/75 mL, enough for one 1-lb/500 g steak.

Flank steak is one of the leanest cuts of beef. It's delicious when marinated, then grilled or broiled and cut diagonally across the grain into thin slices. When served this way, it's also an economical cut of beef because 1 lb will serve four people. (One pound of porterhouse steak of the same thickness looks very skimpy when divided into four portions.)

Father's Day Barbecue Dinner

Ginger Garlic Marinated Flank Steak (page 72)
Yogurt Béarnaise Sauce (page 141)
New Potatoes with Herbs (page 135)
Asparagus
Strawberry Mousse (page 164)
or
Berries with Orange-Honey Yogurt (page 175)
Applesauce-Raisin Squares (page 152)

The flavor of a stew is usually better the second day. Make it a day in advance and refrigerate. Any fat will solidify on top and can easily be removed.

PER SERVING	
calories	235
g fat	5
mg cholesterol	43
mg sodium	325
g protein	20
g carbohydrate	27

GOOD: fiber, iron
EXCELLENT: vitamin A, vitamin C, niacin

Easy Oven Beef and Vegetable Stew

This is the easiest stew to make and tastes wonderful. Make it on the weekend and you'll probably have enough left over for a meal during the week. Or make it during the week to transport to ski cabin or cottage.

1½ lb	stewing beef	750 g
¼ cup	all-purpose flour	50 mL
6	small onions	6
2	large potatoes, cut in chunks (1 lb/500 g)	2
3	large carrots, cut in chunks	3
3	cloves garlic, minced	3
2 cups	diced turnip	500 mL
3 cups	water	750 mL
1¼ cups	beef stock or canned bouillon	300 mL
1	can (7½ oz/213 mL) tomato sauce	1
1 tsp	dried thyme	5 mL
½ tsp	dried oregano	2 mL
¼ tsp	freshly ground pepper	1 mL
1	bay leaf	1
½ tsp	grated orange rind (optional)	2 mL

Remove all visible fat from beef; cut beef into 1-in/2.5 cm cubes.

In large casserole or Dutch oven, toss beef with flour. Add onions, potatoes, carrots, garlic, turnip, water, beef stock, tomato sauce, thyme, oregano, pepper, bay leaf and orange rind; stir to mix.

Bake, covered, in 325°F/160°C oven for 3 hours, stirring occasionally (if you remember). Remove bay leaf. Makes 8 servings.

Compare	mg sodium per serving
This recipe	325
Canned beef and vegetable stew	1064

Compare	Beef Cuts and Portion Sizes					
	3-oz/88 g portion			6-oz/176 g portion		
Cut	g fat	mg cholesterol	calories	g fat	mg cholesterol	calories
Rib roast, roasted lean and fat	18	61	256	36	122	512
Rib roast, roasted lean only	10	60	196	20	120	392
Steak inside (top) round (lean and fat)	5	57	154	10	114	308
Steak inside (top) round (lean only)	3	57	144	6	114	288

Amount to Serve

How do I know what a 3- or 4-oz portion of meat is? The easiest way is to *buy* only that much. For example, if you are cooking for 4 people, buy only 1 lb (500 g) of ground meat, stewing beef, pork chops or boneless chicken breasts. For 4 servings, buy about 1½ lb (750 g) of bone-in meats, 2 lb (1 kg) of chicken.

When you are cooking roasts or bone-in cuts it is more difficult to judge amounts; for a rough estimate, consider a 3½-oz serving of meat to be about the size of a deck of playing cards. Many adults, especially men, are used to larger meat portions than 3 oz/90 g.

How to make the recommended serving size of meat, i.e., 3 oz/90 g, not look skimpy:

*The meat portion should only take up ¼ of the dinner plate. Increase the amount and variety of vegetables you serve.

*Slice meat thinly, it will look like more. For example 3 oz/ 90 g of thinly sliced flank steak will look as if there is more meat than the same weight of sirloin steak in a single piece 1-in/2.5 cm thick.

*Choose dishes in which meat is combined with vegetables, such as stews, stir-frys and casseroles.

*Serve as a sauce over pasta— see Spaghetti Sauce recipes, page 188.

*Canada's Food Guide recommends we have two servings (3 oz/90 g) of meat or meat alternatives a day. If one serving is small, for example a thin slice of meat in a sandwich at lunch, then the serving size at dinner can be larger.

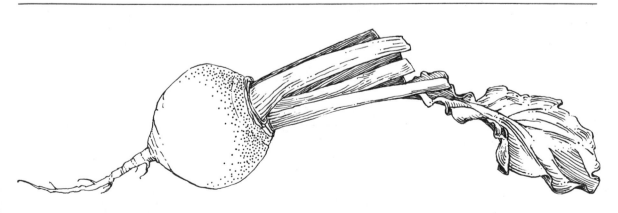

After the Ball Game Supper

Beef and Pasta Casserole for a Crowd (page 76)
Tossed Seasonal Greens (page 54)
French bread
Iced Raspberry Mousse (page 169)

Beef and Pasta Casserole for a Crowd

This is the type of dish to serve to a crowd at the cottage or ski cabin. It's also perfect to take to a potluck supper or for a teenager's party.

1 lb	short pasta (penne, fusilli, rotini)	500 g
1 tsp	vegetable oil	5 mL
2 lb	lean ground beef	1kg
3	onions, finely chopped	3
2	cloves garlic, minced	2
½ lb	mushrooms, sliced	250 g
2	stalks celery, sliced	2
1	sweet green pepper, chopped	1
1	large can (13 oz/369 mL) tomato paste	1
4 cups	water	1 L
1 tsp	each dried oregano and basil	5 mL
¼ cup	chopped fresh parsley	50 mL
1	pkg (10 oz/284 g) fresh spinach, cooked, drained and chopped	1
1 lb	low-fat mozzarella cheese, cut in small cubes	500 g
	Salt and freshly ground pepper	
1 cup	fresh bread crumbs	250 mL
½ cup	freshly grated Parmesan cheese	125 mL

PER SERVING	
calories	378
g fat	13
mg cholesterol	67
mg sodium	295
g protein	29
g carbohydrate	36

GOOD: fiber, riboflavin
EXCELLENT: vitamin A, vitamin C, niacin, calcium, iron

May be prepared up to two days in advance, covered and refrigerated. Remove from refrigerator one hour before baking.

In large pot of boiling water, cook pasta until al dente (tender but firm), about 10 minutes or according to package directions. Drain and rinse under cold running water; drain and set aside.

In large nonstick skillet or Dutch oven, heat oil over medium heat. Add beef, onions and garlic; cook, stirring, for a few minutes or until beef is no longer pink. Drain off fat. Add mushrooms, celery, and green pepper; cook for 5 minutes, stirring occasionally. Stir in tomato paste, water, oregano, basil and parsley; simmer, covered, for 30 minutes.

Combine meat sauce, spinach, pasta and mozzarella cheese; season to taste with salt and pepper. Spoon into lightly greased 16-cup/4 L casserole. Sprinkle with bread crumbs, then Parmesan. Bake, uncovered, in 350°F/180°C oven for 45 minutes or until bubbly. Makes 14 servings.

Grilled Butterflied Leg of Lamb with Lemon and Garlic

I love lamb, and this is one of my favorite ways to cook it. I either barbecue or broil this cut; when it's cooked medium-rare, lamb is delicious cold the next day.

3	cloves garlic, minced	3
½ tsp	grated lemon rind	2 mL
½ tsp	dried crushed rosemary (or 1 tbsp/ 15 mL chopped fresh)	2 mL
¼ tsp	freshly ground pepper	1 mL
2 tbsp	lemon juice	25 mL
2 tbsp	olive or vegetable oil	25 mL
1	boned and butterflied* leg of lamb (about 3 lb/1.5 kg boned)	1

In small bowl or food processor, combine garlic, lemon rind, rosemary, pepper and lemon juice. Gradually pour in oil and mix until blended.

Trim fat from lamb. Place lamb in shallow dish; pour marinade over, turning to coat both sides. Cover and let stand at room temperature for 1 to 2 hours or refrigerate overnight (bring to room temperature before cooking).

Remove lamb from marinade, reserving marinade. On greased grill 4 in/10 cm from hot coals (at high setting if a gas barbecue), or under broiler, grill or broil lamb for 15 minutes, brushing with marinade several times. Turn and cook for 12 minutes longer or until meat is pink inside.

Remove from heat and let stand for 10 minutes. To serve, slice thinly across the grain. Makes 8 servings.

PER SERVING (based on using only lean part of lamb)

calories	196
g fat	10
mg cholesterol	88
mg sodium	63
g protein	26
g carbohydrate	1

GOOD: iron
EXCELLENT: niacin

Cooking Methods to Reduce Fat
*Most of the time, don't fry meats—instead, grill, broil, stew, stir-fry, braise, roast on a rack.

*If you are going to fry, use a nonstick skillet and use as little high-polyunsaturated margarine or vegetable (not palm or coconut) oil as possible.

*Make a stew one day in advance; cover and refrigerate. When cold, remove fat that has solidified on top.

*Butterflied legs of lamb are boned then cut open, but not all the way through, so the meat can be spread apart like two butterfly wings. Be sure to trim all fat from lamb.

Lamb Tenderloins with Rosemary and Peppercorns

Fork-tender lamb tenderloins or loins, often available in the frozen food section of the supermarket, are a special treat and one of the leanest cuts of lamb.

1 lb	lamb tenderloins or loins	500 g
1½ tsp	dried peppercorns, crushed (¼ tsp/mL freshly ground)	7 mL
1 tbsp	fresh rosemary (or 1 tsp/5 mL dried)	15 mL
2 tbsp	chopped fresh mint (optional)	25 mL
2	cloves garlic, minced	2
2 tbsp	dry sherry or red wine vinegar	25 mL
1 tbsp	light soy sauce	15 mL

Place lamb in shallow dish.

In small bowl, combine peppercorns, rosemary, mint, garlic, sherry and soy sauce; mix well and pour over lamb. Cover and marinate at room temperature for 30 minutes or refrigerate for at least 1, or up to 6, hours.

Remove from marinade. Broil or grill over hot coals 3 to 4 minutes for tenderloins; 6 minutes for loins or until meat is still pink inside, turning once or twice. Cut diagonally into thin slices. Makes 4 servings.

PER SERVING	
calories	170
g fat	7
mg cholesterol	90
mg sodium	93
g protein	25
g carbohydrate	0

GOOD: iron
EXCELLENT: niacin

Lamb tenderloins and loins cook quickly and are best served rare or medium-rare. Be careful not to overcook as they will be too dry and sometimes tough.

Compare	per 4 oz/125 g serving	
Grilled Lemon-Garlic Leg of Lamb using:	g fat	calories
Lamb leg, lean and fat	25	354
Lamb leg, lean only	10	196

Pork Chops with Rosemary and Orange

This fast and easy recipe also works well using veal or turkey scallopine. For my son (who doesn't like sauces), I don't pour any over his serving. My daughter quietly scrapes the rosemary off hers. My husband and I like it the way it is, so everyone is happy.

1 lb	fast-fry or thinly sliced pork chops	500 g
2	oranges	2
2 tsp	soft margarine	10 mL
2 tsp	dried rosemary	10 mL
	Salt and freshly ground pepper	

Trim fat from pork chops. Peel and slice one orange; squeeze juice from other and set aside.

Heat heavy-bottomed or non-stick skillet over high heat; add margarine and heat until sizzling. Add pork chops and cook for about 2 minutes or until brown on bottom; turn. Sprinkle with rosemary, and salt and pepper to taste. Cook until brown on other side. Remove chops to side plate.

Add reserved orange juice and slices; cook for 1 to 2 minutes, stirring to scrape up brown bits on bottom of pan. To serve, arrange chops on plates and pour juice and orange slices over. Makes 4 servings.

PER SERVING (made with center loin chops)	
calories	201
g fat	9
mg cholesterol	67
mg sodium	70
g protein	22
g carbohydrate	6

EXCELLENT: vitamin C, thiamin, niacin

Brochette of Pork with Lemon and Herb Marinade

Herbs and lemon add tangy flavor to this easy-to-prepare pork dish. Use pork tenderloin or any other lean cut of pork. Zucchini or blanched slices of carrot can be used instead of the vegetables here. (Recipe pictured on front cover.)

1 lb	boneless lean pork	500 g
	Grated rind and juice of 1 lemon	
2	large cloves garlic, minced	2
2 tsp	dried basil (or 2 tbsp/25 mL fresh)	10mL
1 tsp	dried thyme (or 1 tbsp/15 mL fresh)	5 mL
2 tbsp	chopped fresh parsley	25 mL
1 tbsp	vegetable or olive oil	15 mL
1	sweet green pepper, cut in squares	1
2	onions, quartered and separated into pieces	2
16	cherry tomatoes or fresh pineapple chunks	16

Cut pork into 1-in/2.5 cm cubes. In bowl, combine lemon rind and juice, garlic, basil, thyme, parsley and oil. Add pork and toss to coat well. Cover and marinate in refrigerator for 4 hours or overnight.

Alternately thread pork, green pepper, onions and cherry tomatoes or pineapple onto skewers. On greased grill about 4 in/10 cm over hot coals, or under broiler, grill brochettes, turning often, for 15 minutes or until pork is no longer pink inside. Makes 4 servings.

PER SERVING	
calories	235
g fat	12
mg cholesterol	67
mg sodium	58
g protein	23
g carbohydrate	8

GOOD: fiber, riboflavin, iron
EXCELLENT: vitamin C, thiamin, niacin

Pineapple chunks packed in their own juice can be used instead of fresh pineapple.

Cauliflower and Ham Gratin

Ham and cauliflower are a wonderful combination. Dill adds extra flavor and red pepper adds color and crunch. This recipe is adapted from a Foodland Ontario recipe.

½	head cauliflower	½
1½ tbsp	soft margarine	20 mL
2 tbsp	all-purpose flour	25 mL
1 cup	skim milk	250 mL
¼ cup	freshly grated Parmesan cheese	50 mL
¼ cup	grated low-fat mozzarella cheese	50 mL
¼ cup	chopped fresh dill*	50 mL
	Freshly ground pepper	
½ cup	diced cooked ham (2 oz/60 g)	125 mL
½	sweet red pepper, coarsely chopped	½
⅓ cup	fresh bread crumbs	75 mL

Cut cauliflower into florets, about 2-in/5 cm pieces. In large pot of boiling water, blanch cauliflower for 5 minutes or until tender-crisp; drain and set aside.

In saucepan, melt margarine; add flour and cook over low heat, stirring, for 1 minute. Pour in milk and bring to simmer, stirring constantly. Simmer, stirring, for 2 minutes. Add Parmesan and mozzarella cheeses, dill, and pepper to taste; cook, stirring, until cheese melts.

In lightly greased 11- by 7-in/2 L shallow baking dish, arrange cauliflower, ham and sweet pepper; pour sauce evenly over. Sprinkle with bread crumbs. Bake in 375°F/190°C oven for 30 minutes or until bubbly. Makes 4 servings.

*If fresh dill is unavailable, use ¼ cup/50 mL fresh parsley plus 1 tsp/5 mL dried dillweed.

PER SERVING

calories	219
g fat	10
mg cholesterol	21
mg sodium	533
g protein	15
g carbohydrate	18

GOOD: fiber, vitamin A, thiamin
EXCELLENT: vitamin C, niacin, calcium

Nutrition Notes
Because ham is very high in sodium, it shouldn't be used very often. When you do use it, try to make a little go a long way, as in this cauliflower dish. Don't add any salt.

Use the remaining cauliflower in stir-frys, in salads or soup.

Compare

Ham Dinner 1 (29% of calories from fat)	g fat	mg cholesterol	mg sodium	calories
Cauliflower and Ham Gratin (page 81)	10.1	21	533	219
Green beans	0.1	0	8	17
Sliced tomatoes	0.1	0	5	12
Whole-wheat bun	1.0	1	197	90
Margarine (1 tsp/5 mL)	3.6	0	32	34
Milk, skim (8 oz/250 mL)	0	5	133	90
Totals	15.0	27	908	461

Ham Dinner 2 (47% of calories from fat)	g fat	mg cholesterol	mg sodium	calories
Ham steak	8.7	65	1571	187
Cauliflower	0.1	0	4	14
with cheese sauce	9.9	33	271	126
Green beans	0.1	0	8	17
Whole-wheat bun	1.0	1	197	90
Butter (1 tsp/5 mL)	3.6	11	39	34
Milk, whole (8 oz/250 mL)	9	35	126	159
Totals	32.4	145	2186	627

Barbecued Lemon Chicken

This simple way to cook chicken is one of my husband's favorites—the chicken is moist and juicy and very delicious. In the winter, my friend Janet Dey cooks chicken this way in her fireplace barbecue.

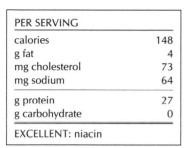

PER SERVING	
calories	148
g fat	4
mg cholesterol	73
mg sodium	64
g protein	27
g carbohydrate	0
EXCELLENT: niacin	

4	boneless chicken breasts	4
	Juice of 1 lemon	
2 tsp	olive oil	10 mL
1	clove garlic, minced	1
½ tsp	dried oregano	2 mL
Pinch	cayenne pepper	Pinch

Remove skin from chicken. In shallow dish, arrange chicken in single layer.

In small dish, combine lemon juice, oil, garlic, oregano and cayenne; mix well. Pour over chicken and turn to coat both sides. Let stand at room temperature for 20 minutes or cover and refrigerate up to 6 hours.

On greased grill, cook chicken over hot coals for 4 to 5 minutes on each side or until meat is no longer pink inside. Makes 4 servings.

Grilled Tandoori Chicken

This Indian yogurt-and-spice marinade makes the chicken moist and full of flavor. Serve with rice and a green vegetable such as asparagus, green beans or broccoli or see the Summer Barbecue menu on this page.

1½ tsp	Dijon mustard	7 mL
2 tbsp	vegetable oil	25 mL
¼ cup	low-fat plain yogurt	50 mL
1½ tsp	minced fresh gingerroot	7 mL
¼ tsp	cumin seeds	1 mL
¼ tsp	coriander seeds	1 mL
¼ tsp	ground turmeric	1 mL
2 tbsp	lemon juice	25 mL
2 tbsp	chopped canned green chili or 1 fresh green chili, seeded and chopped	25 mL
1	chicken, cut in pieces (about 2½ lb/1.25 kg) or chicken breasts	1

Place mustard in mixing bowl or food processor; add oil, drop by drop, whisking or processing until well blended. Stir in yogurt; set aside.

Using mortar and pestle, spice grinder or coffee grinder, pound or grind gingerroot, cumin and coriander seeds, and turmeric to form a paste; add lemon juice and mix well. Stir into yogurt mixture along with chopped chili.

Remove skin from chicken. Using knife, make very small cuts in meat. Arrange in shallow dish or place in plastic bag; pour yogurt-spice mixture over chicken and stir to coat all pieces. Cover and refrigerate for at least 8 hours or up to 24 hours.

On greased grill 4 to 6 in/10 to 15 cm from hot coals, or under broiler, grill chicken for 15 to 20 minutes on each side (15 minutes if top is down on barbecue) or until chicken is tender and juices run clear when chicken is pierced with fork. Watch carefully and turn to prevent burning. Makes 6 servings.

PER SERVING

calories	174
g fat	10
mg cholesterol	59
mg sodium	81
g protein	20
g carbohydrate	2

GOOD: vitamin C
EXCELLENT: niacin

Summer Barbecue

Grilled Tandoori chicken (page 84)
New Potatoes with Herbs (page 135)
Sliced tomatoes with basil
Whole-Berry Blueberry Sherbet (page 170)
Microwave Oatmeal Squares (page 193)

Curried Chicken Crêpes

This is a delicious dish to consider when you want a make-ahead dish for brunch, lunch or dinner. If you keep crêpes in your freezer and have any leftover cooked chicken or turkey, these can be a quick and easy dinner. Cooked turkey, shrimp or pork can be used instead of chicken.

Old-Fashioned Chicken or Turkey Pot Pie If you have leftover cooked chicken or turkey, and any crisp-cooked vegetables such as carrots, green beans, zucchini or leeks, combine them with sliced fresh mushrooms, frozen peas and Cream Sauce (recipe page 140). Season with touch of tarragon and sherry; spoon into baking dish.

Cover with mashed potatoes and bake in 375°F (190°C) oven for 30 minutes or until hot and bubbly and potatoes are golden.

Note: Using mashed potatoes instead of pastry as a topping for a chicken or meat pie reduces the fat by about half.

2 tsp	soft margarine	10 mL
½	medium onion, chopped	½
½ cup	diced celery	125 mL
1 tbsp	all-purpose flour	15 mL
1½ tsp	(approx.) curry powder	7 mL
¼ tsp	salt	1 mL
½ cup	chicken stock	125 mL
1½ cup	diced cooked chicken (about ¾ lb/375 g boneless chicken breasts)	375 mL
¼ cup	sour cream	50 mL
¼ cup	low-fat plain yogurt	50 mL
8	Basic Crêpes (recipe page 160)	8
Garnish:	Yogurt, chutney, green grapes	

In saucepan, melt margarine; over medium heat cook onion and celery, stirring, until onion is softened. Add flour, curry powder and salt; cook, stirring, for 1 minute.

Whisk in chicken stock and bring to simmer while whisking. Reduce heat to low and simmer, stirring, for 2 minutes. Remove from heat and stir in chicken, sour cream and yogurt. Taste and add more curry powder if desired.

Place 2 or 3 large spoonfuls of chicken mixture across center of each crêpe. Roll up and place seam-side-down in lightly greased shallow baking dish.

Bake in 375°F/190°C oven for 20 minutes or microwave at high (100%) power for 2 minutes or until heated through. Top each serving with spoonful of yogurt and another of chutney; garnish plate with grapes. Makes 4 servings of 2 crêpes each.

Curried Chicken and Tomato Casserole

For an easy yet elegant dinner, serve small dishes of raisins, peanuts, coconut, chutney and yogurt, plus rice, along with this casserole. For a particularly delicious fresh flavor, grind the cumin and coriander seeds just before using. You can, however, substitute 2 tbsp/25 mL curry powder or more to taste, for the cumin and coriander seeds, turmeric, aniseed and hot pepper flakes. Don't substitute canned tomatoes. The Sliced Cucumbers with Chives, Yogurt and Basil (page 52) is particularly nice with this.

Make-Ahead Dinner Party

Spiced Meatballs with Coriander Dipping Sauce (page 24)
Tossed Seasonal Greens (page 54)
Curried Chicken and Tomato Casserole (page 86)
Bulgur Pilaf with Apricots and Raisins (page 135)
Sliced Cucumbers with Chives, Yogurt and Basil (page 52)
Oranges in Grand Marnier (page 177)
Easy Oat Bran and Date Cookies (page 154)

Recipe can be prepared in advance, cooled, covered and refrigerated for up to 2 days. To reheat, cook over medium heat, stirring occasionally, for about 20 minutes, or place uncovered in 350°F/180°C oven for 35 to 45 minutes or until heated through.

Photo:
Make-Ahead Paella (page 92)

3 lb	chicken pieces (breasts, thighs)	1.5 kg
2 tbsp	soft margarine	25 mL
4	medium onions, chopped	4
3 tbsp	minced fresh gingerroot	45 mL
¼ cup	water	50 mL
5	cloves garlic, minced	5
2 tbsp	cumin seeds, ground	25 mL
2 tbsp	coriander seeds, ground	25 mL
2 tbsp	turmeric	25 mL
1 tsp	aniseed	5 mL
¼ tsp	(approx.) hot pepper flakes	1 mL
4	large tomatoes, seeded and coarsely chopped	4
1½ cups	low-fat plain yogurt	375 mL
	Salt and pepper	
1 tsp	garam masala*	5 mL
¼ cup	chopped fresh coriander	50 mL

Cut any visible fat from chicken and remove skin.
In large Dutch oven or skillet, heat margarine over medium-high heat; brown chicken pieces a few at a time and remove to plate. Add onions and cook for 3 minutes or until tender, stirring often. Add gingerroot, water, garlic, cumin, coriander, turmeric, aniseed and hot pepper flakes; mix well and simmer for 1 minute. Add tomatoes and simmer for 2 minutes. Stir in yogurt.

Return chicken, including any juices, to pan and stir gently. Season with salt and pepper to taste; add more hot pepper flakes if desired. Cover and simmer for 25 to 30 minutes or until chicken is tender and cooked through.

Just before serving, stir in garam masala and chopped coriander. Makes 10 servings.

*Buy garam masala at specialty food shops, or make this version by using a spice grinder or coffee grinder to combine 4 peppercorns, 2 cardamom seeds, 2 cloves, ½-in/1 cm piece cinnamon stick, pinch each of cumin seeds and grated nutmeg.

Compare

per serving	g fat	calories
This recipe including chicken skin	12	247
This recipe without chicken skin	8	198

To Truss a Chicken
Use a cotton string to tie the legs and wings close to the body. This prevents the legs and wings from becoming overcooked and dried out before the rest of the chicken is cooked.

Winter Sunday Dinner Menu
Tarragon-Roasted Chicken (page 87)
Cranberry sauce
Baked Parsnips and Carrots (page 121)
Garlic-Parsley Potatoes (page 135)
Pear Streusel Cake (page 166)

PER SERVING	
calories	155
g fat	6
mg cholesterol	70
mg sodium	70
g protein	23
g carbohydrate	0
EXCELLENT: niacin	

Photo:
Szechuan Orange-Ginger Chicken (page 90)

Tarragon-Roasted Chicken

This is a delicious and easy way to cook chicken. Be sure to remove the skin when carving as it has a large amount of fat.

2	cloves garlic	2
1	chicken (about 3 lb/1.5 kg)	1
2 tsp	dried tarragon	10 mL
¼ cup	white wine	50 mL
1 tbsp	vegetable oil	15 mL

Cut 1 garlic clove in half. Rub cut sides on outside of chicken; place garlic in chicken cavity. Sprinkle half the tarragon in chicken cavity. Truss chicken with string and place in roasting pan.

Mince remaining garlic and combine with remaining tarragon, wine and oil; drizzle over chicken. Roast in 350°F/180°C oven, basting frequently, for 1¼ hours or until juices run clear when chicken is pierced with fork. Makes 6 servings.

PER SERVING	
calories	59
g fat	1
mg cholesterol	1
mg sodium	122
g protein	2
g carbohydrate	2
GOOD: fiber,	

Variations:
Instead of mushrooms or celery add chopped apple or pear, cooked cranberries or chopped dried apricots; or replace half of the breadcrumbs with cooked wild rice

Stuffing a Chicken or Turkey
Stuff a bird just before cooking. If you stuff it in advance, even if you refrigerate it, the center will take time to become cold and you run the risk of contamination. Fill cavity but don't pack it in, it will expand during cooking. Fasten closed with skewers or sew closed using a needle and string or thread.

Mushroom Onion Stuffing

This stuffing is good with chicken or turkey. Serve with cranberry sauce and nobody will notice if you don't have gravy.

3 cups	fresh whole wheat bread crumbs	750 mL
1½ cups	coarsely chopped mushrooms	375 mL
1 cup	finely chopped celery	250 mL
2	small onions, finely chopped	2
1 tsp	dried thyme	5 mL
1 tsp	dried sage	5 mL
¼ tsp	freshly ground pepper	1 mL

In large bowl, combine bread crumbs, mushrooms, celery, onions, thyme, sage and pepper. Makes 6 cups (1.5 L), enough for a 6 lb/3 kg chicken. (About 8 servings.)

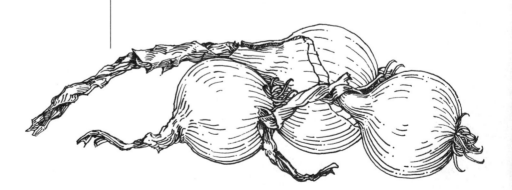

Chicken and Shrimp Creole

To celebrate the publishing of Marg Fraser's *Total Fibre* book we had a potluck dinner at my house. We served a version of this recipe, from Monda Rosenberg, food editor of *Chatelaine* magazine. If preparing in advance, use parboiled (converted) rice as some kinds of rice will get mushy when reheated. Cooked, sliced Italian sausage is a tasty addition or substitute for shrimp in this dish.

1½ lb	boneless chicken	750 g
1 tbsp	vegetable oil	15 mL
2	onions, coarsely chopped	2
3	cloves garlic, minced	3
1	each sweet red and green pepper, coarsely chopped	1
1	can (28 oz/796 mL) tomatoes (undrained)	1
4 cups	chicken stock	1 L
1 tsp	dried thyme	5 mL
1 tsp	dried oregano	5 mL
¼ tsp	cayenne pepper	1 mL
2 cups	parboiled (converted) rice	500 mL
1 lb	medium shrimp (fresh or frozen)	500 g
½ cup	chopped fresh parsley	125 mL

Remove skin from chicken and cut into cubes. In large nonstick skillet or heavy pan, heat oil over medium heat; cook chicken for about 3 minutes or until lightly browned. Add onions and garlic; cook for 3 minutes or until softened. Stir in peppers; add tomatoes, breaking up with back of spoon. Add stock, thyme, oregano and cayenne; bring to boil. Stir in rice; cover, reduce heat and simmer for 25 minutes or until most of the liquid is absorbed.

Meanwhile, in saucepan of boiling water, cook shrimp for 3 minutes; drain. Peel and de-vein if necessary. Add shrimp to rice mixture and cook for 5 minutes or until shrimp are hot. Stir in parsley. Makes 8 servings.

PER SERVING	
calories	321
g fat	5
mg cholesterol	105
mg sodium	638
g protein	30
g carbohydrate	38

GOOD: fiber, thiamin
EXCELLENT: niacin, iron, vitamin C

Buffet Dinner for 16

(Double or triple recipes where needed.)
Spinach-Onion Dip with fresh vegetables (page 18)
Spiced Meatballs with Coriander Dipping Sauce (page 24)
Chicken and Shrimp Creole (page 89)
Tossed Seasonal Greens (page 54)
Hot French bread
Oranges in Grand Marnier (page 177)
Strawberry Mousse (page 164)

For the most flavor, cook shrimp in shells then peel and de-vein (rather than peeling before cooking).

PER SERVING	
calories	220
g fat	10
mg cholesterol	66
mg sodium	58
g protein	24
g carbohydrate	6
EXCELLENT: vitamin C, niacin	

Szechuan Orange-Ginger Chicken

This popular recipe is much easier and faster to make than it looks. Chinese dishes from the Szechuan region of China usually have a spicy, hot flavor; if you prefer a milder taste, use less chili paste — the dish is delicious either way. Serve with rice. (Recipe pictured opposite page 87.)

4	chicken breasts, skinned and boned (about 1 lb/500 g boneless)	4
1	sweet green pepper	1
1	sweet red pepper	1
1	orange	1
1 tsp	bottled chili paste*	5 mL
2 tbsp	sherry	25 mL
1 tsp	granulated sugar	5 mL
1 tsp	cornstarch	5 mL
2 tbsp	vegetable oil	25 mL
1 tsp	minced garlic	5 mL
1 tbsp	minced fresh gingerroot	15 mL

Cut chicken into 1-in/2.5 cm squares; set aside. Halve green and red peppers and remove ribs and seeds; cut into 1-in/2.5 cm squares.

Using vegetable peeler, remove rind from orange (orange part only, no white). Cut rind into thin julienne strips about 1½ in/4 cm long; set aside. Squeeze orange and reserve ¼ cup/50 mL juice.

In small bowl, combine reserved orange juice, chili paste, sherry, sugar and cornstarch; stir until smooth.

In wok, heat oil over high heat; add chicken and stir-fry for 2 minutes or until no longer pink. Remove chicken. Add orange rind, garlic and gingerroot; stir-fry for 10 seconds. Add peppers and stir-fry for 1 minute. Add chili paste mixture and bring to boil. Return chicken to wok and stir until heated through. Makes 4 servings.

*Bottled chili paste is available in some supermarkets and most Oriental grocery stores. You can substitute dried chili peppers or the kind of hot chili sauce found in Oriental grocery stores. The seeds in fresh or dried peppers are very hot; if you want a milder taste omit seeds.

Fresh Gingerroot
I love the flavor fresh ginger gives to cooked dishes and always try to have it on hand. It is far superior to ground ginger. Gingerroot is usually available in the fresh-produce section in supermarkets and at Oriental grocery stores.

To store: Will keep in the refrigerator for 2 to 3 weeks, or wrap tightly in plastic wrap and freeze for up to 4 weeks.

To use: I usually peel the skin from the portion of gingerroot I plan to use with a sharp knife or vegetable peeler, then either chop or finely grate it. I use fresh gingerroot most often in stir-frys such as Szechuan Orange-Ginger Chicken (page 90), and with vegetables, such as Broccoli with Ginger and Lemon (page 122).

To substitute ground ginger in recipes calling for gingerroot: Use ground ginger only if you can't find gingerroot. Use about ½ tsp/2 mL ground ginger in most recipes in this book. Taste, then add another ½ tsp/2 mL if desired. Use ground ginger where called for in baked recipes such as cookies.

Stir-Fried Chicken with Broccoli

Stir-fries are perfect last-minute dishes that can easily be stretched to accommodate extra guests. Just add more broccoli or extra vegetables and cook more rice or noodles. If you have dried Chinese mushrooms on hand, use a few of them (soaked first) instead of fresh.

PER SERVING	
calories	171
g fat	6
mg cholesterol	49
mg sodium	224
g protein	21
g carbohydrate	8

GOOD: iron
EXCELLENT: fiber, vitamin A, vitamin C, niacin

1 ½ lb	boned skinned chicken breasts	750 g
2 tbsp	vegetable oil	25 mL
2 tbsp	minced fresh gingerroot	25 mL
2	onions, sliced	2
6 cups	broccoli florets	1.5 L
1 cup	thinly sliced carrots	250 mL
½ lb	mushrooms, sliced	250 mL
¾ cup	chicken stock	175 mL
2 tbsp	sherry	25 mL
2 tsp	soy sauce	10 mL
2 tsp	cornstarch	10 mL
2 tbsp	water	25 mL
4 cups	sliced Chinese cabbage, or bok choy*	1 L

When stir-frying, it is very important to heat wok or heavy skillet and have oil very hot before adding any food. If food sticks, either the wok wasn't hot enough or you need a little more oil. If food starts to stick after adding vegetables, add a little water to prevent scorching.

Cut chicken into thin strips about 1 ½ in/4 cm long; set aside.

In wok or large heavy skillet, heat oil over high heat. Gradually add chicken to wok with half of the gingerroot; stir-fry for 2 minutes. Remove from wok and set aside. Add onion and stir-fry for 2 minutes; set aside with chicken.

Add broccoli, carrots, mushrooms and remaining gingerroot to wok; stir-fry for 2 minutes, adding a little water to prevent sticking if necessary.

Mix together chicken stock, sherry and soy sauce; pour over broccoli mixture. Cover and let steam for 2 minutes. Stir in reserved onion and chicken. Mix cornstarch with water; stir into wok and bring to boil. Add Chinese cabbage; stir and cook for 1 minute or until tender crisp. Makes 8 servings.

*If bok choy not available use thinly sliced green cabbage.

To store mussels:
Mussels will keep for 1 to 2 days in a bowl or paper bag in the refrigerator. Don't store in a plastic bag.

PER SERVING	
calories	309
g fat	8
mg cholesterol	115
mg sodium	429
g protein	31
g carbohydrate	30

GOOD: fiber, thiamin
EXCELLENT: niacin, vitamin C, iron

Make-Ahead Paella

This is one of my favorite dishes for entertaining—it looks spectacular, tastes delicious and can be mostly prepared in advance. It's great any time of year for a sit-down dinner or special buffet. There are many versions of this Spanish specialty—do vary the seafood to your own tastes and to what's available. Saffron adds a delicate flavor and a beautiful yellow color but is terribly expensive and sometimes hard to find. If unavailable add 1 tbsp/5 mL turmeric. (Recipe pictured opposite page 86.)

12	littleneck or Manila clams (in shells)	12
1 lb	mussels (in shells)	500 g
2 lb	chicken breasts (or 1 lb/500 g boneless)	1 kg
1 tbsp	vegetable oil or margarine	15 mL
½ lb	hot Spanish or Italian sausage	250 g
4	cloves garlic, minced	4
1½ cups	uncooked parboiled rice	375 mL
3 cups	water or clam cooking liquid	750 mL
1½ cups	coarsely chopped tomato	375 mL
1	sweet green pepper, cut in ½-in/1 cm pieces	1
1	bay leaf	1
1 tsp	saffron threads	5 mL
¼ tsp	ground turmeric	1 mL
¼ tsp	freshly ground pepper	1 mL
	Cayenne pepper	
¾ lb	medium shrimp, cooked peeled and de-veined*	375 g
1 cup	peas	250 mL

Scrub clams and mussels under cold running water; cut off any hairy beards from mussels. Discard any clams or mussels that do not close when tapped. Refrigerate mussels until needed. Steam clams** over boiling water until shells open (about 5 minutes); reserve cooking liquid, discard any that don't open. Refrigerate until needed.

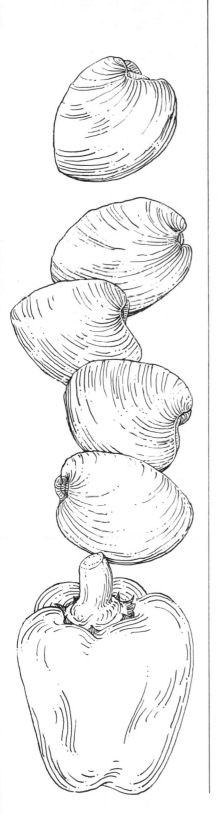

Remove skin from chicken breasts; cut into bite-size pieces. In large nonstick skillet, heat oil over medium-high heat, brown chicken. Transfer chicken to paella pan or large shallow casserole.

Add sausage to skillet and cook (time will vary depending on type of sausage); remove from skillet and cut into ¼-in/5 mm thick slices; add to pan with chicken.

In same skillet, cook garlic for 1 minute; stir in rice. Add clam cooking liquid or water, tomatoes, green pepper, bay leaf, saffron, turmeric, pepper, and cayenne to taste; bring to boil. Reduce heat and simmer for 15 minutes; pour over chicken.

(Recipe can be prepared ahead to this point, covered and refrigerated for up to 1 day. Return all ingredients to room temperature before continuing with recipe.)

Add mussels and bake, covered, in 425°F/220°C oven for 20 minutes. Stir in shrimps, clams and peas; bake for 15 minutes or until heated through and mussels open (discard any mussels that don't open). Makes 8 servings.

*Cook shrimp in boiling water for 3 minutes. Drain and cool under cold water; peel and de-vein.
**Because some clams take much longer to cook than others I cook them in advance. I cook the mussels in the rice because they cook in a short time and I want the liquid from the mussels to flavor the dish.

PER SERVING	
calories	162
g fat	6
mg cholesterol	57
mg sodium	120
g protein	25
g carbohydrate	1
EXCELLENT: niacin	

Grilled Turkey Scallopini with Herbs and Garlic

This is a favorite dish of mine for summer entertaining. It's extremely fast and easy, yet a little different. Because turkey is tender and this is a fairly strong-flavored marinade, it doesn't need hours of marinating and can be prepared at the last minute or an hour or two in advance. Veal scallopini can be used instead of turkey.

3	cloves garlic, minced	3
½ tsp	each dried thyme, rosemary and oregano	2 mL
2 tbsp	olive oil	25 mL
2 tbsp	lemon juice	25 mL
¼ tsp	salt	1 mL
	Freshly ground pepper	
1 lb	turkey scallopini*	500 g

In food processor or small bowl, combine garlic, thyme, rosemary, oregano, oil, lemon juice, salt, and pepper to taste; mix well. Brush over both sides of turkey. (Grill immediately or cover and let stand at room temperature for 30 minutes or refrigerate for up to 2 hours.) On lightly greased grill 4 in/10 cm from hot coals, grill turkey for 2 minutes on each side or just until cooked through. Makes 4 servings.

*If turkey scallopini aren't available in your store, slice partially frozen turkey breast meat thinly, then pound between two pieces of waxed paper into ¼-in/5 mm-thick slices or use veal scallopini.

Spring Barbecue

Grilled Turkey Scallopini with Herbs and Garlic (page 94)
Asparagus
Wild Rice and mushrooms
Spinach Salad with Sesame Seed Dressing (page 55)
Rhubarb-Strawberry Sorbet (page 170)

30-minute Summer Barbecue

Grilled Turkey Scallopini with Herbs and Garlic (page 94)
Corn on the cob
French bread
Sliced tomatoes
Strawberries with Raspberry Sauce (page 172)

Buying Fish

Odor and appearance are the clues to the freshness of seafood. There should be no strong fishy odor, the eyes should be bright and bulging, not sunken into the head. The skin should spring back when pressed lightly. When I buy fish I ask the salesperson what fish came in that day and choose from these.

Storage

Wash, pat dry and cover with an airtight wrapper. Fish can be refrigerated for about two days or in a freezer as long as three months.

Cooking Fish

Fish and shellfish are naturally tender. They should be cooked for a short time at a high temperature. To determine the length of cooking time, measure the thickness of the fish at its thickest part. Cook fresh fish 10 minutes per inch of thickness, adding five minutes if wrapped in foil; frozen fish requires 20 minutes per inch, plus 10 minutes if wrapped in foil. Cooking time may vary depending on the cooking method used. Don't overcook. Overcooked fish becomes dry, tough and rubbery and loses its flavor. Fish is cooked when the flesh is opaque and it flakes easily.

Oven Steaming Fish

This method is the easiest and requires the least cleanup. Place fish on the shiny side of foil and season with lemon juice and/or herbs. Wrap fish in foil and place on cookie sheet. Bake in 450°F/230°C oven for required time (see above), depending on thickness.

FISH

Fish is an original fast food that's easy to cook at home. Not only does it taste good but it is very nutritious. It is an excellent source of high-quality protein, and is high in vitamins A, D and B-complex, and low in fat, particularly saturated fat. Fish contains the beneficial omega-3 type of fat, which according to the latest research helps to reduce the incidence of heart disease. Most fish is lower in cholesterol than meat and poultry.

For many years shellfish were banned on diets prescribed to lower blood cholesterol, because of a supposed high sterol count. But better testing techniques can now discriminate between the different sterols, and show that cholesterol isn't present in shellfish in so large an amount as to be of concern. Shrimp is the shellfish that is highest in cholesterol but as long as you don't have it too often or are on a low-cholesterol diet, it can still be enjoyed.

The two most important factors in preparing tasty fish are, above all, to buy good-quality fish, either fresh or frozen, and not to overcook it. You can substitute one kind of fish for another in the recipes here. Buy whatever kind is freshest and use in the recipe that appeals most to you.

Steaming Fish

If you don't have a fish steamer you can: 1. Use a wok with a lid. Place fish on a heat-proof plate. Add a small amount of water to the bottom of a wok and bring to a boil. Set two chopsticks above water level in the wok and place the plate on the chopsticks. Cover. The steam will circulate around the fish and cook it gently; 2. Use a roasting pan. Place a rack in the roaster and a heatproof plate on top of the rack. Add water to below the level of the plate. To prevent the fish from falling apart, wrap in cheesecloth or lettuce leaves. Cover with a lid or foil.

PER SERVING (analysis based on cod fillets)	
calories	187
g fat	8
mg cholesterol	70
mg sodium	145
g protein	25
g carbohydrate	3
GOOD: iron EXCELLENT: niacin	

Fish Fillets with Herbed Crumbs

Here's an easy-to-make and tasty way to serve fish fillets. It's really quick if you make your bread crumbs and chop the parsley in a blender or food processor, then melt the margarine and cook the fish in a microwave.

1 lb	fish fillets	500 g
⅓ cup	fresh bread crumbs	75 mL
1 tbsp	margarine, melted	15 mL
¼ cup	chopped fresh parsley	50 mL
1 tsp	dried thyme	5 mL
¼ tsp	freshly ground pepper	1 mL

In shallow baking dish or microwave-safe dish, arrange fillets in single layer. Combine bread crumbs, margarine, parsley, thyme and pepper; mix well and sprinkle over fish.

Bake uncovered in 450°F/230°C oven for 10 minutes per inch of thickness (5 to 7 minutes per cm) for fresh fish, 20 minutes per inch (10 to 12 minutes per cm) for frozen or until fish flakes easily when tested with fork. Makes 4 servings.

Microwave Method:

Microwave, uncovered, at high (100%) power for about 4 minutes for fresh fish or until fish flakes easily when tested with fork.

Microwaving Fish

One of the best reasons for owning a microwave is to cook fish. It takes only minutes to cook and is very moist. Arrange fish in a microwave dish with the thickest part facing the outside of the dish. Season with pepper, lemon juice or herbs (always add salt after microwaving not before). Place plastic wrap over dish with a small corner turned back for steam to escape. One pound of fresh or thawed fillets in a single layer at high setting takes about 4 to 5 minutes (10 to 12 for frozen). Times will vary depending on thickness. Rotate dish during cooking.

PER SERVING (using cod)	
calories	164
g fat	6
mg cholesterol	70
mg sodium	112
g protein	25
g carbohydrate	0
EXCELLENT: niacin	

Nutrition note:
Cod is higher in cholesterol than many other fish. If using sole the cholesterol drops to about 60 g, if using halibut to about 55 g per serving.

Fish Fillets with Basil and Lemon

This is so simple and easy, yet results in the best-tasting fish. If buying frozen fillets, try to buy the kind that have been frozen in a single layer or individually wrapped. If using the kind that have been frozen in a block, defrost the fish and separate into fillets before cooking. If buying fresh, choose whatever kind of fillets are freshest. About 1 tbsp/15 mL of any fresh herbs, such as chopped fresh dill, thyme or tarragon, can be substituted for the basil.

1 lb	fish fillets	500 g
1 tbsp	lemon juice	15 mL
2 tsp	margarine, melted	10 mL
½ tsp	dried basil	2 mL
	freshly ground pepper	
Garnish:	Fresh herbs or chopped fresh parsley	

In microwave-safe or conventional baking dish, arrange fillets in a single layer. In small dish, combine lemon juice, margarine and basil; drizzle over fish. Sprinkle lightly with pepper to taste.

Bake, uncovered, in 450°F/230°C oven for 8 to 10 minutes (10 minutes per inch thickness for fresh fish) or until fish is opaque and flakes easily with fork. Sprinkle with fresh herbs or parsley. Makes 4 servings.

Microwave Method:
Cover with plastic wrap and turn back corner to vent. Microwave at high (100%) power for 3½ to 4½ minutes or until fish is opaque and flakes easily with fork.

Quick and Easy Salmon Steaks with Watercress Sauce

Fresh salmon steaks are a wonderful treat and I like them best when simply cooked—either poached, steamed or microwaved, as long as they aren't overcooked. The easiest and fastest is the microwave. In summer, dress them up with this watercress sauce; in winter serve with the Fresh Dill Cream Sauce, page 140. (Recipe pictured opposite page 215.)

4	salmon steaks, 1-in/2.5 cm thick (5 oz/150 g each)	4
2 tsp	lemon juice	10 mL
	Freshly ground pepper	
	Watercress sprigs	

Watercress Sauce:

1 cup	low-fat cottage cheese	250 mL
¼ cup	low-fat plain yogurt	50 mL
¼ cup	chopped fresh watercress leaves	50 mL
2 tbsp	chopped fresh parsley	25 mL
1 tbsp	chopped fresh chives	15 mL
2 tsp	grated Parmesan cheese	10 mL

Oven Steam Method:
On lightly oiled large piece of foil, arrange salmon in single layer. Sprinkle with lemon juice, and pepper to taste. Fold foil over salmon and seal; place on baking sheet. Bake in 400°F/ 200°C oven for about 15 minutes or until fish is opaque and flakes easily with fork.

Microwave Method:
In microwave-safe dish arrange salmon in single layer. Sprinkler with lemon juice, and pepper to taste. Cover with plastic wrap; fold back corner to vent. Microwave at high (100%) power for 5 minutes or until fish is opaque and flakes easily with fork.

Watercress Sauce: In food processor, combine cottage cheese, yogurt, chopped watercress, parsley, chives and Parmesan; process until well mixed. Or pass cottage cheese through a sieve and combine with remaining ingredients.

Arrange salmon on plates and garnish with sprig of watercress. Pass sauce separately. Makes 4 servings.

PER SERVING	
calories	295
g fat	11
mg cholesterol	66
mg sodium	396
g protein	43
g carbohydrate	3

GOOD: thiamin, calcium, iron
EXCELLENT: niacin

The only way to ruin good-quality fish is to overcook it. If fillets or steaks are ¾- to 1-in (2-2.5 cm) thick, you'll be much less likely to overcook them than if they are thin. Cooking times in this recipe are based on 1-in/2.5 cm-thick steaks.

Dilled Snapper Fillets with Cucumber-Yogurt Sauce

Any kind of fish fillets—salmon, sole, sea bass—can be used; just choose whatever is freshest. If at all possible, try to use fresh dill instead of dried because the flavor is quite different.

<table>
<tr><td>4</td><td>red snapper fillets, about 1¼ lb/625 g</td><td>4</td></tr>
<tr><td>1½ tsp</td><td>lemon juice</td><td>7 mL</td></tr>
<tr><td>1</td><td>clove garlic, minced</td><td>1</td></tr>
<tr><td>2 tbsp</td><td>chopped fresh dill (or 1 tsp/5 mL dried)</td><td>25 mL</td></tr>
</table>

Cucumber-Yogurt Sauce:

<table>
<tr><td>¼ cup</td><td>low-fat plain yogurt</td><td>50 mL</td></tr>
<tr><td>¼ cup</td><td>light sour cream</td><td>50 mL</td></tr>
<tr><td>½ cup</td><td>finely chopped cucumber</td><td>125 mL</td></tr>
<tr><td>1 tbsp</td><td>chopped green onion</td><td>15 mL</td></tr>
<tr><td></td><td>Freshly ground pepper</td><td></td></tr>
</table>

On broiler pan or in microwave-safe dish, arrange fillets in single layer with thickest part to outside. Brush with lemon juice; sprinkle with garlic and dill. Broil for 6 to 8 minutes or microwave, covered loosely with waxed paper, at high (100%) power for 4 to 5 minutes or until fish is opaque and flakes easily when tested with fork.

Cucumber-Yogurt Sauce: Meanwhile, in small dish, combine yogurt, sour cream, cucumber, onion, and pepper to taste; mix well. Spread over fish and broil for 2 minutes or microwave at high (100%) power for 1 minute or until sauce is hot. Makes 4 servings.

PER SERVING

calories	127
g fat	3
mg cholesterol	74
mg sodium	134
g protein	21
g carbohydrate	3

EXCELLENT: niacin

Barbecued Skewered Halibut with Red Peppers and Snow Peas

These easy-to-make kabobs look festive, taste great and, as an added bonus, make the fish go further. Serve over rice along with Tomato Salsa Sauce (page 105) or Cucumber-Yogurt Sauce (page 99). Be sure to soak the wooden skewers in water for at least 30 minutes to prevent charring. (Recipe pictured on front cover.)

	PER SERVING	
	calories	164
	g fat	6
	mg cholesterol	64
	mg sodium	109
	g protein	24
	g carbohydrate	3

GOOD: fiber, iron
EXCELLENT: vitamin A, vitamin C, niacin

1 lb	halibut or swordfish steaks	500 g
	Juice of 1 lime	
1 tbsp	olive oil	15 mL
2 tbsp	chopped fresh coriander or parsley or dill	25 mL
	Freshly ground pepper	
1	sweet red pepper	1
20	snow peas	20

Cut fish into 1-in/2.5 cm cubes; place in a single layer in a shallow dish. Sprinkle with lime juice, oil and coriander; cover and refrigerate for at least 30 minutes or up to 4 hours, turning once or twice.

Seed and cut red pepper into 1-in/2.5 cm squares. String snow peas and blanch in boiling water for 1 minute or until bright green and easily bent.

Thread fish on water-soaked wooden skewers alternating with red pepper and snow peas folded in half. Grill over medium-hot coals, turning once or twice, for 12 to 18 minutes or until fish is opaque. Makes 4 servings.

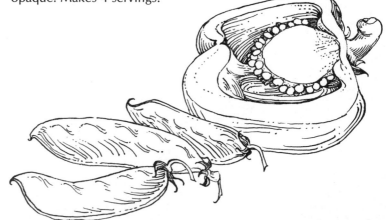

Linguine with Salmon and Chives

Tender-crisp cooked vegetables, such as asparagus, green peas or mushrooms, can be added to this quick and easy supper dish. Green onions can be used instead of chives; cooked fresh salmon instead of canned.

½ lb	linguine or any noodles	250 g
4 tsp	soft margarine	20 mL
1	small onion, chopped	1
2 tbsp	all-purpose flour	25 mL
1 cup	skim milk	250 mL
⅓ cup	chopped fresh chives	75 mL
	Freshly ground pepper	
1	can (7.75 oz/220 g) salmon	1
2 tbsp	grated Parmesan cheese	25 mL

In large pot of boiling water, cook linguine until al dente (tender but firm); drain, reserving ¼ cup/50 mL cooking liquid. Return linguine to pan.

Meanwhile, in saucepan, melt margarine over medium heat; add onion and cook until tender. Stir in flour; mix well. Add milk and cook, whisking, until mixture comes to boil, thickens and loses any raw-flour taste. Stir in chives, pepper to taste, and add reserved cooking liquid.

Flake salmon and add along with juices and chive mixture to pot with linguine; mix lightly. Sprinkle Parmesan cheese over each serving. Makes 4 servings.

PER SERVING	
calories	400
g fat	12
mg cholesterol	23
mg sodium	149
g protein	22
g carbohydrate	49
GOOD: calcium	
EXCELLENT: niacin	

Recipe includes juices from canned salmon. Although this adds to the fat content, these juices are an excellent source of omega 3 fatty acids, which current research indicates may help to reduce heart disease.

Try to time cooking of pasta so it is ready the same time the clams are. If using dried pasta, start it before cooking clams; if using fresh or very fine pasta, cook clams first.

PER SERVING	
calories	293
g fat	7
mg cholesterol	17
mg sodium	78
g protein	10
g carbohydrate	46

GOOD: fiber, niacin
EXCELLENT: vitamin C, iron

Recent research has shown not all shellfish are high in cholesterol. Mollusks— oysters, scallops, clams and mussels—are not as high in cholesterol as are crustaceans —shrimp, crab and lobster.

Tuscan-Style Capellini with Clams and Garlic

In Italy, this popular pasta dish is made with tiny tender clams that have about 1-in/2.5 cm shells. They are available in Canada on the West Coast, but they're harder to find elsewhere. Capellini is the very thin, angel-hair noodle; however, any type can be used.

2 lb	small size clams (in shells)	1 kg
3	cloves garlic, minced	3
2 tbsp	olive oil	25 mL
¼ cup	white wine	50 mL
½ lb	capellini or spaghetti noodles	250 g
1 cup	chopped fresh parsley	250 mL
	Salt and freshly ground pepper	

Scrub clams under cold running water: discard any that do not close when tapped.

In large heavy saucepan, cook garlic and oil over medium-high heat for 1 minute; add wine and clams. Cover and cook until clams open (time will vary from 2 to 10 minutes depending on size of clams); discard any that do not open. Meanwhile, in large pot of boiling water, cook capellini until al dente (tender but firm); drain.

Pour clam mixture over hot pasta and toss with parsley. Season with salt and pepper to taste, Makes 4 servings.

Fettuccine with Mussels, Leeks and Tomatoes

Easy Friday-Night Seafood Dinner for Four

Mushroom Bisque with Tarragon (page 37)
Fettuccine with Mussels, Leeks and Tomatoes (page 103)
French bread
Fresh Pineapple Slices with Rum (page 178)
or Berries with Orange-Honey Yogurt (page 175)

This gorgeous dish is perfect for a special little dinner. As well as being easy to make, it tastes and looks wonderful, too. Choose cultured mussels as they are easy to clean and have lots of meat inside.

3 lb	mussels	1.5 kg
2	leeks	2
¾ lb	fettuccine	375 g
2 tbsp	olive oil	25 mL
4	cloves garlic, chopped	4
½ tsp	dried thyme	2 mL
4	tomatoes, coarsely chopped	4
¼ cup	dry white wine	50 mL
1 cup	coarsely chopped fresh parsley	250 mL
	Freshly ground pepper	

Scrub mussels under cold running water; cut off any hairy beards. Discard any that do not close when tapped.

Trim leeks, discarding dark green parts. Slice in half lengthwise and wash well. Cut into thin 1½-in/4 cm-long strips and set aside.

In large pot of boiling water, cook fettuccine until al dente (tender but firm); drain and return to pot.

Meanwhile, in large heavy saucepan, heat oil over medium heat; cook garlic and thyme for 1 minute. Add mussels, leeks, tomatoes and wine; cover and bring to boil. Reduce heat and simmer for 5 to 8 minutes or until leeks are tender and mussels open (discard any that don't open).

Pour tomato mixture over fettuccine; add parsley, and pepper to taste. Toss to mix and serve on dinner plates or in large individual bowls. Makes 4 servings.

PER SERVING	
calories	540
g fat	10
mg cholesterol	87
mg sodium	527
g protein	29
g carbohydrate	82

GOOD: vitamin A, riboflavin, calcium
EXCELLENT: fiber, vitamin C, thiamin, niacin, iron

PER SERVING	
calories	173
g fat	6
mg cholesterol	76
mg sodium	144
g protein	27
g carbohydrate	1
EXCELLENT: niacin	

Teriyaki Cod Fillets

These fillets are absolutely delicious when microwaved. Any kind of fish can be used in this recipe, but I like cod or salmon the best.

2 tbsp	dry sherry	25 mL
2 tbsp	water	25 mL
1 tbsp	low-sodium soy sauce*	15 mL
1 tbsp	vegetable oil	15 mL
2 tsp	grated gingerroot	10 mL
1 tsp	granulated sugar	5 mL
1	clove garlic, minced	1
1 lb	cod fillets, ¾ in/2 cm thick	500 g

In shallow microwave-safe or conventional dish, combine sherry, water, soy sauce, oil, gingerroot, sugar and garlic; stir to mix. Add fish fillets and arrange in single layer; marinate at room temperature for 20 minutes or refrigerate for up to 4 hours, turning once or twice.

Remove fillets from marinade and transfer marinade to small saucepan. Place fillets in single layer in steamer; cover and steam for 5 to 8 minutes or until fish is opaque and flakes easily when tested with fork. Meanwhile, heat marinade over low heat until warm; drizzle over fish before serving. Makes 4 servings.

Microwave Method:
Cover dish (fish and marinade) with vented plastic wrap and microwave at high (100%) power for 5 minutes or until fish is opaque and flakes easily when tested with fork.

*Soy sauce is very high in sodium. Sodium-reduced soy sauce is available at many supermarkets. If not, make your own by diluting regular soy sauce with an equal amount of water. There are two kinds of light soy sauce. One kind is basically lighter in color and is used in dishes for which you don't want the darker color. Another, newer version, lite soy sauce, is sodium-reduced. Naturally brewed soy sauce is lower in sodium than chemically brewed.

Grilled Halibut Steaks with Tomato Salsa Sauce

As well as its delicious taste when barbecued, halibut is a good choice for grilling because it doesn't fall apart as some fish does. However, other kinds of firm-fleshed fish, such as salmon, can be substituted. Instead of a rich cream sauce, dress grilled fish with a light, fresh Mexican salsa. This fairly mild tomato and cucumber salsa does not overpower the delicate flavor of fish. For extra spiciness, add chopped hot peppers to taste.

	PER SERVING	
calories		234
g fat		10
mg cholesterol		75
mg sodium		176
g protein		32
g carbohydrate		3

GOOD: vitamin C
EXCELLENT: vitamin A, niacin

1½ lb	halibut steaks, about ¾ in/2 cm thick	750 g

Tomato Salsa Sauce:

⅓ cup	finely diced cucumber	75 mL
⅓ cup	finely diced sweet red pepper	75 mL
2 tbsp	finely diced red onion	25mL
1	small ripe tomato, finely diced	1
2 tsp	red wine vinegar	10 mL
2 tsp	chopped fresh coriander (optional)	10 mL
½ tsp	Worcestershire sauce	2 mL
Dash	hot pepper sauce	Dash
1 tsp	olive oil	5 mL

Tomato Salsa Sauce: In bowl, combine cucumber, red pepper, onion, tomato, vinegar, coriander (if using), Worcestershire sauce, hot pepper sauce and oil; stir to mix. In food processor, purée half of the salsa mixture; combine with remaining salsa.

On greased grill or in broiler, grill fish, turning once, for about 4 minutes on each side or until fish is opaque and flakes easily when tested with fork. Place on serving platter or plates and spoon salsa over. Makes 4 servings (1¼ cups/300 mL sauce).

Microwave Method:
Place steaks in single layer in microwave-safe dish; cover with vented plastic wrap and microwave at high (100%) power for 4 to 5 minutes or until opaque.

Swordfish Steaks with Lime and Coriander

PER SERVING	
calories	150
g fat	6
mg cholesterol	64
mg sodium	108
g protein	23
g carbohydrate	0
EXCELLENT: vitamin A, niacin	

Fresh lime juice and coriander complement the flavor of most fish. Swordfish is particularly good for barbecuing because its firm flesh doesn't fall apart. Other fresh fish steaks, such as halibut or salmon, are also delicious cooked this way. If fresh coriander isn't available, substitute other herbs, such as fresh parsley, dill, rosemary or oregano. Serve with Tomato Salsa Sauce (page 105). (Recipe pictured opposite page 214.)

1 lb	swordfish or halibut steaks (about ¾ in/2 cm thick)	500g
	Juice of 1 lime	
1 tbsp	olive oil	15 mL
2 tbsp	chopped fresh coriander (or ½ tsp/2 mL ground)	25 mL
	Freshly ground pepper	
Garnish:		
	Lime wedges	
	Fresh coriander sprigs	

Fish Barbecue Dinner

Swordfish Steaks with Lime and Coriander (page 106)
Peas with Green Onions (page 123)
New Potatoes with Herbs (page 123)
Peaches and Blueberries with Easy Grand Marnier Sauce (page 167)

For other main-course dishes see lifestyle section, page 181.

Place fish in single layer in shallow dish. Sprinkle with lime juice, oil and coriander; cover and refrigerate for at least 15 minutes or up to 4 hours, turning once or twice.

Broil or grill fish for 5 to 8 minutes or until fish is opaque and flakes easily when tested with fork. If grilling, turn halfway through. (Time will vary depending upon thickness of fish, about 10 minutes per in/2.5 cm of thickness.) Sprinkle with pepper to taste. Garnish each serving with lime wedges and sprigs of fresh coriander. Makes 4 servings.

MEATLESS MAIN COURSES

To make our diet more healthy we need to rely more on vegetable protein and less on animal protein. Legumes (beans, peas, lentils), nuts, seeds and grains can also provide protein, vitamins and minerals, and are higher in fiber and lower in saturated fat than animal protein.

Protein is made up of 22 amino acids. Nine of these amino acids can't be produced by the body and must be obtained from food. These are called essential amino acids. All animal products contain all the essential amino acids. Plant foods are missing an essential amino acid. Therefore, it is important to combine a plant food with an animal food or two plant foods that together contain all the essential amino acids. Good combinations of plant foods are:

   legumes and grains (e.g. baked beans and whole-wheat bread)
   legumes and nuts (e.g. tossed salad with chick peas and walnuts)
   legumes and low-fat dairy products (e.g. bean casserole with low-fat mozzarella topping)
   grains and low-fat dairy products (e.g. cereal and skim milk)

When we serve a meatless meal, we can use some cheese and eggs and still keep our saturated fat content down to the recommended level. It's important to consider our diet over a day or week. It's when we eat meats, high-fat cheese and eggs on a daily basis that the fat and cholesterol amounts will be too high. See other sections of this book for more meatless main-course dishes.

Bean Casserole with Tomatoes and Spinach

It seems that something that tastes as good as this should be harder to make. My son, Jeff, really likes this and says the Five-Grain Soda Bread (page 155) is perfect with it. Serve as a quick dinner or lunch along with a green salad. Sometimes I cook a pound (500 g) of ground beef along with the onions and add chili powder.

1 tbsp	soft margarine or vegetable oil	15 mL
1	clove garlic, minced	1
2	onions, sliced	2
1	can (14 oz/398 mL) tomatoes	1
1	can (19 oz/540 mL) red kidney beans, drained	1
1	can (19 oz/540 mL) romano beans, drained	1
½ tsp	dried oregano	2 mL
1	pkg (10 oz/284 g) fresh spinach (or 1 bunch) stems removed	1
	Freshly ground pepper	

PER SERVING

calories	333
g fat	4
mg cholesterol	0
mg sodium	239
g protein	20
g carbohydrate	57

GOOD: thiamin, calcium
EXCELLENT: fiber, vitamin A, vitamin C, niacin, iron

In large heavy saucepan or casserole, heat margarine over medium heat; cook garlic and onions, stirring occasionally, for 3 minutes or until softened.

Add tomatoes, breaking up with back of spoon. Add kidney and romano beans, and oregano; bring to simmer.

Add spinach; cover and simmer until spinach is wilted, about 2 minutes. Season with pepper to taste. Makes 4 servings (1½ cups/375 mL each).

PER SERVING	
calories	304
g fat	14
mg cholesterol	40
mg sodium	615
g protein	16
g carbohydrate	31
GOOD: fiber, vitamin A, iron	
EXCELLENT: vitamin C, niacin, calcium	

Cheese is a good source of protein and calcium; however, it (particularly Cheddar) is high in fat. If this is part of a meatless meal, it can fit into a 30% fat diet. If you are serving this with meat, you should reduce the cheese by half and use a low-fat cheese such as low-fat mozzarella or feta.

Barley, Green Pepper and Tomato Casserole

Serve this as a main course along with a tossed salad and whole-wheat toast or pita bread. Crumbled feta cheese is a nice addition.

1 cup	pot barley	250 mL
3 cups	hot vegetable or chicken stock or water	750 mL
2	onions, chopped	2
1	sweet green pepper, chopped	1
2	large tomatoes, cut in chunks	2
1 tsp	dried oregano	5 mL
	Salt and freshly ground pepper	
2 cups	shredded Cheddar cheese	500 mL

In baking dish, combine barley, stock or water, onions, green pepper, tomatoes, oregano, and salt and pepper to taste; stir to mix. Cover and bake in 350°F/180°C oven for 45 minutes. Stir in cheese and bake, uncovered, for 25 minutes longer or until barley is tender and most liquid has been absorbed. Makes 6 servings.

Tomato, Broccoli and Pasta Salad

The broccoli is added just before serving because the acid in the salad dressing will cause the broccoli to lose its bright green color.

For other main-course salads see salad section (page 47).

This salad is perfect for buffets, with a green salad or soup for a main course. I like it with rigatoni, the large, tubular-shaped pasta, because it goes well with large chunks of tomato and broccoli; however, any other pasta can be substituted.

¼ lb	rigatoni or other pasta	125 g
3 cups	broccoli florets	750 mL
1 cup	chopped green onions	250 mL
3	tomatoes, cut in wedges	3
¼ lb	low-fat mozzarella cheese, cubed	125 g
⅓ cup	minced fresh parsley	75 mL
Mustard Vinaigrette:		
3 tbsp	lemon juice	45 mL
3 tbsp	water	45 mL
2	cloves garlic, minced	2
1 tsp	Dijon mustard	5 mL
¼ cup	vegetable oil	50 mL
	Salt and freshly ground pepper	

In large pot of boiling water, cook pasta until al dente (tender but firm). Drain and rinse under cold water; drain again and set aside.

In another pot of boiling water, blanch broccoli for 2 minutes. Drain and rinse under cold water. Drain again and wrap in paper towel; set aside.

In salad bowl, combine pasta, green onions, tomatoes, cheese and parsley.

Mustard Vinaigrette: In food processor or mixing bowl, combine lemon juice, water, garlic, mustard and oil; mix well. Pour over salad and toss to mix. Add salt and pepper to taste.

Cover and refrigerate for 30 minutes or up to 4 hours. Just before serving, add broccoli and toss to mix. Makes 6 servings.

PER SERVING	
calories	229
g fat	13
mg cholesterol	11
mg sodium	116
g protein	9
g carbohydrate	20

GOOD: fiber, vitamin A, niacin, calcium
EXCELLENT: vitamin C

Easy Summer Dinner

Rotini with Fresh Tomatoes, Basil and Parmesan (page 111)
Tossed Seasonal Greens with Ranch-Style Buttermilk Dressing (page 65)
Hot bread
Fresh Blueberries with Orange-Honey Yogurt (page 175)

Adding chicken, turkey or ham to this dish will increase the protein. Adding ham will also increase the sodium (to 703 mg).

PER SERVING (meatless version)	
calories	368
g fat	11
mg cholesterol	8
mg sodium	198
g protein	14
g carbohydrate	55

GOOD: niacin, calcium, iron
EXCELLENT: fiber, vitamin A, vitamin C

Rotini with Fresh Tomatoes, Basil and Parmesan

You can use any kind of pasta in this easy recipe. To preserve the fresh flavor and texture of the tomatoes they are quickly cooked over high heat. Once you have cooked the pasta, the whole mixture cooks in less than five minutes. (Recipe pictured opposite page 118.)

½ lb	rotini (corkscrew shape) or any tubular pasta	250 g
2 tbsp	vegetable oil or margarine	25 mL
4	green onions, chopped	4
4	tomatoes, coarsely chopped	4
3	cloves garlic, minced	3
1 cup	strips or cubes cooked ham, turkey, chicken (optional)	250 mL
1 cup	coarsely chopped fresh parsley	250 mL
¼ cup	coarsely chopped fresh basil (or 1 tsp/5 mL dried)	50 mL
½ cup	grated Parmesan cheese	125 mL
	Salt and pepper	

In large pot of boiling water, cook pasta until al dente (tender but firm); drain. (If sauce isn't ready, rinse pasta under warm water for a few seconds to prevent it sticking together.)

Meanwhile, in large heavy saucepan or Dutch oven, heat oil over high heat. Add onions, tomatoes and garlic; cook, stirring, for 2 to 3 minutes or until tomatoes are just heated through but still hold their shape. Stir in rotini, ham (if using), parsley, basil and Parmesan. Reduce heat to medium; cook, stirring gently, for about 2 minutes or until heated through. Season with salt and pepper to taste. Makes 4 servings.

Easy July Supper

*Fettuccine with Pesto Sauce
(page 112)*

*Sliced Cucumbers with Chives
and Yogurt (omit Basil) (page
52)*

Raw baby carrots.

Whole-wheat pita bread

*Strawberries with Orange
Honey Yogurt (page 175)*

PER SERVING (MAIN COURSE)	
calories	542
g fat	12
mg cholesterol	10
mg sodium	247
g protein	20
g carbohydrate	88

GOOD: vitamin C, calcium, iron
EXCELLENT: fiber, niacin

Freeze pesto sauce in ice-cube
containers; when frozen
transfer to plastic bag. Use a
cube to flavor soups, salad
dressing and sauces.

Fettuccine with Pesto Sauce

Pesto sauce is a fragrant fresh basil sauce that is absolutely perfect over pasta. This version has a full, pungent basil flavor yet omits the pine nuts and is much lower in oil than the classic recipe.

1 lb	fettuccine	500 g
	Freshly ground pepper	
	Grated Parmesan cheese	

Pesto Sauce:

2	cloves garlic	2
1 cup	fresh basil leaves, lightly packed	250 mL
½ cup	grated Parmesan cheese	125 mL
2 tbsp	olive oil	25 mL

In large pot of boiling water cook fettuccine until al dente (tender but firm). While pasta is cooking, prepare sauce.

Pesto Sauce: In food processor, combine garlic and basil; process until chopped. Add Parmesan and olive oil, process until smooth. Remove ½ cup/125 mL of the pasta cooking liquid and add to sauce; process until smooth.

Drain pasta and toss with pesto sauce. Sprinkle with pepper and Parmesan to taste. Makes 4 main course servings; 8 side dish servings.

Compare	g fat per serving
This recipe	12
Most pesto sauce recipes	20 +

PER SERVING	
calories	332
g fat	11
mg cholesterol	30
mg sodium	664
g protein	22
g carbohydrate	37
GOOD: fiber, iron	
EXCELLENT: vitamin A,	
vitamin C, niacin, calcium	

How Much Pasta to Cook?
For a main course pasta dish
which includes a number of
ingredients along with pasta, I
usually plan on about ½ lb/
500 g for 4 servings. If it is a
dish with only a light sauce
such as pesto with pasta I use
more. One-half pound/250 g
of spaghetti noodles yields
about 4 cups when cooked.

The easiest way to measure
it is to weigh the uncooked
pasta. If you don't have scales
you can estimate by dividing
up the package according to
total weight (i.e. divide a 1 lb/
500 g package in half to get ½
lb/250 g).

I usually try to cook more
pasta than I need and use the
extra to make a pasta salad or I
mix it with any extra sauce
and reheat it for breakfast or
lunch.

Vegetable Lasagna

This is light and easy to make. It can be prepared a day or two
in advance and refrigerated.

1 tbsp	vegetable oil	15 mL
1	small onion, chopped	1
3	cloves garlic, minced	3
1	carrot, chopped	1
1	stalk celery, chopped	1
2 cups	sliced mushrooms	500 mL
1	can (19 oz/540 mL) tomatoes	1
1	can (7½ oz/213 mL) tomato sauce	1
1 tsp	each dried basil and oregano	5 mL
	Salt and freshly ground pepper	
3 cups	small broccoli florets	750 mL
9	lasagna noodles	9
1 cup	low fat cottage cheese	250 mL
3 cups	shredded low-fat mozzarella cheese	750 mL
⅓ cup	grated Parmesan cheese	75 mL

In large saucepan, heat oil over medium heat; add onion and
cook until tender. Stir in garlic, carrot, celery and mushrooms;
cook, stirring often, for 5 minutes.

Add tomatoes, breaking up with fork. Stir in tomato sauce,
basil, oregano; season with salt and pepper to taste. Simmer,
uncovered, for 10 minutes or until thickened slightly. Let cool;
stir in broccoli.

In large pot of boiling water, cook noodles until al dente
(tender but firm); drain and rinse under cold water.

In lightly greased 13- × 9-in/3.5 L baking dish, arrange
3 noodles evenly over bottom. Spread with one-half of the
vegetable mixture then half of the cottage cheese. Sprinkle with
⅓ of the mozzarella cheese.

Repeat noodle, vegetable mixure, cottage and mozzarella
cheese layers once. Arrange remaining noodles over top;
sprinkle with remaining mozzarella and Parmesan. Bake in
350°F/180°C oven for 35 to 45 minutes or until hot and
bubbly. Makes 8 servings.

Cabbage and Potato Pie

Crinkly savoy cabbage, collard greens, kale, chard or a combination of these in light cream sauce with mashed potato topping is a delicious vegetable dish.

PER SERVING	
calories	246
g fat	7
mg cholesterol	1
mg sodium	137
g protein	7
g carbohydrate	40

GOOD: vitamin A, thiamin, niacin, calcium
EXCELLENT: fiber, vitamin C

1 lb	savoy cabbage or 1 bunch collard greens	500 g
4	medium potatoes, peeled and quartered	4
¼ cup	skim milk	50 mL
1 tbsp	soft margarine	15 mL
	Freshly ground pepper	
	Paprika	

Cream Sauce:

1½ tbsp	margarine	22 mL
1	medium onion, chopped	1
2 tbsp	all-purpose flour	25 mL
1 cup	skim milk	250 mL
	Salt, freshly ground pepper and nutmeg	

Separate and trim cabbage leaves or stems from collard leaves. In large pot of boiling water, cover and cook cabbage for 5 to 10 minutes, collards for 10 to 15 minutes, or until tender. Drain thoroughly; chop coarsely and set aside.

In saucepan of boiling water, cook potatoes until tender; drain. Mash potatoes along with milk, margarine and pepper to taste.

Cream Sauce: Meanwhile, in small saucepan, melt margarine over medium heat; add onion and cook for 3 to 5 minutes or until tender. Stir in flour and mix well; cook, stirring, for 1 minute. Add milk and cook, stirring, for 3 to 5 minutes or until mixture comes to simmer and has thickened. Season with salt, pepper and nutmeg to taste.

Mix sauce with cabbage; spoon into 4-cup/1 L baking dish. Cover evenly with mashed potatoes; sprinkle lightly with paprika. Bake in 350°F/180°C oven for 20 to 30 minutes or until heated through. Makes 4 servings.

Winter Meatless Dinner

*Cabbage and Potato Pie
(page 114)
Baked Parsnips and Carrots
(page 121)
Whole-wheat buns with low-fat mozzarella cheese
Fresh-fruit compote
Milk*

Gratin of Fall Vegetables

This cheese-topped vegetable casserole dish is adapted from a Foodland Ontario recipe. It's a nice dish to serve as part of a meatless meal, or with roast chicken, turkey or meats.

2 tbsp	vegetable oil	25 mL
2 cups	thin strips of small yellow turnip or rutabaga	500 mL
½ cup	water	125 mL
1	sweet red pepper, cut in thin strips	1
¾ cup	thinly sliced onion	175 mL
2 cups	thinly sliced zucchini	500 mL
1 cup	sliced mushrooms (about 8)	250 mL
4	medium tomatoes, cut in chunks	4
½ tsp	dried oregano	2 mL
	Salt and freshly ground pepper	
1½ cups	shredded low-fat mozzarella cheese	375 ml
1 tbsp	grated Parmesan cheese	15 mL

In large skillet or Dutch oven, heat oil over medium heat. Add turnip and cover and cook for 10 minutes or until tender, stirring occasionally. If necessary, add more water to prevent burning. Add red pepper and onions; cook, stirring, for 2 minutes.

Add zucchini and mushrooms; cook, stirring, for 3 minutes. Add tomatoes and increase heat to high; cook, stirring occasionally, 5 to 10 minutes or just until excess moisture has evaporated. Stir in oregano; season with salt and pepper to taste.

Spoon vegetable mixture into shallow heatproof baking dish; sprinkle evenly with mozzarella and Parmesan cheeses. Broil for 3 to 5 minutes or until cheese is melted and slightly browned. Makes 8 servings.

Recipe can be prepared in advance, covered and refrigerated. Reheat in 350°F/180°C oven for 20 to 25 minutes or microwave at high for 3 to 5 minutes or until heated through.

Mexican Rice and Bean Casserole

This is a well-liked dish at our house. You may want to add a little less chili or cayenne if you have young children. Serve with a green vegetable, salad and toast.

1 tsp	vegetable oil	5 mL
½ cup	water	125 mL
1	onion, chopped	1
2	cloves garlic, minced	2
1½ cups	mushrooms, sliced (¼ lb/125 g)	375 mL
2	sweet green peppers, chopped	2
¾ cup	long-grain rice	175 mL
1	can (28 oz/796 mL) red kidney beans, drained	1
1	can (19 oz/540 mL) tomatoes	1
1 tbsp	chili powder	15 mL
2 tsp	cumin	10 mL
¼ tsp	cayenne pepper	1 mL
1 cup	shredded low-fat mozzarella cheese	250 mL

In large skillet or Dutch oven, heat oil with water over medium heat. Add onion, garlic, mushrooms and green peppers; simmer, stirring often, until onion is tender, about 10 minutes.

Add rice, beans, tomatoes, chili powder, cumin and cayenne; cover and simmer for about 25 minutes or until rice is tender and most of the liquid is absorbed.

Transfer to baking dish and sprinkle with cheese. Bake in 350°F/180°C oven for 15 minutes or microwave at high (100%) power for 1 to 2 minutes or until cheese melts. Makes 6 servings, 1 cup/250 mL each.

PER SERVING	
calories	268
g fat	5
mg cholesterol	12
mg sodium	371
g protein	14
g carbohydrate	45

GOOD: vitamin A, thiamin, calcium
EXCELLENT: fiber, vitamin C, niacin, iron

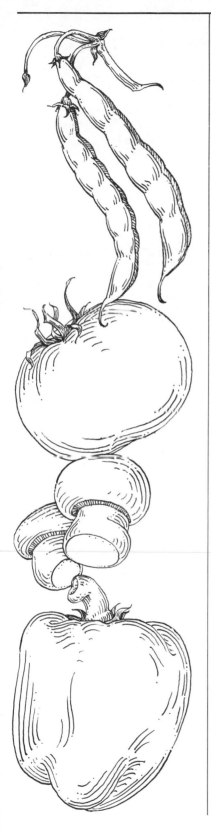

VEGETABLES

When my daughter asks what's for dinner, she can't understand why I often answer by mentioning only the meat course; to her the vegetables are as important and most enjoyable. I, too, love vegetables but often plan meals around the meat or fish because they usually take more time to prepare or cook. For healthy eating, vegetables should cover at least three-quarters of your dinner plate.

Vegetables are an important source of vitamins, minerals, carbohydrates, protein and fiber. They are cholesterol-free and low in fats and calories.

Choose locally grown fresh vegetables that are in season for the best flavor and nutritive value. When out of season, frozen vegetables are often higher in nutritive value than fresh because imported vegetables lose nutrients during transportation and storage. For example, lettuce loses half its vitamin C in one week after it is picked. Canned vegetables are often higher in sodium than fresh or frozen.

Compare Sodium Content

	Fresh	Canned	Frozen
Peas	5 mg	394 mg	147 mg
Green beans	4 mg	361 mg	19 mg

Cherry Tomatoes and Mushroom Sauté

This dish is good any time of year, but especially in the winter when cherry tomatoes are usually less expensive and have better color and flavor than larger ones. Most fresh herbs can be used instead of dried.

1 tbsp	soft margarine	15 mL
1	clove garlic, minced	1
½ lb	medium mushrooms, halved	250 g
2 cups	cherry tomatoes, stems removed	500 mL
½ tsp	dried oregano (or 1 tbsp/15 mL fresh)	2 mL
½ tsp	dried thyme (or 1 tbsp/15 mL fresh)	2 mL
¼ cup	chopped fresh parsley	50 mL
	Salt and freshly ground pepper	

In large nonstick skillet, melt margarine over medium-high heat; cook garlic and mushrooms, shaking pan, for 3 minutes.

Add tomatoes, oregano and thyme; cook for 3 to 5 minutes or until tomatoes are heated through and mushrooms are tender. (Can be prepared an hour or two in advance and reheated.) Sprinkle with parsley; season with salt and pepper to taste. Makes 6 servings.

PER SERVING	
calories	40
g fat	2
mg cholesterol	0
mg sodium	24
g protein	1
carbohydrate	5

GOOD: fiber
EXCELLENT: vitamin C

Squash
I love winter squash and most often serve it very simply— either in wedges still in its skin or mashed with a small amount of margarine and freshly ground pepper. If it is dry, add some orange or apple juice.

Preparation: Cut squash in half and scoop out seeds and interior pulp.

To bake squash: Place cut side down on lightly greased baking sheet. Bake in 375°F/ 190°C oven 50 minutes for acorn or pepper squash, 70 minutes for butternut or until flesh is tender when pierced with a fork.

To steam squash: Cut prepared squash into halves or quarters, hubbard into chunks; peel if desired. Arrange on rack in steamer; add boiling water; cover and steam until tender about 15 to 25 minutes depending on size of pieces. Serve as is or remove squash from skin and mash.

Photo:
Rotini with Fresh Tomatoes, Basil and Parmesan (page 111)

To microwave: Place halves or quarters cut side up on microwave-safe baking dish; cover with plastic wrap. Microwave on high (100%) power approximately 7 to 8 minutes per pound or until flesh is tender when pierced with a fork. (One whole acorn squash, halved will take 12 to 13 minutes, a 14 oz/400 g butternut squash will take 7 minutes.)

Seasonings to add to mashed squash: nutmeg, cinnamon, maple syrup, brown sugar, minced fresh ginger, lemon juice, applesauce, fruit juice.

PER SERVING

calories	55
g fat	2
mg cholesterol	0
mg sodium	41
g protein	1
g carbohydrate	9

GOOD: vitamin C

Note
Recipe can be prepared a day in advance and refrigerated. To serve, bring to room temperature then reheat, covered, in 350°F/180°C oven for 35 minutes, or microwave on high for 8 to 10 minutes or until heated through.

For a very low-calorie meal serve spaghetti squash topped with vegetable mixture in lasagna recipe (page 133).

Photo:
Streusel Plum Cake (page 166)

Spaghetti Squash with Parsley and Garlic

The spaghettilike strands of this unusual squash are very good tossed with garlic and parsley. Be sure to cut the squash crosswise or else you will cut the strands in half.

1	spaghetti squash (4 lb/2 kg)	1
1 tbsp	margarine	15 mL
3	cloves garlic, minced	3
1 cup	coarsely chopped fresh parsley or grated zucchini	250 mL
¼ cup	low-fat plain yogurt (optional)	50 mL
	Freshly ground pepper	

In large pot of boiling water, cook whole spaghetti squash until tender when pierced with skewer, about 30 minutes (some varieties of spaghetti squash may take longer).

In small skillet, melt margarine over medium-low heat; add garlic and cook until tender, about 1 minute.

Drain squash and cut in half crosswise. Scoop out seeds. Run tines of fork lengthwise over squash to loosen spaghettilike strands; scoop out strands into baking dish or serving bowl. Add garlic mixture, parsley, yogurt (if using), and pepper to taste; toss to mix. Makes 8 servings.

Microwave Method:
Pierce spaghetti squash in 10 to 15 places with a fork; place in microwave-safe dish and microwave at high (100%) power for 5 to 7 minutes per lb or until tender when pierced with a fork. Turn over halfway through cooking. Let stand 5 minutes.

To Steam:
Cut squash in half crosswise; scoop out seeds. Steam for 15 to 20 minutes or until tender.

Chinese-Style Vegetables

Any seasonal vegetables can be added to this colorful stir-fry. Consider celery, onion, sweet peppers, mushrooms, green peas, beans, snow peas, tomatoes, asparagus or Brussels sprouts. Instead of red or green cabbage, consider using bok choy or napa cabbage.

1 tbsp	vegetable oil	15 mL
2 cups	cauliflower florets	500 mL
2 cups	broccoli florets	500 mL
4	medium carrots, sliced	4
½ cup	chicken stock	125 mL
¼ lb	snow peas	125 g
1 tsp	minced garlic	5 mL
2 tbsp	minced fresh gingerroot	25 mL
4 cups	chopped red or green cabbage or bok choy*	1 L
1 tsp	soy sauce	5 mL

In wok or large nonstick skillet, heat oil over medium heat. Add cauliflower, broccoli and carrots; stir-fry for 3 minutes. Add chicken stock; cover and steam for 2 minutes.

Add snow peas; stir-fry for 1 minute. Add garlic, gingerroot, and cabbage; stir-fry for 1 minute. Stir in soy sauce. Makes 6 servings.

---

*Bok choy is the Cantonese word for cabbage. We also call it Chinese cabbage. Its mild flavor is a pleasing addition to a stir-fry, soup or salad. Napa cabbage is a crinkly leafed lettuce also good in stir-frys.

PER SERVING	
calories	71
g fat	3
mg cholesterol	0
mg sodium	167
g protein	3
g carbohydrate	10

EXCELLENT: fiber, vitamin A, vitamin C

Baked Parsnips and Carrots

As a child, parsnips were one of the few foods I didn't like; now I love them. I'm not sure if it was because of the parsnips themselves or that they might have been overcooked. In any case, parsnips cooked around a roast, baked or microwaved, are really sweet and delicious. Even my children like them this way.

2	parsnips	2
4	carrots	4
1 tbsp	soft margarine	15 mL
	Salt and freshly ground pepper	
Pinch	Cumin (optional)	Pinch
1 tbsp	water	15 mL

Peel parsnips and carrots; cut in half crosswise, then cut lengthwise into strips. Place in baking dish and dot with margarine. Sprinkle with salt, pepper and cumin (if using) to taste; add water.

Cover and bake in 375°F/190°C oven for 50 to 60 minutes or until vegetables are tender. Makes 4 servings.

Microwave Method:
Prepare as above using a microwave-safe baking dish. Cover and microwave at high (100%) power for 12 to 15 minutes or until vegetables are tender.

PER SERVING	
calories	119
g fat	3
mg cholesterol	0
mg sodium	76
g protein	2
g carbohydrate	23

GOOD: vitamin C
EXCELLENT: fiber, vitamin A

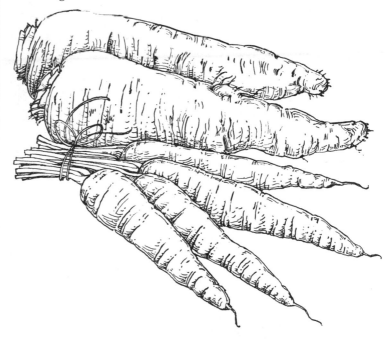

Broccoli is an excellent source of vitamin C and a good source of Vitamin A and fiber.

PER SERVING	
calories	43
g fat	2
mg cholesterol	0
mg sodium	10
g protein	2
g carbohydrate	5
GOOD: fiber, vitamin A	
EXCELLENT: vitamin C	

Make-Ahead Broccoli or Green Beans

If you are entertaining, you might want to partially cook a green vegetable in advance. I find this a big help when serving a first course at a dinner party. It's hard to judge how long it will take everyone to eat the first course, let alone get to the table. If you put the broccoli on to cook before everyone sits down, it'll be overcooked. If you wait until after the first course, it takes too long.

Cook prepared green vegetable in boiling water until tender-crisp when pierced with knife. Immediately drain and plunge into large bowl of ice water. Drain and wrap in paper towels; refrigerate for up to 1 day.

To serve: Blanch vegetable in large pot of boiling water; drain thoroughly. Toss with margarine and lemon juice or other seasonings. Note: Don't add lemon juice to a green vegetable until just before serving. The acid will cause it to turn yellowish.

Broccoli with Ginger and Lemon

Fresh gingerroot is delightful with broccoli; however, using garlic instead of ginger is equally good.

1	bunch broccoli (1¼ lb/625 g)	1
1 tbsp	vegetable oil or soft margarine	15 mL
2 tsp	chopped fresh gingerroot	10 mL
2 tbsp	lemon juice	25 mL
	Freshly ground pepper	

Trim broccoli stalks (peel if tough) and cut into ½-in/1 cm-thick pieces. Separate top into florets. In large pot of boiling water, cook broccoli for 3 to 5 minutes or until tender-crisp when pierced with knife; drain.

Meanwhile, in small skillet, heat oil or margarine over medium-low heat; cook gingerroot for 2 minutes. Add lemon juice.

Transfer broccoli to warmed serving dish; pour lemon-juice mixture over. Sprinkle with pepper to taste and mix lightly. Makes 6 servings.

Skillet Zucchini with Chopped Tomatoes

In the summer and fall when tomatoes are everywhere, this is the way I often prepare zucchini.

1 tsp	soft margarine	5 mL
2	small onions, chopped	2
4	small (6-in/15 cm) zucchini, thinly sliced	4
2	medium tomatoes, chopped	2
	Freshly ground pepper	

In large nonstick skillet, melt margarine over medium heat; add onions and cook, stirring, until softened. Add zucchini and cook for 2 minutes. Add tomatoes and cook for 3 to 5 minutes or until zucchini is tender-crisp. Season to taste with pepper. Makes 4 servings.

PER SERVING	
calories	41
g fat	1
mg cholesterol	0
mg sodium	18
g protein	1
g carbohydrate	8
GOOD: fiber	
EXCELLENT: vitamin C	

Peas with Green Onions

Onions and green peas are a nice flavor combination. I use the white part of green onions or chopped Spanish or regular cooking onions. Tiny pearl onions are lovely if you have the time it takes to peel them.

2 tsp	soft margarine	10 mL
1 cup	chopped green onions (white parts) or Spanish or cooking onion	250 mL
3 cups	frozen peas	750 mL
	Freshly ground pepper	

In nonstick skillet, melt margarine over medium heat; add onions and cook, stirring often, until tender, about 5 minutes.

Meanwhile, blanch peas in boiling water; drain and add to skillet. Sprinkle with pepper to taste and mix gently. Makes 6 servings (about ½ cup/125 mL each).

PER ½-cup SERVING	
calories	68
g fat	2
mg cholesterol	0
mg sodium	89
g protein	4
g carbohydrate	10
GOOD: vitamin A, fiber	
EXCELLENT: vitamin C	

PER SERVING	
calories	106
g fat	2
mg cholesterol	0
mg sodium	69
g protein	4
g carbohydrate	20

GOOD: fiber
EXCELLENT: vitamin C

The Best Brussels Sprouts
When buying: Look for small, compact, firm, bright-green Brussels sprouts. Avoid ones with blemishes or yellowing or a brownish or slimy base.

When cooking: Prepare Brussels sprouts by trimming outer leaves and base. Cut shallow "X" in base for even cooking. Boil, steam, stir-fry or microwave, but remember that it's very important to cook for only a short time—just until tender-crisp. Overcooked Brussels sprouts become strong-flavored and lose their bright-green color.

Brussels Sprouts with Peppers and Potatoes

Wonderful with turkey or roast chicken, this is a tasty, colorful vegetable dish to serve for Sunday or Thanksgiving dinner.

1 tbsp	soft margarine or vegetable oil	15 mL
1	onion, chopped	1
1	large potato, cut in small cubes	1
1	bay leaf	1
1 lb	Brussels sprouts, halved if large	500 g
1	sweet red pepper, cut in ½-in/ 1 cm pieces	1
¼ cup	vegetable or chicken stock	50 mL
	Freshly ground pepper	
2 tbsp	chopped fresh parsley or green onions	25 mL

In large nonstick skillet, melt margarine over medium heat; cook onion, potato and bay leaf, stirring often, for 2 to 3 minutes or until onion is softened.

Add Brussels sprouts, red pepper and stock; cover and cook for 8 to 10 minutes or until sprouts and potatoes are tender (add water if necessary to prevent scorching).

Season with pepper to taste. Serve sprinkled with parsley. Makes 6 servings.

Sunday Family Dinner

*Tarragon Roasted Chicken
(page 87)
Cranberry sauce
Green Beans with Sautéed
Mushrooms (page 125)
Potatoes
Berries with Orange-Honey
Yogurt (page 175) or
Apple and Raspberry Crisp
(page 173)*

Green Beans with Sauteéd Mushrooms

Mushrooms and herbs dress up green beans and add extra flavor. If you want to be really fancy, use wild mushrooms.

¾ lb	green beans	375 g
1 tbsp	margarine	15 mL
1	clove garlic, minced	1
2 tsp	chopped fresh basil (or ½ tsp/ 2 mL dried)	10 mL
¼ tsp	dried crumbled rosemary	1 mL
8	medium mushrooms, sliced	8
Dash	hot pepper sauce	Dash

PER SERVING	
calories	57
g fat	3
mg cholesterol	0
mg sodium	11
g protein	2
g carbohydrate	6
GOOD: fiber, vitamin C	

In saucepan of boiling water, cook beans for 6 to 8 minutes or until tender-crisp; drain.

Meanwhile in small saucepan or microwave-safe dish, melt margarine, add garlic, basil, rosemary, mushrooms and hot pepper sauce; cook over medium heat for 3 to 4 minutes, or cover and microwave at high (100%) power for 1 minute, or until mushrooms are tender.

Transfer beans to warm serving dish; pour mushroom mixture over and toss to mix. Makes 4 servings.

Fresh ginger is a fabulous
seasoning for many vegetables,
such as in the Skillet Greens
recipe presented here. Other
vegetables to stir-fry with
ginger are broccoli, snow
peas, carrots or celery.

PER SERVING	
calories	59
g fat	3
mg cholesterol	0
mg sodium	86
g protein	2
g carbohydrate	8
GOOD: fiber	
EXCELLENT: vitamin A, vitamin C	

Nutrient analysis is based on 1
cup/250 mL of each of the
vegetables listed. The sodium
is mainly from the Swiss chard.

Cabbage, kale and collards
belong to the brassica family
of vegetables. It's now thought
that these vegetables may help
to reduce the risk of cancers of
the colon, stomach and
esophagus.

Skillet Greens with Ginger and Celery

Kale, Swiss chard, spinach and cabbage are all delicious cooked
this way, either on their own or in a combination. Some tougher
greens, such as collard or beet greens, should first be blanched.
Rice vinegar is particularly good but any white vinegar can be
used.

2 tbsp	cider, rice or white vinegar	25 mL
2 tbsp	water	25 mL
2 tsp	cornstarch	10 mL
1 tsp	granulated sugar	5mL
1 tbsp	vegetable oil	15 mL
1	onion, chopped	1
2 cups	sliced celery	500 mL
4 cups	thinly sliced kale, Swiss chard, spinach or cabbage	1 L
1 tbsp	grated fresh gingerroot	15mL

In small dish, mix together vinegar, water, cornstarch and
sugar; set aside.

In large wok or nonstick skillet, heat oil over medium-high
heat. Add onion and stir-fry for 1 minute. Add celery, greens
and gingerroot; stir-fry for 1 minute. Add about 2 tbsp/25 mL
water; cover and steam for 3 minutes or until greens are wilted
and celery is tender-crisp.

Pour in vinegar mixture and stir-fry for 1 minute or until liquid
comes to boil. Serve immediately. Makes 5 servings.

PER SERVING	
calories	74
g fat	2
mg cholesterol	0
mg sodium	71
g protein	2
g carbohydrate	14
GOOD: vitamin C, fiber	
EXCELLENT: vitamin A	

Carrots and Leeks with Parsley

Choose tender, young carrots to combine with delicate-flavored leeks. Chopped fresh dill, thyme or basil is a lovely addition to this dish.

1 lb	carrots (6 medium)	500 g
4	medium leeks	4
2 tsp	water (for microwave method)	10 mL
1 tbsp	soft margarine	15 mL
¼ cup	chopped fresh parsley	50 mL
	Salt and freshly ground pepper	

To Clean Leeks

Trim base and tough green leaves from leeks, leaving tender green and white part.

If you want to use leeks whole, cut lengthwise in half part way down leek; otherwise cut in half lengthwise. Wash under cold running water, spreading leaves apart.

To Bake Leeks

Place leeks on lightly oiled foil, dot with a small amount of high-polyunsaturated margarine and pepper. Wrap in foil. Bake in 350°F/180°C oven for 25 minutes or until tender.

Scrape carrots and cut diagonally into ¼-in/5 mm-thick slices. Clean leeks, discarding tough green parts. Slice white and tender green parts in half lengthwise; cut crosswise into ½-in/1 cm-thick slices.

Microwave Method:

In microwave-safe dish, combine carrots and water; cover with lid or vented plastic wrap and microwave at high (100%) power for 5 minutes. Stir in leeks; dot with margarine. Cover and microwave at high (100%) power for 3 to 5 minutes or until vegetables are tender. Stir in parsley; season with salt and pepper to taste.

To steam:

Place carrots in steamer over boiling water; cover and steam for 5 to 8 minutes or nearly tender-crisp. Add leeks and steam another 5 minutes. Transfer to warmed serving dish; toss with margarine, parsley, salt and pepper. Makes 6 servings.

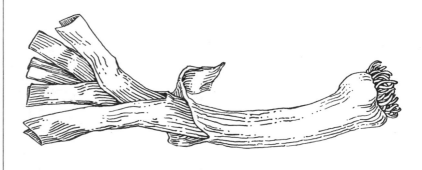

Mushroom-Stuffed Zucchini Cups

This is a delicious vegetable dish for a special dinner. It can be prepared early in the day then reheated in the oven or microwave just before serving. (Recipe pictured opposite page 23.)

2	medium zucchini (about 8–10 in/ 20–25 cm in length)	2
2 tsp	margarine	10 mL
1 cup	finely chopped mushrooms	250 mL
1 tbsp	minced onion or shallots	15 mL
1 tbsp	minced fresh parsley	15 mL
	Salt and freshly ground pepper	
1 tbsp	grated Parmesan cheese	15 mL

PER SERVING	
calories	45
g fat	2
mg cholesterol	1
mg sodium	44
g protein	2
g carbohydrate	6
GOOD: vitamin C, fiber	

Trim ends from zucchini; cut crosswise into 1-in/2.5 cm-thick pieces. Steam zucchini for about 5 minutes or until tender-crisp; let cool. Scoop out small hollow from one end of each piece; set aside.

In nonstick skillet, melt margarine over medium-high heat; cook mushrooms and onion or shallots, stirring, for 2 minutes or until onion is tender. Stir in parsley; season with salt and pepper to taste. Spoon mushroom mixture into zucchini cavities. Arrange in microwave-safe dish or baking dish. Sprinkle with Parmesan cheese.

Just before serving, microwave at high (100%) power for 1 to 2 minutes or bake in 350°F/180°C oven for 15 to 20 minutes or until heated through. Makes 4 servings.

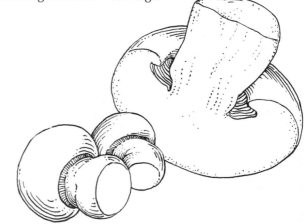

Low-Fat Cooking Tip:
In many recipes vegetables are cooked in margarine or oil to soften and develop flavor. It's important to use as little fat as possible.

If vegetables stick to the pan, or to prevent scorching, add water a spoonful at a time and cook until water evaporates.

Stir-Fry Ratatouille

This version of the colorful Mediterranean vegetable dish is lower in oil and quicker to make than most and is good hot or cold. It's a colorful fall dish to serve with rice and cold meat or grilled lamb chops; for a meatless meal, cover with grated cheese and place under broiler until cheese melts and is golden brown.

2 tbsp	vegetable oil	25 mL
1	medium onion, sliced	1
2	cloves garlic, minced	2
8	medium mushrooms, halved	8
1	small sweet yellow or red pepper, cubed	1
2 cups	cubed (½-in/2.5 cm pieces) unpeeled eggplant	500 mL
1	small zucchini, sliced	1
2	tomatoes, cut in wedges	2
½ tsp	each dried thyme and basil	2 mL
	Salt and freshly ground pepper	

In large nonstick skillet, heat half of oil over medium-high heat; add onion, garlic, mushroom and sweet pepper and stir-fry until tender, about 4 minutes. With slotted spoon remove to side dish and set aside.

Heat remaining oil in skillet; add eggplant, zucchini; stir-fry for 4 minutes or until tender. Return mushroom mixture to pan, add tomatoes, thyme, basil; cover and simmer for 5 minutes. Add salt and pepper to taste. Makes 6 servings.

PER SERVING	
calories	107
g fat	7
mg cholesterol	0
mg sodium	12
g protein	2
g carbohydrate	11

GOOD: fiber, niacin
EXCELLENT: vitamin C

Middle-Eastern Eggplant Baked with Yogurt and Fresh Mint

This is one of the tastiest and easiest ways to prepare eggplant. It's very good with lamb. You can also serve it with pork, beef or chicken or as part of a buffet or meatless dinner.

3 tbsp	vegetable oil	45 mL
2 tbsp	water	25 mL
1	large onion, sliced	1
1	medium eggplant, unpeeled (1 ¼ lb/625 g)	1
1 cup	low-fat plain yogurt	250 mL
3 tbsp	chopped fresh mint and/or parsley	45 mL
2	cloves garlic, minced	2
¼ tsp	salt	1 mL
	Freshly ground pepper	
	Paprika	

PER SERVING	
calories	116
g fat	7
mg cholesterol	2
mg sodium	121
g protein	3
g carbohydrate	10
GOOD: fiber	

Variation
When tomatoes are in season, add slices of tomato between eggplant slices and onion in baking dish. Sprinkle top with grated low-fat mozzarella cheese.

In large nonstick skillet, heat 1 tsp/5 mL of the oil and water over medium heat; cook onion, stirring, for 5 minutes or until softened. Remove onion and set aside.

Cut eggplant into ¼-in-/5 mm-thick slices. Brush remaining oil over eggplant slices. In skillet over medium heat, cook eggplant (in batches) turning once, until tender, about 10 minutes (or arrange in a single layer on baking sheet and bake in 400°F/ 200°C oven for 15 minutes or until tender and soft).

In ungreased shallow baking dish, arrange overlapping slices of eggplant alternating with onion.

In small bowl, stir together yogurt, fresh mint or parsley, garlic, salt, and pepper to taste; drizzle over eggplant slices. Sprinkle liberally with paprika. Bake in 350°F/180°C oven until hot and bubbly, 10 to 15 minutes. Makes 6 servings.

PER SERVING

calories	121
g fat	3
mg cholesterol	0
mg sodium	59
g protein	3
g carbohydrate	22

GOOD: niacin
EXCELLENT: fiber, vitamin A, vitamin C

Steamed Fresh Vegetables

It's easy to add interest and flavor to a dinner by serving a combination of four colorful vegetables. It takes the same amount of time to peel two carrots and two parsnips as it does to peel four carrots. It's also a great way to use up the four mushrooms or half a stalk of broccoli lurking in the back of your refrigerator. Other vegetables to substitute or add: celery, fennel, sweet red or green pepper, snow peas, cauliflower, zucchini, cabbage and Brussels sprouts.

2	medium carrots, peeled and sliced	2
2	medium parsnips, peeled and sliced	2
1	stalk broccoli, cut in florets	1
8	mushrooms	8
1 tbsp	soft margarine	15 mL
	Salt and freshly ground pepper	

Steam carrots and parsnips for 3 to 5 minutes or until tender-crisp. Add broccoli and mushrooms; steam for 3 minutes or until broccoli is bright green. Transfer to warm serving dish and add margarine. Sprinkle lightly with salt and pepper to taste; toss to mix.

Microwave Method:
In microwave-safe dish, combine carrots, parsnips, broccoli and mushrooms. Add 1 tbsp/15 mL water. Dot with margarine; sprinkle with pepper to taste. Cover with lid or vented plastic wrap; microwave at high power for 6 minutes or until vegetables are tender; rotate dish once or twice during cooking. Add salt to taste. Makes 4 servings.

Steamed Fennel with Zucchini and Green Onions The mild licorice flavor of fennel makes a pleasing addition to zucchini and carrots.

Cut about 6 green onions in half lengthwise then cut into 2-inch/5 cm lengths. Steam onions, and 2 cups/500 mL each julienne (thin strips) carrots, fennel, and zucchini for 6 to 8 minutes or until tender-crisp.

Transfer to warm serving platter and toss with a small amount of margarine, salt and freshly ground pepper to taste. Makes 6 servings.

Turnip and Apple Purée

Apple adds a mellow, sweet flavor to yellow turnip or rutabaga. For an equally delicious variation, use pear instead of apple. The recipe can be prepared up to a day in advance, but omit the yogurt and add when reheating.

PER SERVING	
calories	54
g fat	2
mg cholesterol	1
mg sodium	68
g protein	1
g carbohydrate	9
GOOD: fiber, vitamin C	

1	small turnip (about 1¼ lb/625 g), peeled and cubed	1
1	large apple, peeled, cored and cut in chunks	1
¼ cup	low-fat plain yogurt	50 mL
1 tbsp	margarine	15 mL
Pinch	nutmeg	Pinch
	Salt and freshly ground pepper	

Steam turnip for 15 to 20 minutes or until nearly tender. Add apple and cook for 5 to 10 minutes or until turnip and apple are tender. Drain well.

In food processor or blender, purée turnip mixture until smooth (or mash or put through food mill). Add yogurt, margarine and nutmeg; season with salt and pepper to taste and process just until combined. Reheat in saucepan over medium-low heat or in microwave until heated through. Makes 6 servings.

Before the Theater Light Dinner

Fettuccine with Pesto Sauce (page 112)
Tomatoes Broiled with Goat Cheese and Basil (page 133)
Multigrain Date Quick Bread (page 157)
Strawberries with almonds and Amaretto

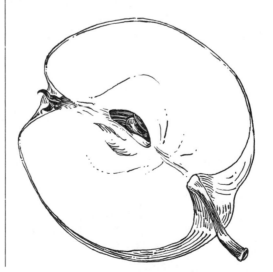

A soft or cream goat cheese, or chèvre, has a distinctive flavor that is lovely with tomatoes. If not available, use fresh mozzarella instead.

PER SERVING

calories	58
g fat	3
mg cholesterol	13
mg sodium	173
g protein	3
g carbohydrate	5

GOOD: fiber, vitamin A
EXCELLENT: vitamin C

Tomatoes Broiled with Goat Cheese and Basil

This simple dish is one of my favorites for entertaining. It goes well with any meat or poultry or as part of a buffet or meatless meal. It tastes best when made in the summer or fall when tomatoes are juicy and full of flavor.

4	medium tomatoes	4
3 oz	soft goat cheese (chèvre)	90 g
	Freshly ground pepper	
3 tbsp	chopped fresh basil	45 mL

Slice each tomato into about 4 thick slices. Arrange in single layer in shallow baking dish or microwave-safe dish.

Thinly slice goat cheese; arrange over tomatoes. Sprinkle with pepper to taste, then basil. Broil for 2 to 3 minutes or microwave at high (100%) power for 2 minutes or until cheese melts. Makes 6 servings.

Compare Fresh vs. Processed Foods for Sodium Content

Fresh Food	mg sodium	Processed Food	mg sodium
Tomatoes, 2 medium	20	Canned (1 cup/250 mL)	683
		Tomato juice (1 cup/250 mL)	931
		Ketchup (1 tbsp/15 mL)	177
Pork chop (3 oz/88 g)	61	Ham, lean (3 oz/88 g)	1319
Beef, round steak (3 oz/88 g)	45	Canned beef and vegetable stew (1 cup/250 mL)	1064
Beets, sliced, boiled (1 cup/ 250 mL)	88	Beets, sliced, canned (1 cup/ 250 mL)	493
Potatoes, boiled (1)	5	Scalloped potatoes (prepared from a dry mix)	883
Oatmeal, regular or quick cooking, cooked (½ cup/ 125 mL)	1	Oatmeal, ready to serve (1 pouch)	323

Fettuccine with Basil and Parsley

Serve this as a side dish with any meats or as part of a meatless meal. Keep a pot of fresh parsley on the windowsill or a bunch in a plastic bag in the refrigerator to give a fresh flavor to this dish. Use any other fresh herbs you have, such as sage, rosemary or thyme (start with 1 tbsp/15 mL and add more to taste), before adding dried.

¼ lb	fettuccine or any pasta	125 g
1 tbsp	soft margarine	15 mL
1	clove garlic, minced	1
⅓ cup	chopped fresh parsley	75 mL
¼ cup	chopped fresh basil (or 1 tsp/5 mL dried)	50 mL
	Freshly ground pepper	

In large pot of boiling water, cook noodles according to package directions or until al dente (tender but firm). Drain in colander.

Add margarine and garlic to pot; cook, stirring, for 1 minute over medium heat. Add hot noodles, parsley, basil, and pepper to taste; toss to mix. Serve hot. Makes 4 servings.

PER SERVING	
calories	237
g fat	4
mg cholesterol	0
mg sodium	28
g protein	7
g carbohydrate	43
GOOD: fiber	

Variation
Add one large tomato, chopped, along with herbs. Sprinkle each serving with grated Parmesan cheese. Make with capellini or vermicelli noodles and serve as a first course.

Starchy foods or complex carbohydrates, such as whole-wheat breads, pastas, rice, potatoes, are not high in fat or calories. They are a good source of B vitamins, iron and trace minerals. It's what we add to these starchy foods that increases the fat content in our diet.

Compare	Per tbsp/15 mL	
Potato toppings	g fat	calories
Yogurt	1 or less	2 or less
Sour cream (14% b.f.)	3	28
Butter or margarine	11	100

Bulgur, or cracked wheat, is available in some supermarkets and most health food stores. It is a good source of fiber.

PER SERVING	
calories	230
g fat	3
mg cholesterol	0
mg sodium	395
g protein	8
g carbohydrate	44
GOOD: iron	
EXCELLENT: niacin, fiber	

Garlic-Parsley Potatoes Boil 1 lb/500 g tiny new potatoes, red-skinned potatoes or any you have on hand until tender. Peel only if skins are old and tough, because the skins add flavor, fiber and vitamins.

In small saucepan or microwave dish combine 2 tsp/10 mL margarine or oil and 2 cloves minced garlic and cook over medium heat, stirring, for 1 minute or microwave on medium power for 30 seconds.

Drain potatoes and cut in half or quarters if large; transfer to warm serving dish. Toss with garlic mixture and ¼ cup/50 ml chopped fresh parsley. Makes 4 servings.

Variation: Instead of potatoes use green beans, carrots, cauliflower, broccoli or peas.

PER SERVING (including oil)	
calories	109
g fat	1
mg cholesterol	0
mg sodium	5
g protein	2
g carbohydrate	23
EXCELLENT: vitamin C	

Bulgur Pilaf with Apricots and Raisins

Bulgur is the rice of the Mediterranean. Its mild nutty flavor and slightly crunchy texture are a nice change from regular rice.

2 tsp	margarine	10 mL
1	onion, chopped	1
1 cup	bulgur or cracked wheat	250 mL
¼ cup	raisins	50 mL
¼ cup	diced dried apricot	50 mL
2 cups	boiling chicken stock	500 mL
¼ cup	chopped fresh parsley (optional)	50 mL
	Salt and freshly ground pepper	

In nonstick skillet, melt margarine over medium heat; cook onion, stirring, until softened. Stir in bulgur and cook, stirring, for 1 minute. Stir in raisins, apricot and stock; cover and simmer over low heat for 15 minutes or until liquid is absorbed. Stir in parsley (if using); season with salt and pepper to taste. Makes 4 servings.

New Potatoes with Herbs

Small new potatoes, boiled in their skins, are delicious. Instead of butter, top with chopped fresh herbs and a dash of lemon juice and oil. These go well with any meats, poultry or fish.

1 lb	tiny new potatoes (about 20)	500 g
1 tbsp	chopped fresh basil or thyme	15 mL
1 tbsp	chopped chives	15 mL
1 tsp	lemon juice	5 mL
1 tsp	olive or vegetable oil (optional)	5 mL
	Freshly ground pepper	

In saucepan, boil unpeeled potatoes until tender, about 15 minutes; drain. Add basil, chives, lemon juice, oil, and pepper to taste. Mix lightly and serve. Makes 4 servings.

Types of Lentils

Split red lentils are used in most soups and cook in 10 to 15 minutes.

Green or brown whole lentils retain their shape when cooked and take about 45 minutes to cook.

PER SERVING	
calories	144
g fat	3
mg cholesterol	0
mg sodium	51
g protein	8
g carbohydrate	23
GOOD: vitamin C, iron EXCELLENT: fiber	

How to Cook Dried Lentils

Lentils are a good source of iron and an excellent source of fiber and vegetable protein. Serve with complementary cereal protein such as bread or rice. One cup/250 mL of dried lentils will yield about 2 to 2½ cups/500 to 625 mL cooked lentils.

Wash and drain dried lentils. In saucepan, combine lentils with 3 times the amount of water (add a quartered onion and bay leaf if desired). Bring to a boil; reduce heat and simmer covered for 10 to 45 minutes depending on type, or until tender; drain. Use in salads, casseroles, soups or as a vegetable.

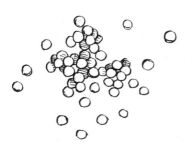

Quick Lentils with Onion and Celery

Keep a can of cooked lentils or a package of dried red lentils on your shelf and you can have a quick vegetable dish in minutes.

1 tbsp	soft margarine or vegetable oil	15 mL
2	onions, chopped	2
2	stalks celery, chopped	2
1	clove garlic, minced	1
1	can (19 oz/540 mL) lentils, drained (or 2 cups/500 mL cooked lentils)	1
Pinch	dried oregano	Pinch
	Salt and freshly ground pepper	
½ cup	chopped fresh parsley	125 mL

In skillet, heat margarine over medium-high heat; cook onions, celery and garlic, stirring, for 3 minutes or until onion is tender. Add lentils and oregano; cook until heated through. Season with salt and pepper to taste; sprinkle with parsley. Makes 4 servings.

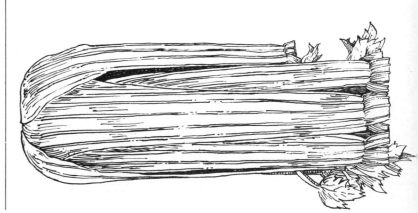

Dish can be prepared a day in advance and refrigerated. Reheat, covered, in 350°F/180°C oven for 30 minutes.

Pot or Pearl Barley?
What's the difference? Pearl is more polished than pot barley. When possible, choose pot barley because it is higher in fiber and more nutritious. They take the same length of time to cook. Use as an alternative to rice or pasta, in soups and casseroles.

PER SERVING	
calories	122
g fat	2
mg cholesterol	0
mg sodium	295
g protein	5
g carbohydrate	21
GOOD: fiber	
EXCELLENT: niacin	

Variation
Rice and Mushroom Pilaf:
Substitute 1½ cups/375 mL parboiled (converted) rice or brown rice for the barley. Stir rice into mushroom mixture. Reduce cooking time to about 40 minutes or until liquid has been absorbed. Makes 8 cups/2 L.

The Canadian Heart Foundation recommends that we reduce the fat, particularly saturated fat, in our diet and increase the complex carbohydrate. One way to do this is to have more rice, pasta or grains.

Barley and Mushroom Pilaf

I like to serve this as an alternative to rice or potatoes. Sometimes I vary it by adding chopped almonds, chopped celery or green onion, chopped fresh dill, thyme or basil. It's nice for a buffet and can be prepared in advance.

1 tbsp	soft margarine	15 mL
1	onion, chopped	1
¾ lb	mushrooms, sliced	375 g
1 cup	pot barley	250 mL
3 cups	hot chicken stock	750 mL
½ cup	chopped fresh parsley	125 mL
	Freshly ground pepper	

In nonstick skillet, melt margarine over medium heat; add onion and cook for about 2 minutes or until softened. Add mushrooms and cook, stirring occasionally, for 5 minutes.

Transfer mixture to 11- × 7-in (2 L) baking dish; add barley and chicken stock. Bake, covered, in 350°F/180°C oven for 1 hour; uncover and bake for 10 minutes longer (or bake in 325°F/160°C oven for 1½ hours). Stir in parsley and pepper to taste. Makes 8 servings (⅔ cup/150 mL each).

Compare   Per 1 cup/250 mL, cooked

	g fat	mg cholesterol	mg sodium	g fiber	g protein	g carbohy-drate	calories
Bulgur, or cracked wheat	1	0	2	4	6	41	191
Rice, parboiled (converted)	0	0	5	0.5	4	41	186
Rice, regular white	0	0	4	0.6	4	50	223
Rice, brown	1	0	6	2	5	50	232
Macaroni	0.5	0	1	1	5	31	150
Spaghetti	0.5	0	1	1	5	31	150

Kinds of Rice
White rice is most common in Canada; during processing the bran is removed.

Parboiled rice is a white rice that has been processed so that when cooked the grains are firm and separate. It is more nutritious than white rice because the thiamin is retained during processing. One manufacturer's brand name for parboiled rice is "converted" rice.

Brown rice is the most nutritious because it contains the bran and germ. It's higher in fiber and B vitamins than other rice.

Instant or pre-cooked rice is white rice that has been cooked then dehydrated. It cooks the fastest but is the least nutritious. Follow package directions for cooking.

Wild rice is not really a rice but we use it as a rice. It has a wonderful nutty flavor and chewy texture. It is expensive and is often served mixed with cooked white or brown rice. To cook: Rinse under running water. Place in a saucepan. For each cup/250 mL of rice add 4 cups/1 L cold water; bring to a boil. Cover and boil for 40 minutes or until grains are firm-tender but not mushy or splayed; drain.

Short- or long-grain rice: Short-grain cooked rice is more sticky. The long-grain rice is more firm and separate after cooking.

To Cook Rice
Rinse under cold water. For each cup/250 mL of rice bring 2 cups/500 mL water or stock to a boil. Stir in rice; reduce heat, cover and simmer for 20 + minutes for white, 45 minutes for brown or until water is absorbed and rice is tender. One cup/250 mL of raw rice yields about 3 cups/750 mL when cooked.

Fresh Tomato Sauce

One of my favorite meals in August and September is a fresh tomato sauce made with plum tomatoes and fresh herbs served over pasta. Sometimes I add some cooked Italian sausage. I don't follow a recipe and the result is slightly different every time.

Cook a few pounds of small plum tomatoes (chopped) in a spoonful or two of olive oil (sometimes I add a chopped onion and garlic) until they are soft, nearly smooth, thick and of a saucelike consistency. This should take about 30 minutes. Add a handful of chopped fresh basil, or a pinch of dried rosemary or oregano, and you will have a wonderful Italian tomato sauce to toss with pasta. Top with freshly grated Parmesan cheese.

Is it necessary to peel and seed tomatoes?

The skin and seeds of tomatoes are high in fiber. I only peel tomatoes if the skin is very tough. When making a sauce using the small plum tomatoes, peeling isn't necessary.

The easiest way to peel tomatoes is to put them in a pot or bowl and cover with boiling water; let stand for about 30 seconds, then drain. The skin can easily be removed using a knife.

SAUCES AND ACCOMPANIMENTS

Sauces are like jewelry: they add the finishing touch to a meal, can dress it up and pull it all together. Many traditional sauces contain large amounts of saturated fat, cholesterol and calories from the butter, cream and egg yolks used.

To Reduce Fat and Cholesterol in Sauces

– Use skim or 2% milk for whole milk.
– Use yogurt or milk instead of cream.
– Use recommended oil or margarine instead of butter and use as little as possible.
– Use low-fat cheese or part-skim instead of high-fat cheese.
– Use flour or cornstarch to thicken instead of egg yolk.
– Use thinner sauces or reduced sauces instead of thick sauces.
– Use meat drippings (au jus) instead of fatty gravies.
– Use a different kind of sauce (cranberry sauce, applesauce or a relish) instead of gravy.
– Use the sauce recipes in this book.

If serving as part of a meatless meal, you could add a little extra low-fat cheese for more protein.

PER ¼-cup/50 mL SERVING	
calories	97
g fat	6
mg cholesterol	12
mg sodium	135
g protein	6
g carbohydrate	4
GOOD: Calcium	

Fresh Dill Cream Sauce
Prepare cheese sauce recipe omitting grated cheese. Instead add ⅓ cup/75 mL (not packed) chopped fresh dill, ¼ tsp/1 mL salt, ¼ tsp/1 mL dried mustard, and freshly ground pepper to taste. Serve with salmon, sole or other fish either whole or in fillets or steaks. It's also very good with cauliflower.

Fresh dill makes this sauce delicious. If unavailable, use ⅓ cup/75 mL chopped fresh parsley and 1 tsp/5 mL dried dill. Other fresh herbs such as basil are also good but the amounts will vary. Add a tablespoon at a time and taste.

Cream Sauce
Prepare cheese sauce recipe, omitting grated cheese.

Cheese Sauce

Cheese sauce is a traditional favorite to serve over cauliflower, broccoli, or other steamed vegetables and pasta. Because it adds extra fat but is a source of protein, it's a good choice to serve with a meatless meal. Using skim milk and a low-fat or part-skim cheese keeps the saturated fat content at a minimum.

1½ tbsp	soft margarine	22 mL
2 tbsp	all-purpose flour	25 mL
1 cup	skim milk	250 mL
1 cup	shredded low-fat mozzarella cheese	250 mL
	Cayenne pepper	

In saucepan, melt margarine over medium-low heat. Stir in flour and mix well; cook for 1 minute.

Stir in milk and cook over medium heat, stirring, 3 to 5 minutes, until mixture comes to a low boil and has thickened. Add cheese and stir until melted. Season with cayenne to taste. Makes about 1½ cups/375 mL.

Compare	per serving	
Cheese sauce made with:	g fat	calories
Skim milk and part-skim cheese	6	97
2% milk and part-skim cheese	7	103
Whole milk and Cheddar cheese	10	134

To serve with fish or seafood, substitute dill for tarragon. To serve with lamb or chicken, you could substitute basil for tarragon.

Yogurt Béarnaise Sauce

In this version of a Béarnaise sauce, the classic accompaniment to steak, I use yogurt instead of butter and half the usual number of egg yolks—so I call it a halfway healthy sauce. Margie Glue, a Mississauga, Ont., cooking school teacher, gave me the idea of using yogurt in a Béarnaise sauce. It's also delicious with grilled chicken, turkey, lamb or fish.

4 tsp	chopped shallots or onions	20 mL
¼ cup	white wine	50 mL
1	small clove garlic, crushed	1
1 tbsp	chopped fresh tarragon (or 1 ¼ tsp/6 mL dried)	15 mL
1 cup	2% plain yogurt*	250 mL
2	egg yolks	2
1 tsp	cornstarch	5 mL
¼ tsp	granulated sugar	1 mL
	Salt, cayenne and freshly ground pepper	

PER 1 tbsp/15 mL SERVING	
calories	26
g fat	1
mg cholesterol	47
mg sodium	16
g protein	2
g carbohydrate	2

Herb Shaker   The Ontario Heart and Stroke Foundation's Cooking for a Healthy Heart Program has a great suggestion for reducing sodium. Instead of salt keep a mixture of herbs handy and use to season meats, poultry, soups, salads or salad dressings.

One pleasing combination is 1 tsp/5 mL each of dried thyme, sage and rosemary mixed with 1½ tsp/7 mL each of dried marjoram and savory.

In small saucepan, combine shallots, wine, garlic and tarragon; bring to boil over medium heat. Boil until liquid is reduced to 1 tbsp (15 mL).

In top of nonaluminum double boiler or saucepan, beat together yogurt, egg yolks, cornstarch and sugar; add wine mixture.

Cook over simmering water, stirring often, until sauce has thickened, about 20 minutes. Remove from heat and season to taste with salt, cayenne and pepper. Serve warm.

Sauce can be prepared in advance and refrigerated for up to 1 week. Reheat over hot water or at low (10%) power in microwave. Makes about 1¼ cups (300 mL), enough for 12 people.

*For best results use a 2% or richer yogurt; a skim-milk yogurt isn't as good.

Compare: per tbsp/15 mL	g fat	mg cholesterol	calories
This recipe	1	47	26
Regular béarnaise sauce	12	98	117

PER ¼-cup/50 mL SERVING	
calories	11
g fat	0
mg cholesterol	0
mg sodium	16
g protein	0
g carbohydrate	3

Cooking Beets

Beets can be steamed, baked or microwaved as well as boiled. Don't peel before cooking beets for they will "bleed" too much. Boiling and steaming take about the same time. Baking takes longer. Large old beets take twice as long to cook as young beets.

To microwave 1½ lb/750 g medium to small beets: Place beets in microwave-safe dish; add ¼ cup/50 mL water. Cover with lid or vented plastic wrap and microwave on high (100%) power for 12 to 15 minutes or until tender.

Beets Vinaigrette

Slice or julienne 1½ lb/750 g cold cooked beets and toss with Mustard-Garlic Vinaigrette (page 64). Makes 6 servings (½ cup/125 mL each). Add chopped onions, chives or parsley. A beautiful addition to salad plates or appetizer salads. Use in late-summer and fall menus.

Old-Fashioned Pickled Beets

These are extremely easy to make, especially if you have any leftover cooked beets. They are a colorful addition to appetizer trays, salad plates, buffets and potluck dinners and are good with hot or cold meats.

9	medium beets (or 1½ lb/750 g trimmed baby beets)	9
1 cup	water	250 mL
1 cup	cider or white vinegar	250 mL
3 tbsp	granulated sugar	45 mL

Trim beets leaving at least 1-in/2.5 cm stems attached. Place in saucepan and cover with warm water; bring to boil and simmer for 40 minutes or until tender.

Drain and rinse under cold running water. Using fingers, slip off skins. Quarter or cut into thick slices and place in clean 4-cup/1 L jar.

In saucepan, combine water, vinegar and sugar; heat until sugar dissolves. Pour over beets; cover and let cool. Refrigerate for up to 1 month. Makes about 4 cups/1 L.

Compare: The Canadian Heart Foundation recommends we limit our sodium intake to 3000 mg per day. Pickles, especially dill pickles, can be very high in sodium; instead choose homemade pickled beets.

	mg sodium
Pickled beets (¼ cup/50 mL)	16
Dill pickle, 1 (4 in/10 cm)	1942

PER 1-tbsp/15 mL SERVING	
calories	19
g fat	0
mg cholesterol	0
mg sodium	28
g protein	0
g carbohydrate	5

Fresh-Tasting Cucumber Relish

This recipe from my friend Evelyn Barrigar in Ottawa makes the best relish I've ever tasted. Serve it with cold meats, chops or hamburgers.

4 cups	coarsely shredded peeled cucumbers*	1 L
2 cups	chopped onions	500 mL
1	sweet red pepper, chopped	1
half	bunch celery, chopped	half
2½ cups	packed brown sugar	625 mL
1½ tsp	salt	7 mL
2⅓ cups	white vinegar	575 mL
6 tbsp	all-purpose flour	90 mL
½ tsp	ground turmeric	2 mL
½ tsp	dry mustard	2 mL

In large heavy saucepan, combine cucumbers, onions, red pepper, celery, sugar, salt and 1½ cups/375 mL of the vinegar. Bring to boil over medium-high heat and boil for 15 minutes.

Meanwhile, in small bowl, blend together flour, turmeric, mustard and remaining vinegar until smooth; whisk into cucumber mixture. Boil for 15 minutes (reduce heat but maintain a boil), stirring and skimming off any foam. Be careful mixture doesn't burn.

Ladle into sterilized jars, leaving ¼-in/5 mm headspace. Immediately cover with sterilized lids and seal tightly. Makes about 8 cups/2 L.

*About 3½ large cucumbers. If cucumbers have large seeds, remove and discard before shredding.

Compare

per tbsp/15 mL	mg sodium
This recipe	28
Sweet relish, store-bought	61
Sour relish, store-bought	117

PER 1-tbsp/15 mL SERVING	
calories	40
g fat	0
mg cholesterol	0
mg sodium	2
g protein	0
g carbohydrate	10

Red Pepper Jelly

One year I make this with red peppers, the next, I use green. It is extremely quick and easy to make, is delicious with roast pork or chicken and is a nice hostess gift.

5 cups	granulated sugar	1.25 L
2 cups	finely chopped or puréed sweet red or green peppers (3 medium peppers)	500 mL
1½ cups	white vinegar	375 mL
1	bottle (170 mL) liquid pectin	1

In large saucepan, combine sugar, red peppers and vinegar; stir and bring to full boil. Boil over medium heat for 15 minutes, skimming off foam. Remove from heat; blend in pectin and stir for 2 minutes.

Pour into sterilized jars, leaving ¼ in/5 mm headspace; seal with paraffin wax. Cover with lids. Store in cool, dry place. Makes about 6 cups/1.5 L.

Use this relish and jelly instead of gravy and rich sauces. Most store-bought condiments have a high salt content.

PER 1-tbsp/15 mL SERVING	
calories	21
g fat	0
mg cholesterol	0
mg sodium	1
g protein	0
g carbohydrate	6

Fresh Mint Sauce

Make this accompaniment to roast lamb in the summer when fresh mint is everywhere because it grows like a weed. Since I'm a lazy gardener, I just keep a pot of it near the back door.

3 tbsp	granulated sugar	45 mL
⅓ cup	cider vinegar	75 mL
¼ cup	water	50 mL
1 ½ tsp	cornstarch	7mL
½ cup	firmly packed fresh mint leaves, finely chopped	125 mL

In small saucepan, combine sugar, vinegar, water and cornstarch; bring to boil over medium heat, stirring constantly. Stir in mint; simmer for 3 minutes.

Transfer to sauce boat and let stand for 30 minutes to develop flavors. Refrigerate any leftovers (up to 2 months). Makes about ½ cup/125 mL.

PER 1-tbsp/15 mL SERVING	
calories	22
g fat	0
mg cholesterol	0
mg sodium	9
g protein	0.5
g carbohydrate	5

Sauce recipes, see also:

Cucumber-Yogurt Sauce (page 99)
Tomato Salsa Sauce (page 105)
Watercress Sauce (page 98)
Cream Sauce (page 140)
Coriander Dipping Sauce (page 24)
Basic Stock Recipes (page 46)
Yogurt-Herb Dressing (page 56)
Vegetable Taco Sauce (page 105)
All-Purpose Quick Spaghetti Sauce (page 188)
Herbed Tomato Tuna Sauce (page 190)
Pesto Sauce (page 112)
Quick Tzatziki Sauce (page 198)

Marinades, see:

Lamb Tenderloins with Rosemary and Peppercorns (page 78)
Teriyaki Cod Fillets (page 104)
Italian Herb Marinade (page 73)
Ginger-Garlic Marinade (page 72)

Homemade Ketchup

This tastes delicious, is a snap to make and is much lower in sodium than commercial ketchup.

1	can (5½ oz/156 mL) tomato paste	1
¼ cup	packed brown sugar	50 mL
¼ cup	water	50 mL
2 tbsp	cider vinegar	25 mL
¼ tsp	dry mustard	1 mL
¼ tsp	cinnamon	1 mL
Pinch	each cloves and allspice	Pinch

In jar or bowl, combine tomato paste, sugar, water, vinegar, mustard, cinnamon, cloves and allspice; mix well. Cover and store in refrigerator for up to 1 month. Makes about 1 cup/250 mL.

Compare

per tbsp/15 mL	mg sodium
This recipe	9
Commercial ketchup	170

Preparing and Sealing Jars for Preserves

Use Mason-type home-canning jars or glass jars with tight-fitting lids. Assemble the number of jars required, plus one extra in case there is a little more preserve than expected.

Wash jars in hot soapy water; rinse and set upright on a metal tray or sturdy baking sheet along with metal tongs, a heatproof measure or ladle and a wide-mouthed metal funnel.

About 20 minutes before the preserve is ready, heat prepared equipment on tray in 225°F/110°C oven for 15 minutes. Leave all equipment in turned-off oven until needed.

Place lids and screw bands in small saucepan; cover with boiling water and boil for 5 minutes just before sealing jars or follow manufacturer's instructions.

Using ladle or measuring cup pour preserve through funnel into jars, leaving ¼ inch/5 mm headspace. Seal immediately. Wipe cooled, sealed jars and label. Store in a cool dark place for up to one year.

To Seal with Paraffin Wax

Melt paraffin wax in an old double boiler over simmering water or in a microwave-safe container with pouring spout using medium (50%) power. Pour thin layer of paraffin over preserve; tilt and rotate jar to extend seal to rim. Let cool and apply second thin layer in similar manner.

DESSERTS AND BAKED GOODS

When I take the time to bake or make a dessert I want it to taste really delicious. Cookies may have to be a little higher in fat than I would like but there is no sense making low-fat cookies that nobody eats. You can make some adjustments to a recipe to make it more nutritious, such as using whole-wheat flour instead of all-purpose and keeping sugar to a minimum. Most homemade cookies, as long as you use a recommended margarine or oil, are probably going to be lower in saturated fat than commercial cookies.

Too many rich desserts can add a huge amount of saturated fat and calories to your diet. There are desserts, however, that taste wonderful and are also low in fat. Instead of trying to make a low-fat chocolate mousse, try a fresh strawberry mousse; instead of an apple pie make an apple crisp. Imitation nondairy creams and toppings could be worse for you, as they usually contain saturated fats (palm and coconut oils). Fresh fruits in season are one of the best desserts for any type of meal.

Recipe Modification for Baked Goods
It is critical to understand the purpose of an ingredient before you change it.
– Flour forms the network of a baked product. In most recipes, to increase the fiber, you can substitute one-half the amount of all-purpose flour for a less refined flour, e.g., whole-wheat.
– Leavening agents are sodium-based (except yeast), but this ingredient can't be modified or the baked goods won't rise.
– Shortening such as lard and other fats add tenderness, crispness, lightness and volume. All sources of animal fat, plus coconut and palm oil and hydrogenated fats, should be avoided and replaced with polyunsaturated products.
– Sugar and other sweeteners add flavor, color, tenderness and crispness and can sometimes be reduced without affecting the quality of a product. Flavors that give the illusion of sweetness (without adding calories) are cinnamon, nutmeg and vanilla.
– Liquids act as solvents for other ingredients as well as activating chemical reactions. Low-fat liquids that can be substituted are water, fruit juice, skim milk or buttermilk.
– Eggs form the network of baked goods, adding flavor, color and moisture. To reduce cholesterol, you can often substitute two egg whites for one whole egg.
– Salt adds flavor and acts as a catalyst that controls chemical reactions. Salt is necessary to the yeast reaction in baking bread but there is no need for salt in baked goods that call for margarine as margarine already contains salt.

Variations
Apple-Raisin:
Instead of cranberry, use
1 cup/250 mL applesauce plus
½ cup/125 mL raisins.

Banana-Date:
Instead of cranberry, use 1
cup/ 250 mL mashed banana
and ½ cup/125 mL chopped
dates.

Zucchini:
Instead of cranberry, use 1
cup/250 mL grated unpeeled
zucchini and ½ cup/125 mL
raisins.

PER MUFFIN	
calories	156
g fat	5
mg cholesterol	23
mg sodium	126
g protein	2
g carbohydrate	27
GOOD: fiber	

Cranberry-Orange Muffins

These moist, high-fiber muffins are the best way I know to use
up leftover cranberry sauce. It's even worth buying or making
cranberry sauce just to use in these muffins.

¾ cup	natural bran	175 mL
1 cup	whole-wheat flour	250 mL
½ cup	granulated sugar	125 mL
1½ tsp	cinnamon	7 mL
1 tsp	baking powder	5 mL
1 tsp	baking soda	5 mL
1 cup	cranberry sauce	250 mL
1	egg	1
½ cup	buttermilk or low-fat plain yogurt	125 mL
¼ cup	vegetable oil	50 mL
1 tsp	grated orange rind	5 mL

In bowl, combine bran, flour, sugar, cinnamon, baking
powder and baking soda; mix well. Add cranberry sauce, egg,
buttermilk or yogurt, vegetable oil and orange rind; stir just until
combined.

Spoon batter into paper-lined or nonstick muffin tins. Bake in
400°F/200°C oven for 25 minutes or until firm to the touch.
Makes 12 muffins.

PER MUFFIN	
calories	165
g fat	5
mg cholesterol	23
mg sodium	102
g protein	3
g carbohydrate	29
GOOD: fiber	

Oat Bran Banana-Raisin Muffins

Oat bran is available in the cereal section in most supermarkets. It is an excellent source of the kind of fiber that helps to lower blood cholesterol; wheat bran doesn't have the same cholesterol-lowering effect. (Recipe pictured opposite page 182.)

1	egg, lightly beaten	1
½ cup	milk	125 mL
¼ cup	vegetable oil	50 mL
½ cup	granulated sugar	125 mL
1 cup	mashed bananas	250 mL
1 tsp	vanilla	5 mL
1 cup	whole-wheat flour	250 mL
1 tsp	baking soda	5 mL
1 tsp	baking powder	5 mL
1 cup	oat bran	250 mL
½ cup	raisins	125 mL

In bowl, combine egg, milk, oil, sugar, bananas and vanilla; mix well. In another bowl, mix together flour, baking soda, baking powder, oat bran and raisins, stir into egg mixture, mixing only until combined.

Spoon into 12 nonstick or paper-lined muffin tins, filling each about ⅔ full. Bake in 400°F/200°C oven for 20 to 25 minutes or until firm to the touch. Makes 12 muffins.

Buttermilk, Bran and Blueberry Muffins

These delicious and healthy low-fat high-fiber muffins are from Pastel restaurants, on the West Coast.

PER MUFFIN	
calories	160
g fat	5
mg cholesterol	31
mg sodium	111
g protein	5
g carbohydrate	29
GOOD: niacin, iron	
EXCELLENT: fiber	

3 cups	natural bran	750 mL
2 cups	whole-wheat flour	500 mL
½ cup	granulated sugar	125 mL
1 tbsp	baking powder	15 mL
1 tsp	baking soda	5 mL
2	eggs, beaten	2
2 cups	buttermilk	500 mL
⅓ cup	vegetable oil	75 mL
½ cup	molasses	125 mL
1 cup	fresh or frozen blueberries	250 mL

In large bowl, mix together bran, flour, sugar, baking powder and baking soda. In another bowl, combine eggs, buttermilk, oil and molasses; pour into bran mixture and stir just enough to moisten, being careful not to overmix. Fold in blueberries.

Spoon into nonstick or paper-lined large muffin tins filling almost to top. Bake in 375°F/190°C oven for about 25 minutes or until firm to the touch. Remove from oven and let stand for 2 minutes before removing muffins from tin. Makes about 20 muffins.

Instead of buttermilk, you can substitute 2 cups/500 mL milk plus 2 tbsp/25 mL white vinegar.

Photo:
Rhubarb Strawberry Sorbet (page 170), Pineapple Orange Sorbet (page 171), Whole-Berry Blueberry Sorbet (page 170)

Oatmeal Carrot Muffins

Jonn Ashlie, baker for Ruffage's, a delightful Canadian fast-and-fresh-food restaurant chain, developed this fabulous muffin recipe that I adapted slightly here.

PER MUFFIN	
calories	176
g fat	5
mg cholesterol	23
mg sodium	307
g protein	4
g carbohydrate	30
GOOD. fiber	

1 cup	buttermilk	250 mL
1 cup	quick-cooking rolled oats	250 mL
½ cup	grated carrots	125 mL
¼ cup	packed brown sugar	50 mL
¼ cup	margarine, melted	50 mL
1	egg, slightly beaten	1
1 tsp	grated orange rind	5 mL
1 cup	all-purpose flour	250 ml
¼ cup	granulated sugar	50 mL
1 tbsp	baking powder	15 mL
1 tsp	salt	5 mL
½ tsp	baking soda	2 mL
¾ cup	raisins	175 mL

In large bowl, pour buttermilk over oats; stir to mix. Cover and let stand for 2 hours or refrigerate overnight.

Mix together carrots, brown sugar, margarine, egg and orange rind; stir into oat mixture. Sift together flour, granulated sugar, baking powder, salt and baking soda; stir in raisins. Stir into batter just until moistened.

Spoon into nonstick or paper-lined large muffin pans filling almost to top. Bake in 400°F/200°C oven for 20 to 25 minutes or until firm to the touch. Let stand for 2 minutes before removing from tins. Makes 12 muffins.

Photo:
Winter Fruit Compote with
Figs and Apricots (page 176)

PER SQUARE	
calories	88
g fat	3
mg cholesterol	11
mg sodium	10
g protein	2
g carbohydrate	14

Applesauce-Raisin Squares

Cinnamon and lemon add extra flavor to these moist, cakelike squares. (Recipe pictured opposite page 182.)

1	egg	1
¼ cup	vegetable oil	50 mL
½ cup	low-fat plain yogurt	125 mL
¾ cup	brown sugar	175 mL
1 cup	applesauce	250 mL
1 tsp	vanilla	5mL
1 tsp	grated lemon rind	5 mL
½ cup	raisins	125 mL
1 cup	whole-wheat flour	250 mL
½ cup	natural bran	125 mL
1 tsp	baking powder	5 mL
2 tsp	cinnamon	10 mL
1 tsp	ginger	5 mL
¼ tsp	ground nutmeg	1 mL
⅓ cup	sliced almonds	75 mL

In large mixing bowl, beat egg; add oil, yogurt, brown sugar, applesauce, vanilla and lemon rind; mix well.

In another bowl, stir together raisins, flour, bran, baking powder, cinnamon, ginger and nutmeg; add to wet ingredients and mix only until combined.

Turn into lightly greased 8-in/2 L square cake pan. Lightly press almonds into top of batter. Bake in 350°F/180°C oven for 45 minutes or until tester inserted in center comes out clean. (Squares will be moist.) Let cool, then cut into squares. Makes 25 1½-in/4 cm squares.

PER COOKIE	
calories	52
g fat	2
mg cholesterol	6
mg sodium	25
g protein	1
g carbohydrate	1

Oatmeal-Apricot Cookies

I test how good cookies are by how long they stay around my house. These passed with flying colors because they were all gone in a few hours. They are much lower in fat and higher in fiber than most cookies.

⅓ cup	margarine	75 mL
1 cup	packed brown sugar	250 mL
1	egg	1
½ cup	2% milk	125 mL
1 tsp	vanilla	5 mL
1 cup	whole-wheat flour	250 mL
1 tsp	baking powder	5 mL
½ tsp	baking soda	2 mL
½ tsp	cinnamon	2 mL
1¼ cups	rolled oats	300 mL
¼ cup	wheat germ	50 mL
1 cup	chopped dried apricots (or dates, raisins or a combination)	250 mL

In large mixing bowl, combine margarine, sugar and egg; beat well. Beat in milk and vanilla. Add flour, baking powder, baking soda, cinnamon, rolled oats, wheat germ and raisins; mix well.

Drop batter a small spoonful at a time onto nonstick baking sheet. Bake in 375°F/190°C oven for 12 to 15 minutes or until golden. Makes about 50 cookies.

Easy Oat Bran and Date Cookies

These easy-to-make, crisp cookies are a favorite in our house. Oat bran is available in the cereal section of most supermarkets. (Recipe pictured opposite page 182.)

Oat bran, an excellent source of soluble fiber, may help to reduce blood cholesterol.

⅔ cup	soft margarine	150 mL
1 cup	packed brown sugar	250 mL
1	egg, slightly beaten	1
1 tbsp	water	15 mL
1 cup	whole-wheat flour	250 mL
1 cup	oat bran	250 mL
¼ cup	wheat germ	50 mL
1 tsp	baking soda	5 mL
1 tsp	baking powder	5 mL
1 cup	chopped dates or raisins	250 mL
½ cup	chopped nuts, chocolate chips or coconut (optional)	125 mL

In large bowl, cream margarine, brown sugar, egg and water together thoroughly. Add flour, oat bran, wheat germ, baking soda and baking powder; mix well. Stir in dates or raisins, and nuts (if using).

Drop batter by spoonfuls onto lightly greased baking sheets; flatten slightly with floured fork. Bake in 350°F/180°C oven for 15 minutes or until light golden. Makes about 3 dozen cookies.

PER COOKIE
(made with coconut)

calories	97
g fat	4
mg cholesterol	8
mg sodium	64
g protein	1
g carbohydrate	14

PER SLICE	
calories	128
g fat	3
mg cholesterol	1
mg sodium	185
g protein	4
g carbohydrate	22
GOOD: fiber	

Instead of buttermilk, you can substitute soured milk. To sour milk add 1 tbsp/15 mL white vinegar to 1 cup/250 mL milk.

Five-Grain Soda Bread

This is a quick and easy bread to make. It's particularly good served hot with brunch or with bean dishes, such as Bean Casserole with Tomato and Spinach (page 108). If you don't have all of these flours, use a combination of what you have to make a total of 3¼ cups/800 mL and add ¾ cup/175 mL rolled oats. (Recipe pictured opposite page 182.)

1 cup	all-purpose flour	250 mL
¾ cup	each whole-wheat flour, rye flour, graham flour and rolled oats	175 mL
2 tbsp	granulated sugar	25 mL
1 tbsp	baking powder	15 mL
1 tsp	baking soda	5 mL
½ tsp	salt	2 mL
3 tbsp	soft margarine or vegetable oil	45 mL
¾ cup	raisins (optional)	175 mL
1¾ cups	buttermilk	425 mL

In bowl, combine all-purpose, whole-wheat, rye and graham flours, rolled oats, sugar, baking powder, baking soda and salt; cut in margarine until well mixed. Stir in raisins (if using), add buttermilk and stir to make soft dough.

Turn out onto lightly floured surface and knead about 10 times or until smooth. Place on greased baking sheet; flatten into circle about 2½ in/6 cm thick. Cut large "X" about ¼ in/5 mm deep on top.

Bake in 350°F/180°C oven for 1 hour or until toothpick inserted in center comes out clean. Makes 1 loaf (about 16 slices).

PER SLICE	
calories	83
g fat	1.5
mg cholesterol	1
mg sodium	40
g protein	3
g carbohydrate	15

Whole-Wheat Oatmeal Bread

Whole-wheat bread has three times the fiber of white bread, more protein and much more flavor.

1 cup	2% milk	250 mL
⅓ cup	packed brown sugar	75 mL
2 tbsp	vegetable oil	25 mL
½ tsp	salt	2 mL
1 tsp	granulated sugar	5 mL
1 cup	warm water	250 mL
1	pkg active dry yeast (or 1 tbsp/ 15 mL)	1
4 cups	(approx.) whole-wheat flour	1 L
1 cup	rolled oats	250 mL
¼ cup	wheat germ (optional)	50 mL
Topping:		
1	egg white	1
1 tbsp	2% milk	15 mL
1 tsp	dill seeds	5 mL
1 tsp	celery seeds	5 mL
2 tbsp	rolled oats	25 mL

Variation

Food Processor Method: Halve recipe, except use the same amount of yeast (1 pkg or 1 tbsp/15 mL). Dissolve granulated sugar and yeast as directed.

In food processor fitted with metal or dough blade, combine flour, rolled oats, and wheat germ (if using), brown sugar and salt; process to combine. Stir oil into dissolved yeast mixture; add to flour mixture and process for 5 seconds.

With machine running, gradually add cold milk; process until dough forms ball, about 45 seconds. If dough is too dry, add more water 1 tbsp/15 mL at a time. If too sticky, add more flour a little at a time and process with off-on turns. Transfer dough to greased bowl and follow above recipe.

In saucepan (or large bowl and in microwave), heat milk until hot; stir in brown sugar, oil and salt until blended and sugar has dissolved. Let cool to lukewarm.

In small bowl, dissolve granulated sugar in warm water; sprinkle yeast over top and let stand for 10 minutes or until foamy.

In large bowl, combine milk mixture and yeast mixture. Using electric mixer or by hand, gradually beat in 3 cups/750 mL of the flour; beat for 2 to 3 minutes or until smooth. smooth.

Gradually mix in rolled oats and wheat germ (if using); add enough of the remaining flour to make medium-stiff dough. Turn out onto lightly floured surface and knead until smooth and elastic, about 10 minutes. (If dough is sticky, knead in more flour.)

Place dough in lightly greased bowl, turning to grease all sides. Cover bowl with greased plastic wrap. Let rise in warm place until doubled in bulk, about 1 hour.

Punch down dough and turn out onto lightly floured surface. Divide in half, forming each half into smooth ball. Cover and let rest for 10 minutes.

Shape each half into round or rectangular shape; place rectangular shapes in 2 greased 8- × 4-in/1.5 L loaf pans; place round shapes on baking sheet. Cover with plastic bag or greased waxed paper; let rise until doubled in bulk, about 1 hour.

Topping: In small bowl, mix egg white with milk; brush over top of dough. Combine dill seeds, celery seeds and rolled oats; sprinkle over dough.

Bake in 400°F/200°C oven for 15 minutes; reduce heat to 350°F/180°C and bake for 20 to 25 minutes longer or until crusts are brown and loaves sound hollow when tapped on bottom. Remove from pans and let cool on racks. Makes 2 loaves, about 16 slices each.

Multigrain Date Quickbread

Serve this dark, flavorful bread for lunch with Tarragon Chicken Salad (page 47) or Pasta and Fresh Vegetable Salad (page 61) and sliced tomatoes. (Recipe pictured opposite page 182.)

1 cup	boiling water	250 mL
1 cup	dates or raisins	250 mL
1 tsp	baking soda	5 mL
¾ cup	natural bran	175 mL
1 cup	whole-wheat flour or graham flour	250 mL
1 cup	rolled oats	250 mL
⅓ cup	granulated sugar	75 mL
1 tsp	baking powder	5 mL
¼ tsp	salt	1 mL
1 cup	2% milk	250 mL

PER SLICE	
calories	81
g fat	1
mg cholesterol	1
mg sodium	82
g protein	2
g carbohydrate	18
GOOD: fiber	

Grease and flour 9- × 5-in/2 L loaf pan.

In large bowl, pour boiling water over dates or raisins; add soda and let stand for 5 minutes.

Add natural bran, flour, rolled oats, sugar, baking powder, salt and milk; mix until combined. Pour into pan. Bake in 350°F/180°C oven for 70 to 80 minutes or until toothpick inserted in center comes out clean. Makes 1 loaf, about 20 slices.

Whole-Wheat Zucchini Bread

This version of zucchini bread is lower in fat and cholesterol than most, yet it is moist and full of flavor.

PER SLICE	
calories	152
g fat	4
mg cholesterol	21
mg sodium	100
g protein	3
g carbohydrate	27

1½ cups	all-purpose flour	375 mL
1½ cups	whole-wheat flour	375 mL
1 tbsp	cinnamon	15 mL
1 tsp	nutmeg	5 mL
1 tsp	baking soda	5 mL
1 tsp	baking powder	5 mL
½ tsp	salt	2 mL
¾ cup	raisins	175 mL
2	eggs	2
⅓ cup	vegetable oil	75 mL
¾ cup	low-fat plain yogurt	175 mL
¼ cup	milk	50 mL
1 cup	packed brown sugar	250 mL
2 tsp	vanilla	10 mL
2 cups	finely shredded unpeeled zucchini	500 mL

In bowl, combine all-purpose and whole-wheat flours, cinnamon, nutmeg, baking soda, baking powder, salt and raisins.

In large bowl, beat eggs until foamy; beat in oil, yogurt, milk, sugar and vanilla. Stir in zucchini. Add flour mixture and stir until combined.

Pour batter into 2 well-greased 8- × 4-in/1.5 L loaf pans. Bake in 350°F/180°C oven for 55 minutes or until toothpick inserted in center comes out clean. Remove from pan and let cool thoroughly before slicing. Makes 2 loaves (about 13 slices each).

If you are on a low-cholesterol diet, you can reduce the cholesterol in Whole-Wheat Zucchini Bread to 0 by substituting 4 egg whites for 2 eggs.

PER 5 PIECES	
calories	96
g fat	4.5
mg cholesterol	1
mg sodium	98
g protein	3
g carbohydrate	12

Flatbread Crackers

Arrange this crisp, thin bread, or crackers, in a wicker basket and serve with salads or soups, or break into small pieces and use instead of chips for dipping.

½ cup	sesame seeds	125 mL
½ cup	cracked wheat	125 mL
1 cup	all-purpose flour	250 mL
1 cup	whole-wheat flour	250 mL
1 tbsp	granulated sugar	15 mL
½ tsp	salt	2 mL
½ tsp	baking soda	2 mL
⅓ cup	soft margarine	75 mL
¾ cup	buttermilk	175 mL
Topping:		
1	egg white	1
1 tbsp	water	15 mL
2 tbsp	poppyseeds	25 mL

In bowl, combine sesame seeds, cracked wheat, all-purpose and whole-wheat flours, sugar, salt, baking soda; cut in margarine. Add buttermilk; mix well.

Shape into 6 balls about the size of a lemon; roll out on lightly floured surface into circles less than ⅛ in/3 mm thick (as thin as you can). Using spatula, transfer to ungreased baking sheet.

Topping: Combine egg white and water; brush over top of circles. Sprinkle with poppyseeds. Bake in 400°F/200°C oven for 10 minutes or until golden brown.

Let cool on wire rack until crisp. Break in smaller pieces and store in airtight container. Makes 24 servings (about 5 pieces each).

PER PLAIN CRÊPE	
calories	39
g fat	0.5
mg cholesterol	1
mg sodium	20
g protein	2
g carbohydrate	7

Variation
Dessert crêpes: For dessert crêpes, add 2 tsp/10 mL granulated sugar, ½ tsp/2 mL each grated orange and lemon rind to batter.

PER DESSERT CRÊPE	
calories	44
g fat	0.5
mg cholesterol	1
mg sodium	20
g protein	2
g carbohydrate	8

Basic Crêpes

This all-purpose crêpe batter is low in cholesterol and fat. If you're on a low-cholesterol diet, use 2 whites instead of a whole egg. Prepare a batch of crêpes when you have time; freeze them and you'll be able to make a main course such as Curried Chicken Crêpes or a luscious dessert of Peach Crêpes with Easy Grand Marnier Sauce at a moment's notice.

½ cup	all-purpose flour	125 mL
Pinch	salt	Pinch
2	egg whites, lightly beaten	2
⅓ cup	2% milk	75 mL
⅓ cup	water	75 mL
½ tsp	soft margarine	2 mL

In bowl, combine flour and salt. Make a well in center and add egg whites. While whisking, gradually add milk and water, whisking until mixture is smooth.

Heat small nonstick skillet or crêpe pan (6 to 8 in/15 to 20 cm) over medium-high heat. Add margarine and brush over bottom of pan. Add 1 to 2 tbsp/15 to 25 mL of batter and swirl to cover bottom of pan. You should have just enough batter to lightly coat bottom of pan; pour off any excess. Shake pan and cook until edges begin to curl and crêpe no longer sticks to pan. Turn crêpe and cook for a few seconds or until golden. Remove from pan and set aside. Repeat with remaining batter. You shouldn't need to add any more margarine.

Crêpes can be made in advance; stack between waxed paper and refrigerate for 1 day or freeze up to 1 month. Makes 8 (8 inch/20 cm) crêpes.

PER PIECE	
calories	232
g fat	6
mg cholesterol	25
mg sodium	89
g protein	5
g carbohydrate	40

Blueberry Cream Flan

No one will ever guess that this cheesecake-type dessert is made with yogurt.

1½ cups	all-purpose flour	375 mL
½ cup	granulated sugar	125 mL
1½ tsp	baking powder	7 mL
⅓ cup	soft margarine	75 mL
2	egg whites	2
1 tsp	vanilla	5 mL
3 cups	blueberries, fresh or frozen (not thawed)	750 mL

Topping:

2 tbsp	all-purpose flour	25 mL
2 cups	low-fat plain yogurt	500 mL
1	egg, lightly beaten	1
⅔ cup	granulated sugar	150 mL
2 tsp	grated lemon or orange rind	10 mL
1 tsp	vanilla	5 mL

In food processor or mixing bowl, combine flour, sugar, baking powder, margarine, egg whites and vanilla; mix well. Press into bottom of 10-in/3 L square cake pan, springform or flan pan; sprinkle with blueberries.

Topping: In bowl, sprinkle flour over yogurt. Add egg, sugar, rind and vanilla; mix until smooth. Pour over berries.

Bake in 350°F/180°C oven for 60 to 70 minutes or until golden. Serve warm or cold. Makes 12 servings.

Lemon Roll with Berries or Fresh Fruit

Serve this light lemon-filled cake roll with whatever fruit is in season—orange and kiwi slices are nice in winter, strawberries in spring, blueberries in summer, peaches or grapes in the fall.

PER SERVING	
calories	198
g fat	2
mg cholesterol	34
mg sodium	95
g protein	4
g carbohydrate	42
GOOD: vitamin C, fiber	

Lemon Filling:

3 tbsp	cornstarch	45 mL
⅓ cup	granulated sugar	75 mL
1 tsp	grated lemon rind	5 mL
⅓ cup	lemon juice	75 mL
¾ cup	water	175 mL
1	egg yolk	1
1 tbsp	margarine	15 mL

Cake:

5	egg whites	5
⅛ tsp	salt	0.5 mL
⅛ tsp	cream of tartar	0.5 mL
½ cup	granulated sugar	125 mL
½ cup	sifted cake-and-pastry flour	125 mL
2 tsp	lemon juice	10 mL
½ tsp	vanilla	2 mL
¼ tsp	almond extract	1 mL
3 tbsp	icing sugar	45 mL

Garnish:

2	oranges, peeled and sliced	2
2	kiwi, peeled and sliced	2
	OR	
4 cups	strawberries or blueberries	1 L

Lemon Filling: In small saucepan, combine cornstarch with sugar: whisk in lemon rind, juice and water. Bring to boil over medium heat, stirring constantly, and cook for 2 minutes or until thickened and smooth. Blend a little of the hot mixture into egg yolk; stir yolk mixture into saucepan. Cook over low heat,

Portable Picnic Dessert Take to picnic a container of sliced strawberries sprinkled with a small amount of sugar, a container of plain yogurt and a small jar of brown sugar. Also pack some clear plastic glasses and spoons. Spoon strawberries into glasses, top with yogurt and sprinkle with brown sugar.

For maximum flavor be sure to serve fruit, including berries, at room temperature, not straight from the refrigerator.

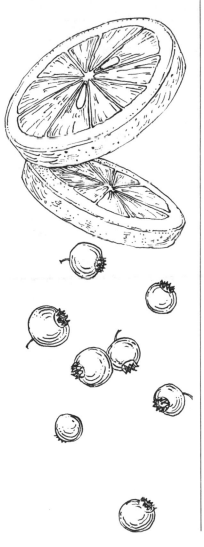

stirring constantly, for 2 minutes. Remove from heat and stir in margarine. Let cool, stirring frequently to prevent skin from forming on top.

Cake: Line 15- × 10-in/2 L jelly-roll pan or baking sheet with foil; thoroughly grease and flour foil.

In large bowl, beat egg whites, salt and cream of tartar just until mixture mounds on spoon (not quite to soft peak stage). Using spatula, fold in granulated sugar, a large spoonful at a time. Sift half of the flour over egg-white mixture and fold in gently; repeat with remaining flour. Fold in lemon juice, vanilla and almond extract.

Spread in prepared pan; bake in 300°F/150°C oven for 25 minutes or until firm to the touch. (Cake will be light in color.)

Sift half of icing sugar over cake; cover with tea towel then inverted baking sheet. Turn cake over and carefully remove jelly-roll pan and foil. Trim any crusty edges. While cake is hot, roll up in towel, starting at long side, jelly-roll fashion; let cool. (Cake and filling can be prepared to this point, covered and refrigerated for up to 1 day.)

Unroll cake and spread evenly with lemon filling. Roll up cake using towel to help roll. Sift remaining icing sugar over top. Place seam-side-down on serving platter. Just before serving arrange slices of fresh orange and kiwi around lemon roll. Makes 8 servings.

PER SERVING (including whipping cream)	
calories	128
g fat	4
mg cholesterol	15
mg sodium	40
g protein	4
g carbohydrate	19
EXCELLENT: vitamin C	

Strawberry Mousse Cake
Prepare Strawberry Mousse, page 164. Cut a sponge cake or a small angel food cake into 2 layers.

Place one layer on serving platter. Spread one-third of strawberry mousse over cake. (If mousse is too firm to spread, let stand at room temperature to soften slightly.) Cover with second cake layer. Spread remaining mousse over top and sides of cake. Refrigerate for up to 8 hours.

Just before serving, arrange fresh strawberries around or over top of cake. Makes 8 servings.

Strawberry Mousse

This is a wonderful dinner-party dessert. It's light yet full of flavor, can be prepared in advance and is easy to make.

1	envelope unflavored gelatin	1
¼ cup	orange juice	50 mL
3 cups	fresh strawberries	750 mL
¼ cup	icing sugar	50 mL
⅓ cup	whipping cream (optional)	75 mL
4	egg whites	4
¼ cup	granulated sugar	50 mL
Garnish:	Fresh strawberries, hulled	

In small microwave-safe dish or saucepan, sprinkle gelatin over orange juice; let stand for 5 minutes to soften. Microwave at medium (50%) power for 30 seconds, or warm over low heat until gelatin has dissolved.

Meanwhile, hull strawberries and place in food processor or blender; add icing sugar and process just until puréed (you should have about 1½ cups/375 mL). Transfer to mixing bowl and stir in gelatin mixture. Refrigerate until mixture is consistency of raw egg whites.

Whip cream (if using) and set aside. In large bowl, beat egg whites until soft peaks form; gradually add granulated sugar, beating until stiff peaks form. Whisk about ¼ of the beaten egg whites into strawberry mixture.

Fold strawberry mixture along with whipped cream into remaining beaten egg whites. Pour into 6-cup/1.5 L glass serving bowl or individual sherbet or stemmed glasses; refrigerate for at least 4 hours or up to 2 days. Garnish with fresh strawberries. Makes 6 servings.

Compare	per serving		
Dessert made with:	g fat	mg cholesterol	calories
No whipping cream	0	0	90
⅓ cup/75 mL whipping cream	4	15	128
1 cup/250 mL whipping cream	13	44	206

Hot Apricot Soufflé

This light dessert is surprisingly easy to make—and no one will guess that it's low in calories and fat. Try to buy the apricots that are canned in a light or a low-sugar syrup.

PER SERVING	
calories	91
g fat	0
mg cholesterol	0
mg sodium	52
g protein	4
g carbohydrate	20
GOOD: vitamin A	

1	can (14 oz/398 mL) apricot halves	1
½ tsp	grated lemon rind	2 mL
1 tsp	lemon juice	5 mL
2 tbsp	granulated sugar	25 mL
4	egg whites	4
¼ tsp	cream of tartar	1 mL
1 tsp	cornstarch	5 mL

   Drain apricots; place between paper towels and pat dry. In food processor, blender or food mill, purée apricots, lemon rind, lemon juice and sugar.

   In large bowl, beat egg whites and cream of tartar until stiff peaks form; sift cornstarch over whites and fold in. Add about ¼ of the beaten whites to apricot mixture and pulse 4 times or mix just until combined. Add apricot mixture to remaining beaten whites and fold together.

   Pour into ungreased 8-cup/2 L soufflé dish. Bake in 350°F/ 180°C oven for 30 to 35 minutes or until puffed and golden brown. Serve immediately. Makes 4 servings.

Streusel Plum Cake

This is a lovely cake to serve for a special Sunday-night dinner or for dessert when you have guests in for bridge or after the movies. I like it because it isn't too sweet, yet it's moist and full of flavor. The glaze is optional—it only takes a minute to prepare, makes the cake look fancy yet adds only a few more calories. (Recipe pictured opposite page 119.)

PER PIECE	
calories	288
g fat	8
mg cholesterol	56
mg sodium	109
g protein	4
g carbohydrate	50

¼ cup	margarine	50 mL
¾ cup	granulated sugar	175 mL
2	eggs, separated	2
1½ cups	all-purpose flour	375 mL
1 tsp	baking powder	5 mL
½ cup	2% milk	125 mL
2	cans (each 14 oz/398 mL) plums, drained (or 2 cups/500 mL halved ripe plums)	2

Streusel Topping:

½ cup	packed brown sugar	125 mL
1 tbsp	soft margarine	15 mL
1 tsp	cinnamon	5 mL

Glaze (optional):

¼ cup	icing sugar	50 mL
1 tsp	2% milk	5 mL
¼ tsp	vanilla	1 mL

Variations

Peach Streusel Cake: Instead of plums use 2 fresh peaches, sliced into wedges or 1 can (14 oz/398 mL) sliced peaches, thoroughly drained.

Apple Streusel Cake: Instead of plums use 2 apples, sliced into thin wedges. (If apples are unpeeled the fiber content is higher.)

Pear Streusel Cake: Instead of plums use 2 pears, sliced into wedges or 1 can (14 oz/398 mL) sliced pears, thoroughly drained.

Grease 9-in/2.5 L square cake pan.* (Or use greased springform or flan pan.)

In large bowl, cream together margarine, sugar and egg yolks until fluffy. Combine flour and baking powder; beat into egg mixture alternately with milk. Beat egg whites until stiff but not dry; fold into batter. Turn into prepared pan. Halve and pit plums and arrange over top.

Streusel topping: In small bowl, combine brown sugar, margarine and cinnamon; mix well and sprinkle over fruit.

Bake in 350°F/180°C oven for 35 to 45 minutes or until top is golden and toothpick inserted into cake comes out clean.

Glaze: Combine icing sugar, milk and vanilla; mix well. Drizzle over cool cake. Makes 10 servings.

*Cake Pan Size:
I sometimes use a 10-in/25 cm cake pan because I like a thinner cake. However, a 9- or 8-inch/22 or 20 cm pan also works well but will take a longer cooking time. If you are using a 10-in/25 cm pan and canned fruit you can use a 19-oz/540 mL can.

Peach Crêpes with Easy Grand Marnier Sauce

This dessert is a favorite any time of year but is particularly good in peach season. For a fancy dessert, it is surprisingly low in calories.

½ cup	low fat plain yogurt	125 mL
1 tbsp	maple syrup or honey	15 mL
3	fresh peaches, peeled and sliced	3
8	Dessert Crêpes (page 160)	8
Grand Marnier Sauce:		
¾ cup	orange juice	175 mL
1 tbsp	cornstarch	15 mL
3 tbsp	Grand Marnier, Drambuie or other orange liqueur	45 mL
Garnish:	Sliced peaches, blueberries or other fresh berries	

PER CRÊPE:	
calories	97
g fat	1
mg cholesterol	2
mg sodium	30
g protein	3
g carbohydrate	20
GOOD: vitamin C	

Variations
Jiffy Peach Dessert: Sweeten yogurt with maple syrup and spoon over sliced peaches.

Peaches and Blueberries with Grand Marnier Sauce: Spoon Easy Grand Marnier Sauce (page 167) over sliced peaches and blueberries.

Bananas and Kiwi with Easy Grand Marnier Sauce: Spoon sauce over sliced bananas and kiwi.

Grand Marnier Sauce: In saucepan, combine orange juice with cornstarch; whisk until smooth. Cook over medium heat, stirring constantly, until mixture thickens and comes to boil; simmer for 2 minutes. Remove from heat and stir in liqueur.

In bowl, combine yogurt with syrup or honey; stir until smooth. Add peaches and mix lightly.

Wrap crepes in paper towels and heat in microwave at high (100%) power for 30 seconds. Or heat in 350°F/180°C oven for 5 to 10 minutes or until warm.

Spoon some peach mixture onto each crêpe; roll up and place on individual plates. Drizzle with warm sauce and garnish with fresh fruit. Makes 8 crêpes (4 large or 8 small servings).

PER SERVING	
calories	140
g fat	1
mg cholesterol	4
mg sodium	49
g protein	5
g carbohydrate	25
GOOD: vitamin A, vitamin C, fiber	

Apricot Yogurt Parfaits

Enjoy this rich-tasting, easy-to-make dessert without any pangs of guilt—it's healthy and low-calorie.

1	can (14 oz/398 mL) apricots	1
1	envelope unflavored gelatin	1
2 tbsp	lemon juice	25 mL
2 tbsp	apricot brandy	25 mL
1 cup	low-fat plain yogurt	250 mL
1 cup	fresh apricot slices, kiwi or berries	250 mL
Garnish:	Yogurt, brown sugar or mint leaves	

Drain apricots, pouring ¼ cup/50 mL of the juice into saucepan or microwave-safe dish. Sprinkle gelatin over juice and let stand for 5 minutes to soften. Warm over low heat or microwave at medium (50%) power for 30 seconds or until gelatin has dissolved.

In food processor or blender, purée apricots; add lemon juice, brandy, yogurt and gelatin mixture and process for 30 seconds or until combined.

Pour into parfait or stemmed glasses or champagne flutes. Cover and refrigerate until set, at least 1 hour or overnight.

Just before serving, arrange fruit on top. Garnish each with small spoonful of yogurt and sprinkling of brown sugar or mint leaf. Makes 4 servings.

Iced Raspberry Mousse

This make-ahead dessert looks very pretty served in small ramekins or a soufflé dish. You can also chill it in a mold, unmold and surround with fresh fruit then garnish with mint leaves and flowers.

2	envelopes unflavored gelatin	2
½ cup	water	125 mL
1	pkg (425 g) frozen raspberries in light syrup or 2 cups/500 mL puréed raspberries	1
¾ cup	low-fat plain yogurt	175 mL
½ tsp	grated orange rind	2 mL
3	egg whites	3
½ cup	granulated sugar	125 mL
Garnish:	Fresh raspberries, mint leaves, flowers	

In saucepan or microwave-safe dish, sprinkle gelatin over water; let stand for 5 minutes to soften. Heat over low heat or microwave at medium (50%) power for 50 seconds or until gelatin has dissolved.

In food processor or blender, purée raspberries (if using unsweetened, add about ¼ cup/50 mL sugar). Transfer to bowl and stir in gelatin mixture, yogurt and orange rind. Refrigerate until mixture begins to set or is consistency of raw egg whites.

In large bowl, beat egg whites until soft peaks form. Gradually add sugar, beating until stiff peaks form. Whisk about ¼ of beaten whites into raspberry mixture; fold in remaining whites.

Divide among prepared dishes. Cover and refrigerate for at least 1 hour before serving. Garnish with raspberries, fresh mint and flowers. Makes 6 servings.

PER SERVING	
calories	169
g fat	1
mg cholesterol	2
mg sodium	49
g protein	6
g carbohydrate	37

GOOD: vitamin C
EXCELLENT: fiber

To serve as a soufflé
Cut 8 pieces of waxed paper 4 in/10 cm wide and slightly longer than circumference of ¾-cup/175 mL ramekins or soufflé dishes, demitasse or espresso coffee cups. (Or cut 1 strip for 4-cup/1 L soufflé dish.) Fold in half lengthwise. Using string, tie each strip around outside of dish so 1 in/2.5 cm extends above rim. Divide raspberry mousse mixture among prepared dishes and refrigerate for at least 1 hour before serving.

Don't strain raspberry purée mixtures. Raspberries, including the seeds, are an excellent source of fiber.

Sherbets, Sorbets, Ices

Whether you call them sherbets, sorbets or ices, a light refreshing frozen mixture of fresh fruit is the dessert I order most often in restaurants. The desserts are extremely easy to make, especially if you have an ice-cream maker. For a special dinner, serve a combination of sherbets plus fresh berries. Here is a selection to make year-round.

Rhubarb-Strawberry Sorbet

(pictured opposite page 150)

1½ cups	sliced fresh rhubarb	375 mL
1 cup	granulated sugar	250 mL
1½ cups	water	375 mL
2 cups	strawberries	500 mL
1 tbsp	lemon juice	15 mL
1 tsp	grated orange rind or 2 tbsp/ 25 mL orange liqueur	5 mL

In saucepan, combine rhubarb, sugar and half of the water; simmer, covered, until rhubarb is very tender. Purée in food processor; transfer to bowl.

In food processor, purée strawberries; stir into rhubarb mixture. Add lemon juice, orange rind and remaining water.

Freeze according to instructions on page 171. Makes 8 servings, ½ cup/125 mL each.

Raspberry Sorbet
In food processor purée 1 package (9 oz/225 g) frozen sweetened raspberries, thawed. Add ½ cup/125 mL water and 1½ tsp/7 mL lemon juice. Freeze according to instructions on page 171. Makes 4 servings.

Variation
Frozen Blueberry Snow:
Prepare Whole-Berry Blueberry Sherbet. When mixture is cold, process in food processor with 1 egg white until frothy and light in color.

Whole-Berry Blueberry Sorbet

(pictured opposite page 150)

2 cups	blueberries (fresh or frozen)	500 mL
½ cup	granulated sugar	125 mL
½ cup	water	125 mL
1 cup	orange juice	250 mL
1 tbsp	lemon juice	15 mL

In saucepan, combine blueberries, sugar, water, orange and lemon juices; simmer for 10 minutes. Chill then freeze according to instructions on page 171. Makes 6 servings, ½ cup/125 mL each.

Kiwi Sorbet

12	kiwifruit	12
1 cup	granulated sugar	250 mL
1 cup	water	250 mL
1 tbsp	lemon juice	15 mL

Using sharp knife, peel kiwi; purée in food processor or pass through food mill and place in bowl.

In saucepan, bring sugar, water and lemon juice to boil, stirring occasionally until sugar has dissolved. Add to kiwi and mix well.

Freeze according to instructions on this page. Makes 10 servings, ½ cup/125 mL each.

Freezing and Serving Instructions for Sorbets
Freeze in ice-cream maker following manufacturer's instructions. Alternatively, transfer to metal pan or bowl and freeze until barely firm. Then either process in food processor or beat with electric mixer until smooth. Transfer to freezer container and freeze until firm.

To Serve:
Remove from freezer 15 to 30 minutes before serving or until mixture is soft enough to scoop. Serve on dessert plates surrounded with fresh berries or in sherbet glasses, each garnished with its own fruit or fresh mint leaf.

Pineapple-Orange Sorbet
(pictured opposite page 150)

½ cup	water	125 mL
½ cup	granulated sugar	125 mL
1	pineapple or 1 can (19 oz/ 540 mL) crushed pineapple	1
2 cups	orange juice	500 mL
2 tsp	grated orange rind	10 mL
1 tbsp	lemon or lime juice	15 mL

In saucepan, combine water and sugar; simmer until sugar dissolves. Peel pineapple and cut into quarters; purée quarters or undrained pineapple in food processor.

In bowl, combine sugar syrup, orange juice, pineapple, orange rind and lemon juice. Freeze according to instructions on this page. Makes 10 servings, ½ cup/125 mL.

PER SERVING	
calories	213
g fat	1
mg cholesterol	0
mg sodium	27
g protein	3
g carbohydrate	52
EXCELLENT: fiber, vitamin C	

Sorbet, Fresh Fruit and Fruit Sauce Combinations
There are countless variations of sorbet (sherbets), fresh fruit and sauces you can use. Consider:
Kiwi Sorbet (page 171); fresh sliced kiwi and peaches, Raspberry Sauce
Whole-Berry Blueberry Sorbet (page 170); fresh blueberries and Blueberry Wine Sauce (page 178)
Pineapple-Orange Sorbet (page 171); sliced oranges, Blueberry Wine Sauce (page 178) or Raspberry Sauce
Rhubarb-Strawberry Sorbet (page 170); blackberries or blueberries (or any other berry), Raspberry Sauce

Strawberry Sauce
Make Raspberry Sauce but substitute strawberries for raspberries. If sweetened, omit honey or sugar. Use fresh or frozen strawberries.

Strawberry Meringue Parfait
If you have extra meringue, make this wonderful, easy dessert. Break meringue into pieces and mix with Frozen Strawberry Yogurt (page 193). Spoon into parfait glasses and drizzle with Strawberry Sauce recipe (page 172). Garnish with fresh berries if in season —either strawberry, raspberry, blueberry or blackberry.

Strawberry Meringue Tarts with Raspberry Sauce

Individual meringue shells filled with fresh fruit sherbet, covered with juicy berries or sliced fruit and a drizzling of fruit sauce make a delicious and glamorous dessert that is also light and refreshing. (Recipe pictured on back cover, made with Frozen Strawberry Yogurt, page 193.)

Meringue Shells:

3	egg whites, at room temperature	3
Pinch	cream of tartar	Pinch
⅔ cup	granulated sugar	150 mL
½ tsp	vanilla	2 mL

Filling:

2 cups	Strawberry-Rhubarb Sorbet (page 170) or Frozen Strawberry Yogurt (page 193)	500 mL
2 cups	sliced fresh strawberries or other fruit	500 mL

Raspberry Sauce:

1	pkg (300 g) frozen unsweetened raspberries	1
1 tbsp	(approx) honey or icing sugar	15 mL

Meringue Shells: In bowl, beat egg whites with cream of tartar until soft peaks form. Gradually add sugar a tbsp at a time, beating until stiff peaks form. Beat in vanilla.

Spoon meringue onto foil-lined baking sheet in six 4- to 5-in/10 to 12 cm rounds. Using spoon, shape into nests. Bake in 250°F/120°C oven for 2 hours or until meringues are crisp but not browned and can be removed from foil. If foil sticks, continue baking. Cool, then store in airtight container up to 2 days; freeze for longer storage.

Raspberry Sauce: In food processor, blender or food mill, purée raspberries. Stir in honey or sugar, adding more to taste. Cover and refrigerate for up to 2 days.

To serve: Spoon sherbet into meringue shells; spoon fresh fruit over. Pass sauce separately. Makes 6 servings.

PER SERVING	
calories	219
g fat	7
mg cholesterol	0
mg sodium	77
g protein	2
g carbohydrate	39
GOOD: vitamin C	
EXCELLENT: fiber	

This recipe uses the minimum amount of fat—less than half of a standard crisp recipe—while extra flavor is gained through fruits and cinnamon. Oatmeal adds fiber and flavor. Fruit crisps have less fat than fruit pies. For example, see Sunday-Night Chicken Dinner menu (page 174).

Variations
Apple-Cranberry Crisp:
Prepare Apple and Raspberry Crisp, substituting 1 cup/250 mL fresh cranberries for raspberries and increase granulated sugar to ⅔ cup/150 mL.

Apple, Pear and Apricot Crisp:
Prepare Apple and Raspberry Crisp using 4 cups/1 L sliced peeled apples, 2 cups/500 mL sliced peeled pears and ½ cup/125 mL coarsely chopped dried apricots.

Maple Yogurt Sauce for Fruit Crisps: Combine ½ cup/ 125 mL plain yogurt with 2 tsp/10 mL maple syrup and mix well. Drizzle over individual servings of fruit crisp.

Apple and Raspberry Crisp

Combining two fruits, such as apple and raspberry, in a crisp adds more flavor and color to the crisp than if you use one fruit. Depending on the sweetness of the apples you might want to add more sugar.

6 cups	sliced peeled apples	1.5 L
1	pkg (300 g) unsweetened frozen raspberries (1½ cups/375 mL, fresh)	1
⅓ cup	granulated sugar	75 mL
2 tbsp	all-purpose flour	25 mL
2 tsp	cinnamon	10 mL
Topping:		
1 cup	quick-cooking rolled oats	250 mL
¼ cup	packed brown sugar	50 mL
1 tsp	cinnamon	5 mL
¼ cup	soft margarine	50 ml

In 8 cup/2L baking dish, combine apples and raspberries (thawed or frozen). In small bowl, combine sugar, flour and cinnamon; add to fruit and toss to mix.

Topping: Combine rolled oats, sugar and cinnamon. With pastry blender or 2 knives, cut in margarine until crumbly. Sprinkle over top of fruit mixture.

Bake in 350°F/180°C oven for 55 minutes or microwave at high (100%) power for 15 minutes or until mixture is bubbling and fruit is barely tender. Serve warm or cold. Makes 8 servings.

Rhubarb Stewed with Apple and Strawberries

Combine spring rhubarb with apple and orange, then add some dried fruit such as raisins or apricots during cooking. Or after cooking, add any other fresh fruit such as kiwi, grapes, banana or strawberries.

PER SERVING	
calories	85
g fat	0.5
mg cholesterol	1
mg sodium	14
g protein	2
g carbohydrates	20

GOOD: fiber
EXCELLENT: vitamin C

1	orange	1
1 lb	fresh or frozen rhubarb	500 g
1	large apple	1
1 cup	water	250 mL
¼ cup	(approx.) granulated sugar	50 mL
2 cups	fresh strawberries (optional)	500 mL
½ cup	low-fat plain yogurt	125 mL
2 tbsp	packed brown sugar	25 mL

Grate rind and squeeze juice from orange. Cut rhubarb into 1-in/2.5 cm lengths. Peel, core and thinly slice apple.

In saucepan, combine orange rind and juice, rhubarb, apple, water and sugar; cover and bring to boil. Reduce heat and simmer for 10 minutes or until fruit is tender, stirring occasionally. Remove from heat and stir in strawberries. Add more sugar to taste. Serve warm or at room temperature. Top each serving with a spoonful of yogurt and sprinkle with brown sugar. Makes 8 servings, ⅔ cup/150 mL each.

Compare Dinner 1 and Dinner 2:

A few easy choices in everyday foods can make a big difference in the amount of fat and cholesterol in our diet.

Sunday-Night Chicken Dinner 1	g fat	mg cholesterol	mg sodium	calories
Roast Chicken (no skin)	8	101	98	215
Cranberry sauce	0	0	7	38
Baked potato	0	0	16	220
with sour cream and yogurt	1	3	8	16
Baked squash	1	0	1	38
Steamed broccoli	0	0	10	26
Apple and Raspberry Crisp (page 173)	7	0	77	219
Totals	17	104	217	772

Calories from fat = 20%

Fruits to Combine with or Substitute for Berries

Winter: sliced oranges, bananas, kiwi, pineapple, cantaloupe or honeydew melon

Spring: strawberries, stewed rhubarb

Summer: raspberries, blackberries, blueberries

Fall: peaches, plums, grapes

Suggested berry or fruit combinations

grapes and melon; melon and blueberries; blackberries and sliced peaches; raspberries and blueberries, strawberries and kiwi; bananas and kiwi or sliced oranges.

PER SERVING	
calories	126
g fat	3
mg cholesterol	4
mg sodium	43
g protein	5
g carbohydrate	24
GOOD: fiber	
EXCELLENT: vitamin C	

Berries with Orange-Honey Yogurt

Any kind of fresh fruit is wonderful with this tasty, easy-to-make sauce. Choose the fruits depending on the season. This looks nice served in stemmed glasses.

4 cups	strawberries or combination of berries	1 L
Garnish:	Fresh mint leaves, thin strips of orange rind or 1 tbsp/15 mL toasted sliced or slivered almonds	

Orange-Honey Yogurt:

1 cup	low-fat plain yogurt	250 mL
1 tsp	grated orange rind	5 mL
1 tbsp	orange juice	15 mL
2 tbsp	liquid honey	25 mL
½ tsp	vanilla or almond extract	2 mL

Orange-Honey Yogurt: In bowl, combine yogurt, orange rind, orange juice, honey and vanilla; mix well.

Wash berries and hull; slice if large.

Either mix fruit with sauce, cover and refrigerate for 1 hour or, alternatively, at serving time spoon fruit into individual bowls or stemmed glasses and pour sauce over. Garnish each serving with fresh mint leaves, orange rind or almonds. Makes 4 servings.

Sunday-Night Chicken Dinner 2	g fat	mg cholesterol	mg sodium	calories
Roast Chicken (with skin)	15	100	93	271
Gravy	3	1	249	34
Mashed potatoes	0	0	10	182
with butter and milk	8	21	80	70
Baked squash	1	0	1	38
Steamed broccoli	0	0	10	26
Apple pie	18	0	478	406
Totals	45	122	921	1027
Calories from fat = 44%				

Winter Fruit Compote with Figs and Apricots

Figs, apricots and prunes spiked with rum are a delicious base for an easy compote. Add the fresh fruits suggested here or any you have on hand such as pineapple or kiwi. You can substitute orange juice for the rum, if desired. For a stronger rum flavor add it to the cooled mixture. (Recipe pictured opposite page 151.)

¾ cup	each dried figs, apricots and prunes	175 mL
½ cup	rum	125 mL
1½ cups	orange juice	375 mL
2 cups	seedless green grapes	500 mL
1 cup	purple or red grapes, halved and seeded	250 mL
1	can (10 oz/284 mL) mandarin oranges, undrained	1
1	grapefruit, peeled and sectioned	1

In saucepan, combine dried figs, apricots, prunes, rum and orange juice; cover and bring to boil. Simmer for 10 minutes; remove from heat and let stand for 20 minutes or until fruit is plump and tender. Let cool.

In serving dish, combine fig mixture, green and purple grapes, mandarin oranges and grapefruit. Serve immediately or cover and refrigerate up to 3 days. Makes 8 servings.

PER SERVING	
calories	148
g fat	1
mg cholesterol	0
mg sodium	6
g protein	2
g carbohydrate	38

EXCELLENT: fiber, vitamin C

PER SERVING	
calories	196
g fat	0
mg cholesterol	0
mg sodium	11
g protein	1
g carbohydrate	45
GOOD: fiber	
EXCELLENT: vitamin C	

Oranges in Grand Marnier

This very elegant dessert is one of my favorites. It's a good choice in February and March when navel oranges are so sweet and juicy. Serve with cake or wafer-thin cookies.

6	oranges	6
½ cup	granulated sugar	125 mL
1 cup	water	250 mL
¼ cup	corn syrup	50 mL
2 tbsp	lemon juice	25 mL
¼ cup	(approx) Grand Marnier or Triple Sec liqueur	50 mL

Using zester or vegetable peeler, peel thin strips of orange rind from 2 of the oranges, being careful not to include any white part. Cut into wispy thin strips and place in saucepan. Pour in enough cold water to cover and bring to boil (this removes bitter flavor); drain and set aside.

Using sharp knife, cut peel, including any white pith and membrane, from oranges. Cut oranges into round slices and place in glass bowl or in overlapping slices on platter.

In saucepan, combine sugar, water and corn syrup; bring to boil, stirring only until sugar has dissolved. Add strips of orange rind; simmer, uncovered, for 25 minutes or until syrup is slightly thickened. Remove from heat, stir in lemon juice and liqueur. Let cool, then pour over oranges.

Refrigerate for 2 to 8 hours, turning oranges once or twice. Taste and add more liqueur if desired. Makes 6 servings.

PER SERVING	
calories	87
g fat	0
mg cholesterol	0
mg sodium	3
g protein	0
g carbohydrate	18
EXCELLENT: vitamin C	

Fresh Pineapple Slices with Rum

Juicy, sweet, fresh pineapple spiked with a touch of rum is a quick and easy dessert. For a special occasion, cut pineapple carefully so you can present it in pineapple quarters garnished with strawberries, purple grapes, kiwi or other fresh fruits. Serve with a crisp cookie.

1	pineapple	1
3 tbsp	packed brown sugar	45 mL
3 tbsp	rum, preferably dark	45 mL
Garnish:	Sliced kiwi fruit, orange segments, grapes or strawberries	

Cut top and bottom from pineapple. Cut down sides to remove peel and eyes. Cut pineapple into quarters. If core is tough or pithy, remove. Slice quarters into cubes.

In bowl, toss pineapple with brown sugar and rum; cover and let stand for 30 minutes or refrigerate up to 3 hours.

Serve in frosted sherbet or wine glasses and garnish with fresh fruit. Makes 6 servings.

Blueberry Wine Sauce

Rich with blueberries, this easy-to-make sauce is delicious over ice cream, sherbets or angel-food cake.

½ cup	granulated sugar	125 mL
1 tbsp	cornstarch	15 mL
1 cup	dry white wine	250 mL
1 tbsp	lemon juice	15 mL
1½ cups	blueberries (fresh or frozen)	375 mL

PER ⅓ cup (75 mL) SERVING	
calories	69
g fat	0
mg cholesterol	0
mg sodium	3
g protein	0
g carbohydrate	18

In small saucepan, stir together sugar and cornstarch; stir in wine and lemon juice. Cook, stirring constantly, over medium heat until mixture thickens, clears and comes to boil.

Stir in blueberries and simmer, stirring, for 1 minute or until at least half of the berries burst. Let cool and refrigerate. Makes 2 cups/500 mL, about 6 servings.

PER SERVING	
calories	82
g fat	0
mg cholesterol	0
mg sodium	13
g protein	1
g carbohydrate	20
GOOD: fiber, vitamin C	

Fresh Peaches with Banana Cream Whip

For a quick, low-cal, family dessert, serve this on sliced peaches, berries or other fruits or instead of whipped cream. It's best to make it about an hour or less before serving because it will darken upon standing.

1	egg white	1
1	large banana, mashed	1
1 tbsp	icing sugar	15 mL
1 tsp	lemon juice	5 mL
2 cups	sliced fresh peaches	500 mL

In small bowl, beat egg white until foamy. Add banana, icing sugar and lemon juice; beat until mixture forms stiff peaks. Spoon peaches into individual dishes; top with Banana Cream. Makes 4 servings.

Buttermilk Apple Cake

This coffeecake-type cake stays moist and is great for brunch, with fruit desserts or packed lunches. I don't peel the apples because the skin adds fiber. (Recipe pictured opposite page 182.)

¼ cup	soft margarine	50 mL
⅔ cup	packed brown sugar	150 mL
1½ cups	buttermilk	375 mL
1 cup	all-purpose flour	250 mL
1 cup	whole-wheat flour	250 mL
1 tsp	baking powder	5 mL
1 tsp	baking soda	5 mL
1 tbsp	cinnamon	15 mL
½ tsp	salt	2 mL
2	medium apples, cored and finely chopped (about 2½ cups/625 mL)	2

Topping:

¼ cup	packed brown sugar	50 mL
2 tsp	cinnamon	10 mL
2 tbsp	chopped nuts or ¼ cup/50 mL coconut (optional)	25 mL

Lightly grease and flour 8- or 9-in/2 or 2.5 L square cake pan or Bundt pan.

In large bowl, beat together margarine and sugar until combined; beat in buttermilk. Add flours, baking powder, baking soda, cinnamon, salt and apples; mix until combined. Spread batter evenly in pan.

Topping: Combine sugar, cinnamon and nuts or coconut; sprinkle over batter. Bake in 350°F/180°C oven for 40 to 45 minutes or until toothpick inserted in center comes out clean. Let cool in pan. Makes 12 servings.

PER PIECE
(including coconut)

calories	192
g fat	5
mg cholesterol	1
mg sodium	168
g protein	4
g carbohydrate	35

GOOD: fiber

LIFESTYLE

Canadian Heart Foundation's Dietary Recommendations and Children

The Canadian Heart Foundation's dietary recommendations are designed for healthy adults. Most school-age children can also follow the recommendations, keeping in mind that it's most important to eat a balanced diet, choosing foods from the four food groups: milk and milk products; breads and cereals; fruits and vegetables; meats and alternates. Children don't need to limit their fat, sodium and cholesterol content to the same extent as adults, and they can choose 2% or whole milk and eat more eggs. They should, however, follow the other suggestions in the book for healthy eating. Families with a history of heart disease may want to consult their doctor to see if a more restrictive diet is necessary for their children.

Young babies to the age of one year should be on full-fat milk if not on breast milk or formula. Babies shouldn't be given high-fiber foods. Consult your doctor for further dietary advice.

Feeding Your Family

One of the primary responsibilities of parents is to see that their children are well fed and develop good eating habits. Sometimes this can take all your wits and patience, but it is worth every bit of thought and effort. The sooner children develop good eating habits the healthier they'll be, and the more likely it will be that they'll continue eating well throughout life.

Now that our three children are teenagers, we get a great deal of pleasure from trying new foods together, eating out at ethnic restaurants, and having a nice dinner in the dining room as often as everyone can be home. But this wasn't alway the case: I can remember the children screaming with 2-year-old rage because I wouldn't give them a cookie 20 minutes before dinner; or as 5-year-olds refusing homemade soup but loving it out of a can; or saying "Yuck" to what I thought was delicious homemade stew.

Unhealthy eating can cause behavior problems, lack of concentration and drowsiness in children. Poor nutrition can be the result of skipping breakfast and eating too many fast foods, too few fruits, vegetables and whole-grain breads and cereals, too much sugar and fat. It means a lack of necessary nutrients and fiber, as well as too many calories.

The unbalanced meals shown below are ones that many children might enjoy. They are fine for energy, protein and carbohydrates but are lacking in milk, whole grain cereals, fruits and vegetables. Children who follow this eating pattern are not getting enough vitamins, minerals and fiber.

Unbalanced, Less-Healthy Meals	Balanced Healthy Meals
Breakfast	*Breakfast*
Cereal, high in sugar, low in fiber	Bran flakes
Milk	Milk
Orange juice	Orange
Toast and jam	Toast and peanut butter
Lunch	*Lunch*
Hot dog, or jam or bologna sandwich on white bread	Tuna fish sandwich on whole-wheat bread
1 small bag potato chips	Raw carrots
4 chocolate cookies	2 oatmeal cookies
Soft drink	Milk
Dinner	*Dinner*
Fried chicken	Roast chicken
French fries	Baked potato
Roll	Green beans
Strawberry Jello	Cantaloupe (or any fresh fruit)
Milk	Milk

Developing Good Eating Habits in Your Family

1.   If you prepare good-tasting nutritious foods and don't let children snack too close to meal times, the rest is up to them. Don't nag, don't tell them that it is good for them or that other children around the world are starving—they couldn't care less. Make mealtimes enjoyable.

2.   If you don't have potato chips, candy, or soft drinks in the house, you won't have to argue with your kids about whether or not they can have some. Healthy, nutritious food doesn't take long to prepare and young children like simple food best. What is faster for snacks than a banana, apple, carrot or yogurt?

3.   Children will learn most from the example you set. If you don't like a certain food, there is a pretty good chance your

Photo:
Easy Oat Bran and Date Cookies (page 154), Oat Bran Banana-Raisin Muffins (page 149), Multigrain Date Quickbread (page 157), Buttermilk Apple Cake (page 180), Five Grain Soda Bread (page 155), Applesauce Raisin Squares (page 152)

child won't either. If you snack on potato chips just before dinner, so will your child.

4.   If kids don't like a particular food or dish, try to figure out why. Young children usually don't like hot, spicy food, mixtures of foods, sauces, or unfamiliar foods. Don't give up on new foods and don't make a fuss. Eventually they will be curious and want to try them. Sometimes young children will say they don't like a food because they are angry at you and they know this will upset you. Don't let a child's poor eating habits be an attention-getter.

For more information on feeding children you can refer to these two excellent books:

Brownridge, Eleanor. *I'm Hungry, Your Guide to Nutritious and Tasty Food for Young Children*. Mississauga, Ont.: Random House, 1987.

Lagace, Louise-Lambert. *Feeding Your Child*. Don Mills, Ont.: Stoddart Publishing, 1986.

Feeding Your Teenager

The main challenge to feeding teenage boys is keeping enough food in the house. I concentrate on stocking wholesome foods rather than junk foods. I keep a large bowl of fruit out on the counter and they usually grab a banana or apple because they are there.

With teenage girls, eating problems are more complex and eating disorders such as anorexia nervosa are becoming distressingly prevalent. If you are worried about your daughter in this respect, don't hesitate to seek outside help from health professionals specializing in the field.

Iron and calcium deficiencies are common among teenagers, especially if they don't eat red meat or drink milk. Milk and milk products are the best sources of calcium. Most meats and meat alternates are good sources of iron. Many of the recipes in this book are high in calcium and/or iron. For example pizza is often a good source of calcium.

Here are some recipes with particular appeal to teenagers, which they may enjoy preparing. All of the recipes in this section are quick and easy to prepare and have been chosen with kids' preferences in mind. (See also menu and recipes for beginner cooks, pages 191–4.)

Photo:
Mushroom, Broccoli, and
Onion Pizza (page 186)

PER SERVING (made with 1 tbsp/15 mL cheese)	
calories	295
g fat	14
mg cholesterol	39
mg sodium	742
g protein	19
g carbohydrate	24

GOOD: vitamin C, iron, fiber
EXCELLENT: niacin

Instead of bottled taco sauce, you can make your own by adding chopped fresh hot peppers or hot pepper sauce and dried hot pepper flakes to homemade tomato sauce. Alternatively, to keep the salt at a minimum, use Tomato Salsa, page 105, and add hot chilis to taste.

Keep the fat down by avoiding high-fat toppings. Avocado, or guacamole, is a popular taco topping, but avocado is extremely high in fat: 1 raw avocado has about 30 g of fat, nearly half the daily requirement of a small woman.

Compare tacos with toppings of regular sour cream, avocado and cheddar cheese to one without avocado, with reduced-fat cheese and with light sour cream in the chart on the next page.

Mexican Beef Tacos or Tostadas

A tostada is a flat tortilla with toppings. A taco is a folded tortilla filled with a variety of foods such as grated cheese, shredded lettuce and meat sauce. Use this meat sauce as a basis for either and let each person top or fill his or her own taco or tostada.

1 lb	lean ground beef	500 g
1	medium onion, chopped	1
1	clove garlic, minced	1
1/3 cup	tomato paste	75 mL
2/3 cup	water	150 mL
2 tsp	chili powder	10 mL
1 tsp	dried oregano	5 mL
1/2 tsp	cumin	2 mL
1/4 tsp	hot red pepper flakes	1 mL
	Salt and freshly ground pepper	
16	6-in/15 cm corn tortillas (tacos or tostadas)	16

Toppings:

Shredded lettuce	
Chopped tomato	
Chopped sweet green pepper	
Bottled or homemade taco sauce or Tomato Salsa Sauce (page 105)	
Yogurt or light sour cream	
Grated part-skim mozzarella	

In large skillet, cook beef over medium heat until brown; pour off fat. Add onion and garlic; cook until tender. Stir in tomato paste, water, chili powder, oregano, cumin and hot red pepper flakes. Simmer for 5 to 10 minutes. Taste and add salt, pepper, and hot pepper flakes to taste. (If mixture becomes dry, add a little water.) Spoon into serving dish.

Toppings: Place bowls of various toppings on table. Serve packaged crisp tortillas cold, or warm in 300°F/150°C oven for 5 minutes. Soft tortillas are usually fried in hot oil, but to keep fat content down, instead crisp them in a 400°F/200°C oven for 10 minutes.

To make tacos or tostadas, let each person spoon some meat mixture into tortilla then top with cheese, lettuce and other toppings of their choice. Makes 6 servings, 2 tacos each.

Compare	g fat	mg cholesterol	mg sodium	calories
Mexican Beef Tacos (2 tacos)	14	39	742	295
Mexican Beef Tacos or Tostadas with avocado, olives, Cheddar cheese toppings (2 tacos)	27	59	1440	410

Variation

Instead of taco shells serve Vegetable Taco Sauce over toasted whole-wheat bread or hamburger buns.

Nutrition note

To reduce the sodium to 90 mg use corn tortillas instead of commercial taco shells or tostadas.

Vegetable Taco Sauce

Kidney beans make a tasty and nutritious change from meat in a taco or tostada filling. Add other seasonal vegetables, such as chopped zucchini, broccoli, sweet peppers or corn, that you might have on hand. Use the same toppings and procedure as in Mexican Beef Tacos or Tostadas, page 184.

2 tsp	vegetable oil	10 mL
2	onions, chopped	2
1	clove garlic, minced	1
2	carrots, minced	2
2	tomatoes, chopped	2
1	can (19 oz/540 mL) red kidney beans, drained	1
1	green chili (canned or fresh), chopped (optional)	1
2 tsp	chili powder	10 mL
1 tsp	cumin	5 mL
¼ tsp	hot red pepper flakes	1 mL
	Salt and freshly ground pepper	

PER SERVING
(of sauce plus 2 taco shells)

calories	168
g fat	5
mg cholesterol	0
mg sodium	687
g protein	5
g carbohydrate	26

GOOD: vitamin C
EXCELLENT: fiber, vitamin A, niacin

In large nonstick skillet or saucepan, heat oil over medium heat; add onions, garlic and carrots and cook for 5 minutes or until tender, stirring often. Add tomatoes, beans, green chili (if using), chili powder, cumin and hot pepper flakes. Season to taste with salt, pepper, and more hot pepper flakes, if desired.

Simmer, uncovered, for 15 to 20 minutes or until sauce is thickened and flavors blended. Makes 3½ cups, enough for 12 tacos, along with other toppings.

PER 2-PIECE SERVING	
calories	424
g fat	16
mg cholesterol	42
mg sodium	658
g protein	25
g carbohydrate	46

GOOD: riboflavin vitamin A, iron
EXCELLENT: fiber, vitamin C
thiamin, niacin, calcium

Nutritious Pizza
Good-tasting pizza can also be very nutritious. If you choose vegetables such as broccoli, onion, sweet peppers, tomatoes, zucchini, mushrooms and reduced-fat cheese for toppings, your pizza will be a good source of calcium, vitamins A and C, and fiber.

If, instead, you choose anchovies, olives, pepperoni, and regular mozzarella cheese, you will double the fat and sodium. The pizza will still be a good source of calcium but it will be too low in fiber and vitamins.

If your children don't like broccoli, don't assume they won't like it on pizza. They might be receptive to it in this way.

One serving (2 pieces) of Mushroom, Broccoli and Onion Pizza provides the following percentage of daily recommended intake: protein 42%, vitamin A 22%, vitamin C 65%, thiamin 33%, riboflavin 40%, niacin 45%, calcium 50%, iron 22%.

Mushroom, Broccoli and Onion Pizza

Keep some homemade or store-bought pizza dough rounds in your freezer so you can easily make your own fast food. Depending on the toppings you choose, your pizzas can be nutritious as well as delicious. (Recipe pictured opposite page 183.)

1	round (12-inch/30 cm) pizza dough	1
½ cup	tomato sauce	125 mL
1 tsp	dried oregano (or 2 tbsp/25 mL fresh)	5 mL
½ tsp	dried basil (or 1 tbsp/15 mL fresh)	2 mL
10	mushrooms, sliced	10
3 cups	small broccoli florets	750 mL
1	small onion, thinly sliced	1
½	sweet red and/or yellow pepper, chopped	½
2½ cups	shredded low-fat mozzarella cheese	625 mL
Pinch	red pepper flakes	Pinch

Place pizza dough on baking sheet. Combine tomato sauce, oregano and basil; mix well and spread over pizza dough. Arrange mushrooms, broccoli, onion and red pepper on top. Sprinkle with cheese and red pepper flakes, if using. Bake in 475°F/240°C oven for 12 minutes or until cheese is bubbling. Cut into 8 pieces. Makes 4 servings (2 pieces each).

Compare (2 pieces)	g fat	mg cholesterol	mg sodium	calories
Pizza in this book	16	42	658	424
Regular homemade pizza (made with regular mozzarella, pepperoni, anchovies, green olives)	29	73	1343	541

Feeding a Family on the Run

Today every family has a busy schedule. Mothers who work outside the home and single parents are particularly hard-pressed to find the time and energy to make meals. Once you get in the habit, though, you'll find it is not difficult to make a delicious and healthy meal for four in 30 minutes, if you have the ingredients in the house. Here are some tips for mealtimes in busy households:

*If getting a meal on the table is a problem, discuss meal planning with the whole family and try to divide up the jobs, from shopping to putting groceries away to cooking and cleaning up. Younger family members like to help and they can set the table, peel carrots, wash lettuce—don't worry about the mess, they eventually get tidier.

Don't give up if you meet some resistance. In our house, every year—sometimes every month—we come up with new ways to divide the jobs. We have just started a system in which each person makes dinner one night a week. Even if it only lasts for two weeks it's worth it to me.

*Cook extra on the weekends: double whatever you make on Saturday and Sunday and eat it again during the week. Many of the recipes in the book are suitable for reheating or can be eaten cold throughout the week: Easy Oven Beef and Vegetable Stew (page 74); Split Pea, Bean and Barley Soup (page 44); Chunky Vegetable-Bean Soup (page 36); Mexican Rice and Bean Casserole (page 116); Beef and Pasta Casserole for a Crowd (page 76); Pasta and Fresh Vegetable Salad (page 61). Or, cook a number of vegetables and a large roast, chicken or turkey on Sunday, then on Monday have it cold and reheat the vegetables. On Tuesday use the meat in a casserole or soup.

*Do a little meal preparation before you go out in the morning; for example, chop up meat and maybe a vegetable for a stir-fry (page 71), or get a chicken out of the freezer and leave a note or make arrangements for someone else in the family to put it in the oven at a certain time.

*Hire someone to do some cooking as an alternative to fast foods, eating out and using many prepared foods. If you are constantly eating meals at fast-food chains or using prepared and convenience foods (which are usually high in fat and sodium and low in fiber), examine the reasons why and consider alternatives.

It might not be any more expensive to hire someone to do some cooking for you: a student, a cleaning lady, your own child or your housekeeper. This person could help you on a regular basis either daily, weekly or monthly—or just occasionally. Consider spending an evening cooking with the fill-in chef and show him or her how to make a few of your favorite dishes, or prepare some of the recipes in this book. When I'm really under the gun for work, I hire someone to make huge quantities of All-Purpose Quick Spaghetti Sauce (page 188) and freeze it in 2- or 4-cup (500 mL to 1 L) containers. I then use it as a base for chili, tacos, casseroles and lasagna, as well as spaghetti.

Recipes for Family Suppers

Here are some quick and easy solutions to last-minute meal preparation.

All-Purpose Quick Spaghetti Sauce

I make this sauce in large amounts then freeze it in 2-cup/500 mL containers. You can double or triple this recipe. Sometimes I add chopped carrot, green pepper, celery or mushrooms. My kids like it best over spaghetti noodles sprinkled with Parmesan cheese. It's also good as a base for lasagna, tacos, chili or casseroles.

1 lb	ground beef	500 g
2	onions, chopped	2
1	large clove garlic, minced	1
1	can (5½ oz/156 mL) tomato paste	1
1	can (28 oz/796 mL) tomatoes (or 2 cups/500 mL water)	1
1tsp	dried oregano	5 mL
1 tsp	dried basil	5 mL
½ tsp	dried thyme	2 mL
¼ tsp	freshly ground pepper	1 mL

In large heavy skillet, cook beef over medium heat until no longer pink, breaking up with spoon. Pour off fat. Stir in onion and garlic; cook until softened. Stir in tomato paste, tomatoes (breaking up with back of spoon), oregano, basil, thyme and pepper.

Bring to boil, reduce heat and simmer for 10 minutes; thin with water if desired. Taste and adjust seasonings if necessary. Makes 6 servings (6 cups/1.5 L total).

PER SERVING:

calories	195
g fat	9
mg cholesterol	38
mg sodium	280
g protein	17
g carbohydrate	14

GOOD: fiber, vitamin A
EXCELLENT: vitamin C, niacin, iron

Quick Chili
In saucepan, combine 2 cups/ 500 mL All-Purpose Quick Spaghetti Sauce, one 19 oz/ 540 mL can each kidney beans (drained) and beans with pork, and 1 tbsp/15 mL chili powder.

Bring to a simmer over medium heat, stirring occasionally. Add chili powder and hot pepper flakes to taste.

PER SERVING	
calories	247
g fat	5
mg cholesterol	21
mg sodium	187
g protein	14
g carbohydrates	37

GOOD: fiber, iron
EXCELLENT: vitamin C, niacin

Last-Minute Pasta Casserole

This is another of my kids' favorites. If there are any leftovers, my son John heats them up in the microwave for breakfast or snacks. It's a good dish for small children who don't like to chew meat. I never seem to make this exactly the same way twice, and I add what vegetables I have on hand: fresh tomatoes and zucchini in the summer, celery and carrots in the winter. Add fresh basil if you have it.

4 oz	macaroni (1 cup/250 mL) or shell pasta	125 g
2 cups	All-Purpose Quick Spaghetti Sauce (p. 188)	500 mL
1	small sweet green or yellow pepper, chopped	1
4	large mushrooms, sliced	4
1 cup	kernel corn or green peas	250 mL
2 tbsp	grated Parmesan cheese	25 mL

In large pot of boiling water, cook macaroni until al dente (tender but firm); drain.

Meanwhile, in flameproof casserole or heavy saucepan over medium heat, combine Spaghetti Sauce, sweet pepper, mushrooms and corn or peas; simmer for 5 minutes. Stir in hot cooked pasta; sprinkle each serving with Parmesan cheese. Makes 4 servings.

Stocking the Basics

Sometimes we eat out at food chains or order in because we don't have the ingredients in the house to make a fast meal. There are a few simple tips for always having the makings of a fast, healthy meal at home.

Keep your kitchen stocked with staple foods, such as whole-wheat pastas, cereals, rice, tomato paste, canned beans, tuna, salmon, peanut butter and low-fat yogurt. Keep whole-wheat pita bread, muffins, peas, corn, and juice in your freezer, along with chicken and fish fillets.

Vegetables such as cabbage, cauliflower, turnip, cucumber, and carrots, and reduced-fat cheeses and eggs will keep for three to four weeks in the refrigerator.

Below are a few recipes for which you can keep the ingredients on your shelf or in the freezer. Even when the refrigerator looks bare you'll still be able to make these nutritious dishes.

Linguine with Salmon and Chives (page 101)
Fish Fillets with Basil and Lemon (page 97)
Fish Fillets with Herbed Crumbs (page 96)
Barbecued Lemon Chicken (page 83)
Herb-Breaded Chicken (page 195)
Bean Casserole with Tomatoes and Spinach (page 108)
Mexican Rice and Bean Casserole (page 116)

Penne with Herbed Tomato-Tuna Sauce

You'll probably have all the ingredients for this popular economical family dish right in your own cupboard. My kids gobble it up and, at first, didn't know if it was tuna or chicken in the sauce.

1 tbsp	soft margarine or olive oil	15 mL
1	small onion, chopped	1
1	clove garlic, minced	1
1	can (14 oz/398 mL) tomatoes	1
½ cup	chicken stock	125 mL
1 tsp	dried basil (or 2 tbsp/25 mL chopped fresh)	5 mL
½ tsp	dried rosemary (or 2 tsp/10mL fresh)	2 mL
1	can (7 oz/198 g) tuna, packed in water, drained	1
	Salt and freshly ground pepper	
⅓ cup	chopped fresh parsley (optional)	75 mL
½ lb	penne or macaroni (about 3 cups/ 750 mL dried pasta)	250 g

In heavy saucepan, heat oil over medium heat; cook onion and garlic for 5 minutes or until tender, stirring occasionally.

PER SERVING

calories	328
g fat	4
mg cholesterol	22
mg sodium	502
g protein	23
g carbohydrate	49

GOOD: fiber, iron
EXCELLENT: vitamin C, niacin

Add tomatoes and break up using back of spoon. Stir in chicken stock, basil and rosemary; simmer, uncovered, for 10 minutes. Stir in tuna and simmer for 5 minutes. Season with salt and pepper to taste; add parsley (if using).

Meanwhile, in large pot of boiling water, cook penne until al dente (tender but firm); drain. Toss with tomato mixture and serve immediately. Makes 4 servings.

The Beginner Cook

Often we get tied up at work and can't get home or are just too tired at the end of a day to make a meal. Instead of ordering in a pizza, here are some suggestions for meals that teenagers or a beginning cook can make for themselves or for the family.
– Hamburger, raw carrots, milk, apple or pear
– Canned pork and beans, green pepper strips, whole-wheat bread, milk, banana (tip: for half the fat content, buy canned beans with tomato sauce, not beans and wieners)
– Scrambled eggs, peas, salad, toast, milk, sherbet, cookies
  Roast chicken, baked potatoes, any frozen vegetables (or fresh if they know how to prepare and cook them), or salad, milk, fresh or canned fruit (light or low-sugar syrup)

Recipes for the Beginner Cook

One of the most difficult tasks for young cooks is to have everything ready at once. It's a good idea to choose a menu with one or two cold dishes, or foods for which timing isn't critical. Try this one.
Hamburgers
Oven-Baked French Fries (page 192)
Red and Green Cabbage Slaw (page 192)
Frozen Strawberry Yogurt (page 193)
Microwave Oatmeal Squares (page 193)

PER SERVING	
calories	179
g fat	3
mg cholesterol	0
mg sodium	11
g protein	3
g carbohydrate	35

GOOD: fiber, niacin, iron
EXCELLENT: vitamin C

Oven-Baked French Fries

These good-tasting french fries are much healthier and easier to make than the ones that you deep-fry in fat.

4	medium potatoes (1½ lb/750 g)	4
1 tbsp	vegetable oil	15 mL
	Paprika	
	Grated Parmesan cheese (optional)	

Wash potatoes but don't peel; slice into ½-in/1 cm-thick strips. Toss potatoes with oil in a bowl until coated; sprinkle with paprika. Spread on baking sheet and bake in 475°F/240°C oven for 25 to 30 minutes, or until golden, turning occasionally.
Toss with parmesan (if using). Makes 4 servings.

Red and Green Cabbage Slaw

This colorful, easy-to-make salad goes well with hamburgers, toasted cheese sandwiches and many summer barbecue menus. If red cabbage is hard to find, use only green cabbage and add 1 or 2 shredded carrots. Chopped sweet red or green pepper, celery, zucchini, onion, apple or raisins are nice additions.

PER SERVING	
calories	49
g fat	4
mg cholesterol	6
mg sodium	105
g protein	1
g carbohydrate	4

GOOD: fiber
EXCELLENT: vitamin C

2 cups	shredded green cabbage	500 mL
1 cup	shredded red cabbage	250 mL
¼ cup	chopped green or red onion	50 mL
¼ cup	light mayonnaise	50 mL
¼ cup	low-fat plain yogurt	50 mL
¼ cup	chopped fresh parsley	50 mL
	Salt and freshly ground pepper	

In salad bowl, combine green and red cabbage, onion, mayonnaise, yogurt, parsley, and salt and pepper to taste. Mix well, cover and refrigerate for up to 4 hours. Makes 6 servings.

Microwave Oatmeal Squares

These are very easy and the fastest squares I know how to make. Use any crumbs left in the pan with yogurt as a topping over fruit.

½ cup	margarine	125 mL
½ tsp	almond or vanilla extract	2 mL
½ cup	packed brown sugar	125 mL
2 cups	rolled oats	500 mL

In 8-in/2 L square glass or microwave-safe dish, microwave margarine at high power for 40 to 60 seconds or until melted. Stir in extract and sugar; mix well. Stir in rolled oats; mix well.

Firmly press mixture into pan. Microwave at high power for 5 minutes. Let cool and cut into 25 squares.

To Bake in Conventional Oven:
Melt margarine, combine with extract and sugar, then add oats; mix well. Press into pan; bake in 350°F/180°C oven for 15 minutes or until bubbling and golden brown.

PER SQUARE	
calories	71
g fat	4
mg cholesterol	0
mg sodium	32
g protein	1
g carbohydrate	8

Frozen Strawberry Yogurt

Creamy and full of flavor, this frozen dessert is a refreshing finale to any meal and a favorite of my daughter Susie. In strawberry season serve with fresh berries and a crisp cookie.

2 cups	strawberries or 1 pkg (10 oz/ 300 g) frozen, thawed	500 mL
1 cup	low-fat plain yogurt	250 mL
⅓ cup	icing sugar	75 mL
1 tbsp	lemon juice	15 mL

In food processor or blender, purée strawberries; you should have about 1⅓ cups/325 mL. Add yogurt, sugar and lemon juice; process for 1 second or until mixed.

Pour into pan or ice cream machine and freeze according to instructions on page 171. Makes 5 servings (½ cup/125 mL each).

PER SERVING	
calories	81
g fat	1
mg cholesterol	3
mg sodium	35
g protein	3
g carbohydrate	17
EXCELLENT: vitamin C	

Fast Food At Home

Instead of ordering in a pizza or takeout chicken, here are a few tasty and healthy alternatives.

20-Minute Home-Cooked Chicken Dinner for Four

per serving	g fat	mg cholesterol	mg sodium	calories
Herb Breaded Chicken (page 195)	3	70	240	162
Rice (½ cup/125 mL)	—	0	5	80
Peas with Green Onions (page 123)	2	0	89	68
Sliced tomato (½)	—	0	5	12
Milk (2%, 8 oz/250 mL)	5	19	129	128
Total Calories from fat = 20%	10	89	468	450
Total with 2 pieces chicken	13	159	702	612

Compare this with:

Kentucky Fried Chicken Dinner*

per serving	g fat	mg cholesterol	mg sodium	calories
1 piece side breast per person (95 g)	17	96	654	276
French fries (119 g)	13	2	81	268
Coleslaw (79 g)	6	4	171	105
Milk (2%, 8 oz/250 mL)	5	19	129	128
Total Calories from fat = 47%	41	121	1035	777
Total with 2 pieces of chicken	58	217	1689	1053

*Six pieces of Kentucky Nuggets have about the same amount of fat (17 g) as one piece of Kentucky Fried breast meat.

Swanson Fried Chicken Breast Dinner**	g fat	mg cholesterol	mg sodium	calories
10¾ oz portion (chicken, potatoes, corn, sugar, margarine, eggs, salt, monosodium glutamate, butter)	32	80	1425	650
Milk (2%, 8 oz/250 mL)	5	19	129	128
Total Calories from fat = 43%	37	99	1554	778

**This is a smaller portion than the above two dinners. Frozen dinners vary considerably in their content; read the labels carefully.

Single Serving
For one boneless chicken breast, use about ¼ cup/50 mL of crumb mixture (freeze remaining for another time). Bake or microwave, uncovered, on high power for 2 minutes; let stand 1 minute.

I always use the leaf form of dried herbs, not the powdered, and find most recipes are better with this form. Also, the more finely ground the herbs the quicker they will lose flavor under storage.

PER SERVING	
calories	162
g fat	3
mg cholesterol	70
mg sodium	240
g protein	26
g carbohydrate	6

Other quick-to-make chicken recipes as alternatives to takeout chicken:
Barbecued Lemon Chicken (page 83)
Grilled Turkey Scallopini with Herbs and Garlic (page 94)
Stir-Fried Chicken with Broccoli (page 91)

Herb-Breaded Chicken

My son John likes to make this when it is his turn to cook dinner. I try to keep chicken breasts and a jar of these seasoned bread crumbs in my freezer so I can make this in a jiffy. Don't worry if you don't have all the herbs, just use a little more of the ones you have. I also use these crumbs on pork tenderloin, fish fillets and broiled tomato halves.

1½	slices whole-wheat bread	1½
¼ tsp	each dried basil, thyme, oregano, tarragon, paprika and salt	1 mL
	Freshly ground pepper	
1 lb	boneless skinless chicken breasts (about 4 breast pieces) (or 2 lb/ 1 kg bone-in chicken breasts*)	500 g

In food processor or blender, process bread to make crumbs. Add basil, thyme, oregano, tarragon, paprika, salt, and pepper to taste; process to mix.
Rinse chicken under cold running water; shake off water. Transfer crumb mixture to plastic bag; add chicken a few pieces at a time and shake to coat.
Place chicken in single layer in microwave-safe dish or on baking sheet. Bake in 400°F/200°C oven for 18 to 20 minutes for boneless breasts, 40 minutes for bone-in or until no longer pink inside.

Microwave Method:
Microwave, uncovered, at high power for 5 minutes for boneless, 9 minutes for bone-in; let stand for 1 minute. Makes 4 servings.

*When using bone-in chicken breasts, double the amount of bread and herbs.

Compare Home-Cooked and Fast-Food Hamburgers

Home-Cooked Hamburger Dinner	g fat	mg cholesterol	mg sodium	calories
Hamburger (medium grind, broiled) includes bun	18	66	102	404
Pickle relish (1 tbsp/15 mL)	0	0	107	21
Lettuce, onions, tomatoes	0	0	3	8
Raw carrot (1)	0	0	25	31
Milk (2%, 8 oz/ 250 mL)	5	19	129	128
Total	23	85	366	592

McDonald's Hamburger Dinner				
Quarter Pounder (160 g)	24	81	718	427
Small french fries (68 g)	12	9	109	220
Vanilla shake (10.2 oz/291 g)	8	31	201	352
Total	44	121	1028	999
Total with 2% milk (no shake)	41	99	956	775
Total with Big Mac instead of Quarter Pounder	52	101	1289	918

NOTE: The most notable difference between home-cooked and fast-food hamburgers is their sodium content. The extra fat and calories in a McDonald's meal come from the fries and shake. *If you eat at a fast-food burger chain, omit the fries, choose skim or 2% milk, and make a salad from the salad bar using only a small amount of dressing.*

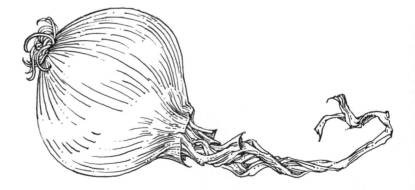

PER PATTY	
calories	169
g fat	10
mg cholesterol	59
mg sodium	54
g protein	17
g carbohydrate	1
GOOD: iron	
EXCELLENT: niacin	

To broil, place frozen patties on grill 3 to 4 inches (8 to 10 cm) from broiler. Broil for about 5 minutes on each side or until browned and to desired doneness.

Frozen Hamburger Patties

Until I was assigned an article on using frozen hamburger patties for *Canadian Living's Food* magazine, I didn't realize what a convenience it would be to have these on hand. It doesn't take long to make hamburger patties, and they are much easier to use than a block of frozen meat. Lean ground pork or lamb also make tasty patties, and they can be combined with beef.

4 lb	lean ground beef	2 kg
3	onions, finely chopped	3
1	sweet green pepper, finely chopped (optional)	1
1	egg	1
1 tsp	dry mustard	5 mL
1 tsp	Worcestershire sauce	5 mL
½ tsp	freshly ground pepper	2 mL
Dash	hot pepper sauce	Dash

In large bowl, combine beef, onions, green pepper (if using), egg, mustard, Worcestershire sauce, pepper and hot pepper sauce; with spoon or hands, mix just until combined.

Using ice-cream scoop or hands, divide mixture into 20 portions; shape each portion into round patty. Place patties on baking sheets and freeze until solid, 4 to 5 hours. Stack patties with foil or paper plates between them. Package in freezer bags and store up to 4 months in freezer. Makes 20 patties.

PER SERVING	
calories	357
g fat	13
mg cholesterol	63
mg sodium	436
g protein	28
g carbohydrate	36

GOOD: fiber, vitamin C, thiamin, riboflavin, calcium, iron
EXCELLENT: niacin

Best Tzatziki Sauce
If you have time to make tzatziki sauce in advance, use this method for a longer lasting thicker sauce. Line a sieve with cheesecloth or muslin; add yogurt and let drain for 2 to 4 hours. Place chopped cucumber in a colander and sprinkle with ¼ tsp/1 mL salt, let stand for 30 minutes then rinse under cold water and pat dry. Combine drained yogurt, cucumber and garlic; mix well. Cover and refrigerate up to 2 days.

Middle-Eastern Burgers

For a nice change, try beef or lamb patties in whole-wheat pita bread pockets topped with garlicky Greek Tzatziki Sauce, which is so delicious any extra can be used as a dip with pita bread.

4	hamburger patties	4
4	whole-wheat pita rounds (6 in/15 cm)	4
	Shredded lettuce	

Quick Tzatziki Sauce:

1 cup	low-fat plain yogurt	250 mL
½	English cucumber, peeled and finely chopped	½
1	large clove garlic, minced	1

Quick Tzatziki Sauce: In small bowl, combine yogurt, cucumber and garlic; mix well.

Broil hamburger patties to desired doneness. Cut slice off each pita bread about 1 in/2.5 cm from edge; pull apart to form opening. Heat pitas in microwave or oven until warm. Place hot hamburger patty and shredded lettuce inside pita; spoon about ¼ cup/50 mL Tzatziki Sauce over each hamburger. Makes 4 servings.

Takeout and Fast Foods

Grabbing a quick bite on the way home from work or ordering in a pizza is part of today's lifestyle. Since these foods are often high in fat and sodium but adequate in protein, the other foods or meals you eat at home should be low in fat and high in vitamins and fiber. If your dieting daughter eats lunch at fast-food chains and often has a hamburger for lunch, she can balance it out with homemade soup, raw vegetables, bread and an apple for dinner. The following table offers some excellent suggestions for making a fast-food meal more nutritious.

*Takeout	Nutritional Considerations	Nutrient Boosters
Chicken	• choose barbecued, baked or broiled • remove the skin, hold the sauce/gravy, forget the fries • low in vitamins A and C, iron and fiber	• add a whole-wheat bun, glass of skim or 2% milk and a salad • choose a baked potato for added nutrients and fiber • hold the butter and sour cream
Chinese	• high in salt and MSG • choose stir-fried dishes, include a vegetable dish and steamed rice • low in calcium and vitamin C	• boost vitamin C—include a dish with broccoli or Chinese greens • add milk to your meal or try a tofu stir-fry. You can even catch up on your calcium later in the day
Pizza	• order a cheese and vegetable pizza, leave off the ham, bacon and pepperoni—these are high in fat and salt • lots of calcium here, but low in vitamins A, C, iron and fiber	• start with a spinach/orange salad and finish with some fruit for added fiber • some pizza parlors offer whole-wheat crust—ask when you order
Tacos	• high in fat • low in vitamins A, C and calcium	• have a glass of skim or 2% milk and fruit for dessert • try a bean or chicken taco for less fat and lots of iron; bean tacos also provide fiber
Souvlaki	• cubed lamb or pork in a pita bread with tomatoes and yogurt/garlic sauce • low in vitamins A, C, calcium and fiber	• extra tomatoes boost the vitamin A and C • for added fiber and calcium, choose whole-wheat pita bread and a glass of skim or 2% milk
Hamburgers	• choose broiled or barbecued hamburgers • hold the mayo, sauce and fries • usually low in vitamins A, C, calcium and fiber	• stay away from the condiments and choose lots of lettuce and tomatoes for added vitamins A and C • choose a salad for added fiber • ask for a whole-wheat bun • add a glass of skim or 2% milk to your meal for calcium and/or have a cheeseburger—you'll boost your calcium even more

*Produced by Public Health Nutritionists in Metropolitan Toronto and regions of Peel and York

Eating Out and Travelling

Recent studies have shown that lifestyle is the important factor in determining how healthily you eat. Men and women who travel and eat out frequently are much more likely to have a high-fat diet than those who don't travel.

If you only eat out for special occasions or once a month, enjoy your meal and order what you want. If, however, you eat out often it's important to make nutritious menu choices. Too often we eat more than we would at home, more high-fat foods and not enough fruits and vegetables.

Tips for Healthy Restaurant Eating

*Choose a restaurant where you can make nutritious choices such as salads, soups, vegetables and fruits. Some restaurants mark low-fat and low-cholesterol dishes on the menu.

*Have a glass of water as soon as you are seated in order to control your urge to eat, as well as to ensure you get enough fluids.

*Avoid buffets and all-you-can-eat specials if you tend to overeat.

*Order salad dressings and sauces on the side and add only a small amount.

*If you eat the breads and rolls, pass on the butter. Don't fill up on crackers and pretzels.

*Avoid gravies and sauces made with cream and butter.

*Avoid fried, sautéed and deep-fried foods; instead, choose broiled, poached, baked, roasted or boiled dishes.

*Trim all visible fat from meat, skin from poultry.

*Choose chicken or fish; avoid duck and goose.

*Choose baked potato over french fries. Avoid butter and go easy on the sour cream, or choose yogurt instead. Ask for extra vegetables and small portions of meat.

*If you have dessert, order fresh fruit or sherbet; avoid pastries and whipped-cream desserts.

*Don't feel you have to eat everything on your plate because you are paying for it. Some restaurant portions are very large and can easily be shared.

*Avoid nondairy creamer, which is high in saturated fat; for coffee or tea choose milk instead.

*If a restaurant or hotel room-service menu doesn't offer many healthy choices, make a special request. They are in the business to please; if enough people ask for nutritious dishes, they might change their menus.

*In Chinese restaurants ask for dishes without MSG (monosodium glutamate) to reduce your sodium intake.

Healthy Breakfast	fat	cholesterol	calories	Less Healthy Breakfast	fat	cholesterol	calories
Orange or fresh fruit	trace	0	62	Croissant or danish	12	13	235
Whole-grain cereal or bran muffin	trace	0	95	Fried eggs (2) and bacon (2 slices)	18	567	241
Yogurt or milk, skim	trace	5	90	Coffee with cream	3	9	28
Healthy Lunch				**Less Healthy Lunch**			
Spinach salad (minimum dressing)	7	0	93	Cream soup	14	21	215
Pasta with tomato-based sauce and Parmesan cheese	11	8	368	Quiche	48	285	600
Raspberry sorbet	0	0	109	Chocolate pudding	10	trace	191
Healthy Dinner				**Less Healthy Dinner**			
Consommé with vegetables	3	32	91	House pâté	5	28	59
Most fish or chicken dishes (4 oz/125 g) (easy on the sauce)	4	73	148	12-oz steak	36	256	752
Rice (½ cup/125 mL) or potato (no butter and not fried)	trace	0	101	Potato with butter or french fries (10)	8	7	158
Asparagus or green beans	trace	0	15	Tossed salad	trace	0	11
with lemon and 1 tsp/ 5 mL margarine	4	0	33	with 2 tbsp/25 mL Thousand Island dressing	12	8	128
Fresh strawberries, 1 cup/250 mL	trace	0	47	Strawberry cheesecake	8	0	222
Total	29	118	1252		174	1194	2840

Calories from fat = 21%   Calories from fat = 55%

Note: For healthy meals, to gain extra calories choose larger portions and nutritious snacks. The Canadian Heart Foundation recommends not more than 30% of our daily calories should come from fat and that we moderate our intake of high cholesterol foods.

Cooking for One

When I lived by myself I would come home from work, open the refrigerator and start to eat. Unless I invited someone for dinner, I lived on cheese and crackers, scrambled eggs, sandwiches, soups, raw vegetables and fruit. This diet can be nutritious but it does become boring. Because sometimes I didn't even bother to put the food on a plate but would snack on the run, I ate more than I needed and gained weight. Finding the motivation to cook and learning how to shop for one are the two key problems confronting people who live alone.

It's difficult to discuss cooking for one or two in a few pages because people's eating patterns vary widely. A single 22-year-old male's nutritional requirements and eating preferences will be different from those of a 70-year-old widow. Following Canada's Food Guide (page 213) and eating foods from the four main food groups each day is an easy way to ensure that everyone eats healthily.

Tips for Shopping and Cooking for One

*Shop at a store where you can buy small portions and everything isn't prepackaged.
*When possible, buy only what you can use. It's more economical to buy a small can and use it all than to buy a larger size and throw half away.
*When you can't buy a small portion of a vegetable, think up different ways to use it. For example, use broccoli in a salad, soup, omelet, stir-fry, over pasta, with cheese or just simply boiled.
*The microwave oven is an advantage not only for speed, but it means you don't have to warm up a large oven to cook or reheat a small portion. A toaster oven is also great for reheating small portions.
*If you eat out often at lunch, make it your main meal of the day; you will only need to prepare a light meal in the evening.
*Because you don't have to buy large amounts you can treat yourself to special foods and more expensive foods, such as an out-of-season vegetable or a pint of strawberries, or a salmon steak.
*Many of the recipes (such as the pasta dishes) in this book are for four servings. You can easily halve them and either freeze one portion or refrigerate the leftovers and use the next day.

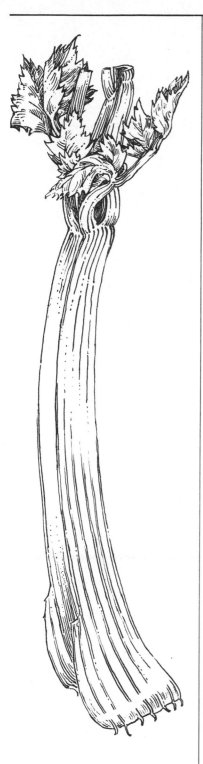

Nutrition for Seniors

Many people who live alone are also older and have some special nutritional needs. The Heart and Stroke Foundation's nutritional recommendations are particularly important for the elderly, whose energy or calorie needs are often less but whose nutrient needs are not. This means that the foods that older people eat should be high in nutrients and that there isn't much room for empty-calorie foods, such as sweets, and alcohol. Most communities have Meals-on-Wheels programs for elderly people who have trouble shopping and preparing food for themselves. Make sure the elderly people you care about aren't making do with tea and toast.

* Fatigue and apathy can be the result of poor nutrition, especially too little protein and iron.
* Complex carbohydrates and fiber-rich foods such as fruits, vegetables, whole-grain breads and cereals should be emphasized.
* Some medications, either prescription or over-the-counter drugs and laxatives, can cause vitamin and mineral deficiencies. Consult your doctor about whether you need a vitamin-mineral supplement.
* As you get older your taste buds and thirst signals aren't as strong. It's important to drink six to eight glasses of fluids and not to oversalt foods.

Recipes for Solo Diners

These two recipes for Sole with Tomatoes and Stir Fry for One are simple and quick. The trick is always to keep such basic ingredients as tomato paste, oil, lemon juice and seasonings in your cupboards so that you can prepare delicious meals on short notice.

Chicken for One

*See Herb-Breaded Chicken
(page 195).*

PER SERVING (with chicken)	
calories	292
g fat	13
mg cholesterol	70
mg sodium	259
g protein	31
g carbohydrate	15

GOOD: iron
EXCELLENT: vitamin C, fiber,
niacin, vitamin A

Stir-Fry for One

Stir-fries are a quick and easy meal for one or two people and an excellent way to use up a piece of broccoli or half a red pepper lurking in the refrigerator—add a few more vegetables and they can easily be stretched to make an extra serving. Don't be put off by the long list of ingredients—they only take a minute or two to put together and taste delicious. Serve over hot rice or noodles.

¼ lb	boneless chicken, beef, or pork	125 g
1 tsp	cornstarch	5 mL
1 tbsp	sherry or white wine	15 mL
1	stalk broccoli or celery or ½ sweet pepper	1
2 tsp	vegetable oil	10 mL
1	clove garlic, minced	1
1 tsp	minced fresh gingerroot	5 mL
Seasoning sauce:		
1 tbsp	water	15 mL
1 tbsp	sherry or white wine	15 mL
½ tsp	cornstarch	2 mL
½ tsp	soy sauce	2 mL

Cut meat into very thin strips about 2 inches/5 cm long. In bowl, mix cornstarch and sherry; stir in meat and let stand for 10 minutes or up to 2 hours. Cut vegetables into thin strips or florets. In small bowl, combine seasoning sauce ingredients and mix well.

In wok or non-stick skillet, heat oil over high heat. Add garlic, ginger and meat and stir-fry for 1 minute. Add broccoli or other vegetable and stir fry 2 minutes or until crisp tender; add water if necessary to prevent scorching. Stir in seasoning sauce and stir fry for another minute. Makes 1 serving.

PER SERVING	
calories	141
g fat	4
mg cholesterol	71
mg sodium	132
g protein	22
g carbohydrate	6

GOOD: fiber, vitamin A
EXCELLENT: vitamin C, niacin

Sole with Tomatoes

This is an absolutely delicious and easy-to-make dish for one. Serve with a green vegetable along with potatoes, rice or bread. For two servings, double the ingredients and place on one plate before microwaving for 4 to 5 minutes.

1	medium tomato, thickly sliced	1
1	fillet sole, about 5 oz/140 g	1
½ tsp	olive oil	2 mL
½ tsp	lemon juice	2 mL
2 tsp	chopped fresh basil, dill or parsley (or ¼ tsp/1 mL dried)	10 mL
	Freshly ground pepper	

On microwave-safe plate, arrange tomato slices in single layer. Arrange fish to cover tomatoes; drizzle with oil and lemon juice. Sprinkle with basil, and pepper to taste. Cover with vented plastic wrap; microwave at high (100%) power for 3 minutes or until fish is almost opaque and flakes easily when tested with fork. Remove from oven and let stand for 1 minute. If necessary, pour off excess liquid from plate. Makes 1 serving.

Conventional Oven Method:
In shallow baking dish arrange fish; cover with sliced tomato. Drizzle with oil and lemon juice. Sprinkle with basil and pepper to taste. Bake in 400°F/200°C oven for 12 minutes or until fish is almost opaque and flakes easily when tested with a fork.

Grocery Shopping

The grocery store is the first place to start thinking about healthy eating. It doesn't matter how well you cook if you haven't bought the right foods in the first place. Some of the new products on the shelves make it much easier to cook in a fast and healthy way than it was 30 years ago, but the opposite can also be true. Spend a few minutes reading labels, especially the first time you buy a new product or brand. As a rule, the more processed or prepared the food, the fewer the nutrients and the more salt, or sodium, and sugar it contains.

Choose	Avoid (or choose less often)
Milk and Milk Products	
2%, 1% or skim milk	Whole milk
Plain yogurt (1 or 2% B.F. [butter fat] or M.F. [milk fat])	Yogurt 4% or higher butter fat
Cottage cheese (1 or 2% B.F.)	
Low-fat cheeses, i.e., skim or part-skim milk mozzarella, ricotta cheese, farmer's cheese, feta	Use less of high-fat cheese, such as Cheddar, Brie
Light sour cream (occasionally)	Cream, regular sour cream
Meat, Fish, Poultry	
Lean cuts of beef—round, flank; medium and lean ground beef	Fatty cuts—prime rib, regular ground beef, bacon, spareribs
Fish, chicken, turkey	Duck, goose, self-basting turkeys, or those with added fat; breaded and fried frozen meats, fish
Tuna packed in water, canned salmon	Tuna packed in oil, luncheon meats, wieners, sausage
Fruits and Vegetables	
Fresh fruits and vegetables	Avocados
Frozen fruits and vegetables	Canned vegetables (with salt or high-sodium compounds)
Low-sodium canned tomato juice and vegetables	
Unsweetened juices	Sweetened juices
Tomato paste	Tomato sauce
Canned whole tomatoes	Canned stewed tomatoes
Fruits canned with juice or light syrup	Canned fruits in heavy syrup
Breads and Cereals	
100% whole-wheat bread	White bread
Whole wheat flour	
Prepared cereals without sugar, with 2 g or more fiber/serving	Sugar cereals, with less than 2 g fiber/serving
Whole-wheat buns, pita bread, English muffins, pasta	Granola cereals made with palm or coconut oil
Fats, Seasonings, Desserts, Snacks	
High-polyunsaturated soft margarines (p. 216)	Butter, lard, hard margarines
Oils: sunflower, safflower, canola, olive (p. 217)	Palm or coconut oils, partially hydrogenated vegetable oils
Light mayonnaise	Mayonnaise
Light or low-fat salad dressings	Regular salad dressings
Ice milk, fruit sorbets	Ice cream
Frozen juice bar, frozen yogurt bar	Ice cream bar
Angel food cake, arrowroot cookies	Chocolates, many types of cakes, pies, peanuts, potato chips
	Cream substitutes

A Guide to Food Labels

Don't be deceived by misleading food labels: the words "light" or "lite" may mean light in color or light in calories, but not necessarily low in fat. Read the list of ingredients and nutrients per serving. Remember that ingredients are listed on the label in order of amounts by weight, beginning with the largest amount. Compare several different brands of the same product and choose the one that is lowest in fat and salt.

*The word "fat" may not appear on the label, but the following words all indicate fat: glycerides, glycerol, esters, shortening, hydrogenated oils.

*Foods containing large amounts of sugar should also be used sparingly. The word "sugar" may not appear, but the following words all mean sugar: fructose, sucrose, lactose, maltose, sorbitol, mannitol, dextrose, honey, syrups, molasses, sweeteners. Although foods may be labelled "no sugar added" or "unsweetened", they may still have a high content of natural sugar.

*Food high in sodium should be consumed carefully. Again, the word "salt" may not appear on the label, but such terms as brine, baking powder, baking soda, and other sodium compounds such as monosodium glutamate (MSG), sodium benzoate, disodium phosphate may be listed.
   Terms such as "salt-free" mean that no salt was added during processing, but salt or sodium could still be present naturally or added as another sodium compound. Check the sodium content per serving.

*Check the list of ingredients on bread packages to be sure that whole wheat is the first ingredient listed. Labels such as "bread with whole grain" or "whole-wheat goodness" may not mean whole wheat.

*"No cholesterol" is a meaningless claim often used on margarines or shortenings: foods from vegetable sources (i.e., vegetable oils) never contain cholesterol. However, they could have a high level of saturated fat, which raises the level of cholesterol in the blood.

---

*Foods advertised on a healthy theme might not be healthy and often may be high in sugar and fat; for example, granola bars have as much sugar and fat as many chocolate bars, and some cereals have as much food value as sugar and a vitamin pill.

Packed Lunches

Brown-bag lunches allow you to control what you eat, save money and have good-tasting foods. With all the new vacuum-packed containers and insulated lunch bags the choice is unlimited. Some of the salads in this book, such as Pasta and Fresh Vegetable Salad or White Bean, Radish and Red Onion Salad are easy to pack and keep well. Also consider packing any of the soups from this book, either hot or cold.

When making sandwiches use a minimum of a high-polyunsaturated margarine (avoid butter because it is high in saturated fat) or light mayonnaise, not both. To keep sandwiches moist I add sliced cucumber or tomato. To prevent the bread from going soggy I pack sliced tomatoes separately and add them to the sandwich just before eating.

I used to pack lunches for my children but after I got a few complaints and didn't remember who liked what, they decided to pack their own. I do try to make sure there is a good supply of the kinds of nutritious food they like. I keep whole-wheat buns and bagels in the freezer; carrots, celery, lettuce, cucumber, alfalfa sprouts, cheese and sliced turkey in the refrigerator; canned tuna and salmon, peanut butter and jam on the shelf, plus a good selection of fresh fruit.

My children don't often take raisins or dried fruit because they are too sweet, but my son often likes popcorn for a treat. Dried fruit rolls are not recommended; they are high in sugar and stick to the teeth, causing tooth decay.

Tips When Using Frozen Dinners

*Choose broiled, baked and stir-fry dishes; avoid ones with butter and cream sauces. Read the label and select ones with the lowest amount of fat, cholesterol and salt.
*Watch your salt intake and choose low-salt foods the rest of the day.
*Frozen dinners are usually low in fiber. Add fiber by eating whole-wheat bread, split pea, lentil or vegetable soup, and a raw or cooked vegetable, and finish off with fruit.

The Morning Meal

Some people are conditioned to eat breakfast while others aren't. The most important reasons for eating a good breakfast are:
*Studies have shown that children who have breakfast perform better than children who haven't.
*If you don't have breakfast it is more difficult to get all the nutrients you need in a day.
*People who maintain an ideal weight eat breakfast; overweight people tend to skip breakfast. If you miss breakfast and have a bran muffin and orange at coffee break, you are eating nutritiously; if you have a danish and coffee you are adding extra fat and calories without vitamins or fiber.

This doesn't mean you should be wolfing down fried eggs and bacon (too high in fat and cholesterol), but you should have some fruits or vegetables, milk, yogurt or low-fat cheese, and whole-grain toast or muffins. There's no need to limit your scope of breakfast foods. Dinner leftovers, a piece of pizza, fish or salad can be as good in the morning as at night.

Breakfast Cereals. It's important to read the labels, as some are much more nutritious than others. Read the ingredients per serving and the list of ingredients. Look for a short list of ingredients and one that begins with a whole grain, bran or oats. I let my children pick whatever cereals they like as long as they aren't high in sugar and have at least two grams of fiber per serving.

Many commercial granolas are high in sugar and saturated fat from coconut oil. An alternative is to add dried fruits, such as raisins, chopped dates or apricots, and nuts to bran flakes or other low-sugar cereal. If you are on a sodium-restricted diet, read the labels for salt and sodium, as many cereals are high in these.

Fruit, fruit juices or fruit drinks. Choose fruit juices over drinks; fruit drinks are fortified with vitamin C but don't have the other nutrients that juices have. Choose fruit instead of juice for more fiber. Children don't need more than two drinks of juice a day; after that they are mainly getting sugar and might as well be drinking soft drinks. Instead, make sure they are drinking enough milk; after that give them water.

Eggs. Egg yolks have 274 mg cholesterol per egg. The Canadian Heart Foundation recommends you moderate your intake of high cholesterol foods. This means you can have two to three eggs per week as long as you follow their dietary recommendations. The Canadian Heart Foundation suggests you be more liberal in this respect with children and seniors because eggs are an easily digested and excellent source of protein and other nutrients.

Bacon. Bacon is high in saturated fat, salt and nitrates and should be avoided or eaten only occasionally.

PER SQUARE	
calories	104
g fat	5
mg cholesterol	0
mg sodium	15
g protein	2
g carbohydrate	15
GOOD: fiber	

"Birdseed" Granola Squares

They're great for school lunches. For an alternative to commercial granola bars try these tasty, easy-to-make squares that have a minimum of saturated fat and a maximum of fiber.

⅓ cup	margarine	75 mL
¾ cup	liquid honey	175 mL
½ cup	lightly packed brown sugar	125 mL
2 cups	rolled oats	500 mL
1 cup	natural bran	250 mL
1 cup	sunflower seeds	250 mL
1 cup	chopped dried apricots, dates or raisins, or a combination (about 6 oz/170 g)	250 mL
½ cup	chopped nuts (walnuts, pecans)	125 mL
¼ cup	sesame seeds	50 mL

In small saucepan, melt margarine over low heat. Add honey and sugar; stir and bring to boil. Simmer for 5 minutes; remove from heat and let cool slightly.

In large bowl, combine rolled oats, bran, sunflower seeds, dried fruit, nuts and sesame seeds. Gradually stir in sugar mixture. Firmly press into lightly greased 11- × 7-in/2 L baking dish; bake in 350°F/180°C oven for 15 minutes or until golden. Let cool and cut into squares. Makes about 40.

Snacks

Snacks are part of our lifestyle and an important part of most children's daily food intake. Healthy snacking doesn't mean never having potato chips or soft drinks, but rather saving them for special occasions and more often having fruit, yogurt, a muffin, certain cereals, or a glass of milk. It's not fair never to let children taste the latest popular snack foods, but they don't need to have them every day. If you keep raw carrots, celery, cauliflower and green peppers ready in the refrigerator, I think you'll be surprised at how often children will choose them. To prevent loss of vitamins, keep raw vegetables in a plastic bag, not in water.

Pita Pizzas are a healthy snack that the whole family will enjoy. The topping is low-calorie; see the comparison after the recipe for how it stacks up against a more conventional topping.

PER 2-PITA SERVING	
calories	286
g fat	6
mg cholesterol	15
mg sodium	718
g protein	23
g carbohydrate	41

GOOD: vitamin A, thiamin, riboflavin, calcium, fiber, iron
EXCELLENT: vitamin C, niacin

Pita Pizzas

A quick snack, lunch or light supper is easy to make using pita bread rounds as a base. Instead of mushrooms, you can add a topping of a combination of sweet red, yellow or green peppers, sliced onion, sliced tomatoes, sliced artichokes, chopped fresh basil and broccoli. Instead of pitas you can substitute English muffins, split in half, hamburger buns, tortillas, tostadas or zucchini, halved lengthwise.

4	whole-wheat pitas (6- to 8-in/15 to 20 cm rounds)	4
¾ lb	fresh mushrooms, thickly sliced	375 g
½ cup	water	125 mL
1⅓ cups	low-fat cottage cheese (small curd)	325 mL
½ cup	grated low-fat mozzarella	125 mL
1 tsp	dried thyme	5 mL
1 tsp	dried oregano	5 mL
⅓ cup	tomato paste	75 mL
⅔ cup	water	150 mL
1 tsp	granulated sugar	5 mL
½ cup	chopped fresh chives or parsley	125 mL

Cut around edge of each pita to separate into 2 rounds; place on baking sheet. Broil for 1 to 2 minutes on each side or until crisp.

In skillet, simmer mushrooms with water over medium heat, covered, for 5 minutes or until tender; drain and set aside.

In bowl or food processor, combine cottage cheese, mozzarella, thyme and oregano; set aside.

Combine tomato paste, water and sugar; mix well. Spread tomato mixture over pitas; top with cheese mixture. Spoon mushrooms over pitas and bake in 400°F/200°C oven for 10 to 15 minutes or until heated through. Sprinkle with chives or parsley. Makes 4 servings of 2 pizzas each.

Compare	g fat	mg cholesterol	mg sodium	calories
Pita Pizzas (2 pita halves) (This serving of 2 pitas will supply the following percentage of daily requirements—protein 38%, Vit A 13%, Vit C 30%, thiamin 21%, niacin 41%)	6	15	718	286
Pita Pizzas (2 pita halves) (with tomato sauce, pepperoni, olives and regular cheese)	37	65	2644	556

Comparisons of Snack Foods	g fat	mg sodium	calories
Popcorn, plain (1 cup/250 mL)	trace	0	23
Popcorn (1 cup/250 mL, 1 tsp/5 mL oil plus salt)	5	233	68
Popcorn, sugar-coated (1 cup/250 mL)	1	0	142
Mixed nuts dry roasted, unsalted (¼ cup/50 mL)	17	4	197
Mixed nuts, oil roasted plus salt (¼ cup/50 mL)	19	222	210
Potato chips (10)	7	94	105
Pretzels, bread stick (5)	trace	252	59
Doughnut, yeast type	11	98	174
Chocolate-chip cookies (2)	6	70	103
Milk-chocolate bar (30 g)	10	28	156
Ice cream, 10% B.F. (½ cup/125 mL)	8	61	142
Frozen fruit yogurt, 6.3% B.F. (½ cup/125 g)	5	63	148
Fruit yogurt, 1.4% B.F. (½ cup/125 g)	2	81	131
Apple	0	0	84
Banana	0	1	105

Appendices

Canada's Food Guide

Follow this healthy eating guide to obtain all the nutrients your body needs. For additional energy, increase the number and size of servings from the various food groups and/or add other foods.

Choose different kinds of foods from within each group to maintain your ideal weight. Select and prepare foods with limited amounts of fat, sugar and salt.

Milk and Milk Products

Children up to 11 years	2–3 servings
Adolescents	3–4 servings
Pregnant and nursing women	3–4 servings
Adults	2 servings

Some examples of one serving:
1 cup/250 mL milk
¾ cup/175 mL yogurt
1½ oz/45 g Cheddar or process cheese

Breads and Cereals
3 to 5 servings, whole-grain or enriched whole-grain products recommended

Some examples of one serving:
1 slice whole-wheat bread
½ cup/125 mL cooked cereal
¾ cup/175 mL ready-to-eat cereal
1 roll or muffin, ½ hamburger bun
½ to ¾ cup/125 mL to 175 mL cooked rice, macaroni, spaghetti

Fruits and Vegetables:
4–5 servings, choose a variety of fruits and vegetables (including at least 2 vegetables), cooked, raw or in their juices; include yellow and green vegetables

Some examples of one serving:
½ cup/125 mL fruits or vegetables or juice
1 medium-size potato, carrot, tomato, peach, orange or banana

Meat, Fish, Poultry and Alternates
2 servings
Some examples of one serving:
2 to 3 oz/60 to 90 g cooked lean meat, fish, poultry or liver
¼ cup/50 mL peanut butter*
1 cup/250 mL cooked dried peas, beans, or lentils
2 oz/60 g cheese*
½ cup/125 mL cottage cheese
2 eggs*
½ cup/125 mL nuts or seeds*
*These should be used less often because of their higher fat or cholesterol content.

Cholesterol Content of Some Foods

	Approx. milligrams cholesterol/3 oz/90 g serving
Egg yolk	280/yolk
Organ meats: heart, kidney, liver, sweetbreads	300+
Shrimp	135
Sardines	118
Crab, mackerel	88
Lobster	78
Meats: lamb, pork, beef, veal, poultry with skin, wild game, cod	65 to 80
Clams, oysters, scallops, sole halibut, perch, trout, tuna	45 to 55
Salmon	35
Dairy: whipping cream (1 cup/250 mL; 1 tbsp/15 mL)	322
2% milk (1 cup/250 mL)	19
whole milk (1 cup/250 mL)	35
cheese (approx. 1½ oz/45 g)	41
ice cream-16% butter fat (½ cup/125 mL)	46
Fats: butter (1 tbsp/15 mL)	31
lard (1 tbsp/15 mL)	12
mayonnaise (1 tbsp/15 mL)	8

Reminder: Cholesterol is not found in plant foods, only from animal or fish sources.

To reduce your cholesterol intake:
1) When possible substitute a food lower in or without cholesterol such as margarine for butter or skim milk for whole milk;
2) Use foods that are high in cholesterol in small amounts or less often.

Photo:
Swordfish Steaks with Lime and Coriander (page 106)

Foods High in Potassium

Dry beans and peas — white, lima, kidney, chickpeas, lentils, soybeans, split peas
Cereals — bran cereals
Nuts and seeds — almonds, peanuts, pistachio nuts, pumpkin seeds, sunflower seeds
Vegetables — asparagus, beets, beet greens, Brussels sprouts, celery, Swiss chard, parsnips, potatoes, pumpkin, rutabaga, spinach, winter squash, sweet potatoes, tomatoes, tomato juice, artichokes, bamboo shoots
Fruits — bananas, dried apricots, avocados, dates, cantaloupe, honeydew melon, orange, papaya, prunes, watermelon, raisins
Fish — scallops, sardines, mackerel, halibut
Calf's liver*
Blackstrap molasses

*Although calf's liver is high in potassium it is also very high in cholesterol.

Foods High in Fiber

As a general guide, choose one or two servings from the list of foods highest in fiber and six to eight servings from the good sources of fiber. It's important to have at least eight glasses (8 oz/250 mL each) of liquid a day.

Foods Highest in Fiber (over 4 g fiber/serving)
Cereals (⅓ cup/75 mL): bran and bran cereals, cereal with more than 4 g of fiber per serving
Legumes (½ cup/125 mL, cooked): baked beans, kidney beans, lima beans, split peas, lentils
Fruits (6 pieces): dried dates, figs, prunes, raisins (¼ cup/50 mL)
Nuts* (½ cup/125 mL): peanuts, almonds, Brazil nuts

Good Fiber Sources (over 2 g fiber/serving)
Breads and Cereals: cereals with 2 g or more fiber per serving, 2 slices whole-wheat, rye or cracked wheat bread, whole-wheat rolls, bran muffins, bulgur or cracked wheat

Fruits (1 whole or ½ cup/125 mL): apple, avocado,* banana,

*Are also high in fat, therefore choose less often or in small amounts

Photo:
Quick and Easy Salmon Steaks with Watercress Sauce (page 98)

blackberries, blueberries, cantaloupe, dates, orange, papaya, pear, raspberries, strawberries, dried apricots (6)

Vegetables (½ cup/125 mL or 1 whole): beans (green or yellow), broccoli, Brussels sprouts, carrots, corn, green peas, baked potato, parsnips, spinach, sweet potato, turnip

Recommended Margarines

This is only a partial list of recommended margarines because stores in each province carry different brands. Hard margarines aren't recommended because they are too high in saturated fats.

Check the label and choose margarines that have at least 40 percent polyunsaturated fatty acids and not more than 18 percent saturated fatty acids, or ones with 55 percent or more polyunsaturated fatty acids and not more than 25 percent saturated fatty acids. These figures are based on recommendations from the Lipid Clinic at St. Michael's Hospital in Toronto.

Brand Name (soft tub)*	% Poly-unsaturates	% Saturates
Becel–87% sunflower oil	55	25
Fleischmann's–84% sunflower oil	55	25
*Fleischmann's Light–84% sunflower oil	55	25
A & P–100% corn oil	40	18
Chef Gaston–100% soya oil	40	17
*Country Crock–100% soya	40	19
Fleischmann's–100% corn oil, regular and unsalted	40	18
G. Blanchet–soft soya	40	17
Lactantia–100% soya oil, regular and unsalted	40	17
Monarch–100% soya oil	40	18
Monarch–100% corn oil	40	18
No Name (Loblaws)–100% corn oil	40	18
Pantry Shelf Soft–100% soya	40	18

*Calorie-reduced, light or diet margarines (50% less fat and calories) are generally not recommended for frying or baking.

Buying Guide for Vegetable Oils

Look for oils with a high percentage of monounsaturated or polyunsaturated fatty acids and a low amount of saturated fatty acids. Keep in mind that coconut and palm oil have a higher saturated fat content than some animal fats and that no vegetable oil contains cholesterol. Canola, safflower and sunflower oils are the best all-purpose oils.

| TYPE | FATTY ACID CONTENT | | | UNSATURATED/ SATURATED FAT RATIO | COMMENT |
	POLY- UNSATURATED (%)	MONO- UNSATURATED (%)	SATURATED (%)		
Canola	32	62	6	15.7:1	best fatty acid ratio
Safflower	75	12	9	9.6:1	highest in polyunsaturates
Sunflower	66	20	10	8.6:1	sometimes used in place of olive oil, but blander
Corn	59	24	13	6.4:1	heavy taste, often used for deep frying
Soybean	59	23	14	5.9:1	most commonly used oil — in baked goods, salad dressings, margarine, mayonnaise
Olive	9	72	14	5.8:1	highest in monounsaturated fat; expensive
Peanut	32	46	17	4.6:1	more pronounced flavor than most oils
Sesame seed	40	40	18	4.4:1	used in Oriental and Middle Eastern cooking; flavorful
Cottonseed	52	18	26	2.7:1	comparatively high in saturated fat; used in processed foods and salad dressings
Palm kernel	2	10	80	0.2:1	the only vegetable oils high in saturated fat. Used in baked goods and candies; not recommended
Coconut	2	6	87	0.1:1	

Note: Other substances, such as water and vitamins, make up the total composition (100%).

Excerpted from an article in the *University of California, Berkeley Wellness Letter*, Volume 3, Issue 6, March 1987.

Average Energy Requirements for Canadians

Age	Sex	Average Height		Average Weight		Cal/Day
		cm	in	kg	lb	
Months						
0–2	Both	55	22	4.5	10	500
3–5	Both	63	25	7.0	15	700
6–8	Both	69	27	8.5	19	800
9–11	Both	73	29	9.5	21	950
Years						
1	Both	82	32	11	24	1100
2–3	Both	95	37	14	31	1300
4–6	Both	107	42	18	40	1800
7–9	M	126	50	25	55	2200
	F	125	49	25	55	1900
10–12	M	141	56	34	75	2500
	F	143	56	36	79	2200
13–15	M	159	63	50	110	2800
	F	157	62	48	106	2200
16–18	M	172	68	62	136	3200
	F	160	63	53	117	2100
19–24	M	175	69	71	156	3000
	F	160	63	58	128	2100
25–49	M	172	68	74	163	2700
	F	160	63	59	130	1900
50–74	M	170	67	73	161	2300
	F	158	62	63	139	1800
75 +	M	168	66	69	152	2000
	F	155	61	64	141	1500

Source: Ottawa. Department of National Health and Welfare. *Recommended Nutrient Intake for Canadians*. Ontario: 1983.

The Canadian Diabetes Association Food Choice System

People with diabetes have the same nutritional needs as anyone else. A qualified dietitian-nutritionist can show them how to balance the kind and amount of food they eat with their activity and/or medication, by using an individualized eating plan based on the Food Choice System of The Canadian Diabetes Association.

The following CDA Food Choice values have been assigned to the recipes in this book in accordance with the *Good Health Eating Guide*. It is hoped that by providing these values, this will be a treasured book for people with diabetes and their families. Numerous recipes carry high FRUITS & VEGETABLES choices which make them impractical to include in most diabetic meal plans. Alcohol calories were also counted as FATS & OILS choices.

For more information on Diabetes and the complete *Good Health Eating Guide*, contact the National Office, Canadian Diabetes Association, 78 Bond Street, Toronto, Ontario M5B 2J8 for the address of your local Branch or Division.

Recipe	Food Choice Per Serving		
Appetizers*			
Broccoli and Mushroom Dip (5 tbsp/75 mL)	1	◆	milk (2%)
Curried Chicken Croustades (3 pieces)	1	◢	protein;
	½	◻	starchy
Italian Tomato Bruschetta	1	◻	starchy;
	½	◢	fruits & vegetables
Low-Salt Bagel Thins (8 thins)	1	◻	starchy;
	1	▲	fats & oils
Marinated Spiced Carrots	½	◢	fruits and vegetables

*The serving sizes for the Appetizers have been adjusted from the original recipes to fit the Diabetic meal plan better.

Recipe	Food Choice Per Serving	
Marinated Mushrooms	½ ◨	fruits & vegetables;
	1 ▲	fats & oils
Mussels on the Half Shell,	1 ⊘	protein;
	½ ◨	fruits & vegetables;
	1 ▲	fats & oils
Salmon Spread (3 tbsp/45 mL)	1 ⊘	protein
Seafood Lettuce Rolls	2 ⊘	protein;
	½ ◨	fruits & vegetables
Shrimp Mousse (4 tbsp/60 mL)	1 ⊘	protein
Spiced Meatballs (2 meatballs)	1 ⊘	protein
Spinach Onion Dip (6 tbsp/90 mL)	1 ◆	milk (2%)

Soups

Recipe	Food Choice Per Serving	
Asparagus and Potato Bisque	1 ◻	starchy;
	½ ◆	milk (2%)
Basic Chicken Stock	Free	
Carrot with Coriander Soup	1 ◨	fruits & vegetables
Chilled Cucumber-Chive Soup	1 ◆	milk (2%);
	1 ▲	fats & oils
Chunky Vegetable-Bean Soup	1 ⊘	protein;
	1 ◻	starchy;
	½ ◨	fruits & vegetables
Cream of Parsnip Soup	1 ◻	starchy;
	1 ▲	fats & oils
Fresh Beet Soup	1 ◨	fruits & vegetables;
	1 ▲	fats & oils
Fresh Corn Bisque	1 ◨	fruits & vegetables;
	1 ▲	fats & oils
Fresh Tomato Soup Provençal	1 ◨	fruits & vegetables
Harvest Pumpkin and Zucchini Soup	1 ◻	starchy;
	1 ▲	fats & oils

Recipe	Food Choice Per Serving		
Mussel, Clam and Fish Chowder	3	⊘	protein;
	1	▢	starchy
Mushroom Bisque	1	◆	milk (2%);
	½	◪	fruits & vegetables;
	1	▲	fats & oils
Split Pea, Bean and Barley Soup	1	⊘	protein;
	1½	▢	starchy
Turkey Noodle Soup	1½	⊘	protein;
	½	◪	fruits & vegetables
Zucchini and Watercress Soup	1	▢	starchy
Salads			
Carrot and Cracked Wheat Salad	1	▢	starchy;
	½	◪	fruits & vegetables;
	1	▲	fats & oils
Classic Tuna Salad	1	⊘	protein
Curried Vermicelli Noodle Salad	1	▢	starchy;
	1	◪	fruits & vegetables;
	2	▲	fats & oils
Danish Potato Salad	2	▢	starchy;
	1	▲	fats & oils
Fettuccine and Mussel Salad	1	⊘	protein;
	2	▲	starchy;
	1	◪	fruits & vegetables;
	1	▲	fats & oils
Italian Rice and Mozzarella Salad	1	▢	starchy;
	1	◪	fruits & vegetables;
	1	▲	fats & oils
Pasta and Fresh Vegetable Salad	1	▢	starchy;
	1	◪	fruits & vegetables;
	1	▲	fats & oils
Roasted Red Pepper, Chèvre and Arugula Salad	½	◪	fruits & vegetables;
	1	▲	fats & oils
Shell Pasta Salad with Salmon and Green Beans	2	⊘	protein;
	1½	▢	starchy

Recipe	Food Choice Per Serving		
Sliced Cucumbers with Chives	½	◨	fruits & vegetables
Snow Pea and Red Pepper Buffet Salad	½	◨	fruits & vegetables;
	1	▲	fats & oils
Spinach Salad	½	◨	fruits & vegetables;
	2	▲	fats & oils
Tossed Seasonal Greens	1	++	extra vegetables;
	½	▲	fats & oils
Tortellini with Tuna Salad	2	⊘	protein;
	2	▢	starchy;
	1	◨	fruits & vegetables
Tarragon Chicken Salad	3	⊘	protein
Warm Vegetable Salad	½	◨	fruits & vegetables;
	2	▲	fats & oils
White Bean, Radish and Red Onion Salad	1	⊘	protein;
	½	▢	starchy
Salad Dressings			
Creamy Herb Dressing (1 tbsp/15 mL)	1	++	extras
Fresh Tomato-Chive Dressing	1	++	extras
Mustard-Garlic Vinaigrette	1	▲	fats & oils
Ranch-Style Buttermilk Dressing	1	++	extras
Yogurt-Orange Dressing	½	◨	fruits & vegetables;
	1		fats & oils
Poultry			
Barbecued Lemon Chicken	3	⊘	protein
Chicken and Shrimp Creole	3	⊘	protein;
	2	▢	starchy;
	½	◨	fruits & vegetables

Recipe	Food Choice Per Serving		
Curried Chicken and Tomato Casserole	2	⬭	protein;
	1	◩	fruits & vegetables;
	½	◆	milk (2%)
Curried Chicken Crêpes	3	⬭	protein;
	1	◻	starchy
Grilled Tandoori Chicken	3	⬭	protein
Grilled Turkey Scallopini	3	⬭	protein
Stir-Fried Chicken	3	⬭	protein;
	½	◩	fruits & vegetables
Szechuan Orange-Ginger Chicken	3	⬭	protein;
	½	◩	fruits & vegetables
Tarragon-Roasted Chicken	3	⬭	protein
Mushroom Onion Stuffing	1	◻	starchy
Beef			
Beef and Pasta Casserole	4	⬭	protein;
	2	◻	starchy;
	1	◩	fruits & vegetables;
	1	▲	fats & oils
Beef and Tomato Stir Fry	3	⬭	protein;
	1	◩	fruits & vegetables
Easy Oven Beef and Vegetable Stew	2	⬭	protein;
	1	◻	starchy;
	1	◩	fruits & vegetables
Family Favorite Shepherd's Pie	2	⬭	protein;
	2	◻	starchy;
	½	◩	fruits & vegetables;
	1	▲	fats & oils
Ginger-Garlic Marinated Flank Steak	3	⬭	protein

Recipe	Food Choice Per Serving		
Lamb			
Grilled Butterflied Leg of Lamb	3	▨	protein;
	1	▲	fats & oils
Lamb Tenderloins with Rosemary	3	▨	protein
Pork			
Brochette of Pork	4	▨	protein;
	½	◨	fruits & vegetables
Cauliflower and Ham Gratin	2	▨	protein;
	1	◨	fruits & vegetables
	1	▲	fats & oils
Pork Chops with Rosemary	3	▨	protein;
	½	◨	fruits & vegetables
Fish			
Barbecued Skewered Halibut	3	▨	protein
Dilled Snapper Fillets	3	▨	protein
Fettuccine with Mussels	3	▨	protein;
	4½	☐	starchy;
	1	◨	fruits & vegetables
Fish Fillets with Basil and Lemon	3	▨	protein
Fish Fillets with Herbed Crumbs	3	▨	protein;
	⅓	☐	starchy
Grilled Halibut Steaks	4	▨	protein;
	1	++	extra vegetables
Linguine with Salmon	2	▨	protein;
	3	☐	starchy;
	½	◆	milk (2%)
	1	▲	fats & oils
Make-Ahead Paella	3	▨	protein;
	2	☐	starchy

Recipe	Food Choice Per Serving		
Penne with Herbed Tomato Tuna Sauce	2	⬗	protein;
	3	◻	starchy
Quick and Easy Salmon Steaks	5	⬗	protein
Swordfish Steaks with Lime	3	⬗	protein
Teriyaki Cod Fillets	3	⬗	protein
Tuscan-Style Capellini with Clams	1	⬗	protein;
	3	◻	starchy;
	1	▲	fats & oils
Meatless Main Courses			
Barley, Green Pepper and Tomato Casserole	2	⬗	protein;
	1	◻	starchy;
	1	◩	fruits & vegetables;
	2	▲	fats & oils;
	1	++	extra vegetables
Bean Casserole with Tomatoes and Spinach	2	⬗	protein;
	2	◻	starchy;
	½	◩	fruits & vegetables
Cabbage and Potato Pie	1	◻	starchy;
	1½	◩	fruits & vegetables;
	1	◈	milk (2%);
	1	▲	fats & oils
Fettuccine with Pesto Sauce (1½ cups cooked)	3	◻	starchy;
	1	▲	fats & oils
Vegetables			
Baked Parsnips and Carrots	2	◩	fruits & vegetables;
	1	▲	fats & oils
Barley and Mushroom Pilaf	1	◻	starchy;
	½	◩	fruits & vegetables
	1	▲	fats & oils
Broccoli with Ginger	1	◩	extra vegetable;
	1	▲	fats & oils
Brussels Sprouts with Peppers	1	◻	starchy;
	1	▲	fats & oils

Recipe	Food Choice Per Serving		
Bulgur Pilaf with Apricots and Raisins	2	▢	starchy;
	1	◪	fruits & vegetables
	1	▲	fats & oils
Carrots and Leeks	1	◪	fruits & vegetables;
	1	▲	fats & oils
Cherry Tomatoes and Mushrooms Sauté	1	++	extra vegetables
	1	▲	fats & oils
Chinese-Style Vegetables	½	◪	fruits & vegetables;
	1	▲	fats & oils
Fettuccine with Herbs and Garlic	3	▢	starchy;
	1	▲	fats & oils
Green Beans with Sautéed Mushrooms	1	++	extra vegetables
	1	▲	fats & oils
Quick Lentils with Onion and Celery	1	⊘	protein;
	1	▢	starchy
Middle-Eastern Eggplant	½	◪	fruits & vegetables;
	½	◆	milk (2%);
	1	▲	fats & oils
Mushroom-Stuffed Zucchini Cups	1	++	extra vegetables;
	1	▲	fats & oils
New Potatoes with Herbs	1½	▢	starchy
Peas with Green Onions	1	◪	fruits & vegetables
Skillet Greens	1	++	extra vegetables;
	1	▲	fats & oils
Gratin of Fall Vegetables	1	⊘	protein;
	½	◪	fruits & vegetables;
	1	▲	fats & oils
Mexican Rice and Bean Casserole	1	⊘	protein;
	2	▢	starchy;
	½	◪	fruits & vegetables;
	1	▲	fats & oils
Rotini with Fresh Tomatoes	1	⊘	protein;
	3	▢	starchy;
	½	◪	fruits & vegetables;
	2	▲	fats & oils

Recipe	Food Choice Per Serving		
Tomato, Broccoli and Pasta Salad	1	⊘	protein;
	1	▢	starchy;
	½	◩	fruits & vegetables;
	2	▲	fats & oils
Vegetable Lasagna	3	⊘	protein;
	2	▢	starchy;
	½	◩	fruits & vegetables
Skillet Zucchini	1	◩	fruits & vegetables
Spaghetti Squash with Parsley	½	◩	fruits & vegetables;
	½	▲	fats & oils
Steamed Fresh Vegetables	1½	◩	fruits & vegetables;
	1	▲	fats & oils
Stir-Fry Ratatouille	1	◩	fruits & vegetables;
	1	▲	fats & oils
Tomatoes Broiled with Goat Cheese	1	⊘	protein;
	1	⧺	extra vegetables
Turnip and Apple Purée	½	◩	fruits & vegetables;
	1	▲	fats & oils
Sauces and Accompaniments			
Cheese Sauce	½	⊘	protein;
	½	◆	milk (2%);
	1	▲	fats & oils
Fresh Mint Sauce	½	◩	fruits & vegetables
Fresh-Tasting Cucumber Relish	½	◩	fruits & vegetables
Homemade Ketchup	½	◩	fruits & vegetables
Old-Fashioned Pickled Beets	1	⧺	extras
Red Pepper Jelly	1	◩	fruits & vegetables
Yogurt Béarnaise Sauce (2 tbsp/25 mL)	1	◆	milk (2%)

Recipe	Food Choice Per Serving	
Desserts		
Apple and Raspberry Crisp	1 ▢	starchy;
	2 ◪	fruits & vegetables;
	1 ▲	fats & oils
Apricot Yogurt Parfaits	2 ◪	fruits & vegetables;
	1 ▲	fats & oils
Berries with Orange-Honey Yogurt	2 ◪	fruits & vegetables;
	½ ◆	milk (2%)
Blueberry Cream Flan	1 ▢	starchy;
	2 ◪	fruits & vegetables;
	1 ▲	fats & oils
Blueberry Wine Sauce	1½ ◪	fruits & vegetables
Buttermilk Apple Cake	1 ▢	starchy;
	1½ ◪	fruits & vegetables
	1 ▲	fats & oils
Fresh Peaches with Banana Cream Whip	1 ◪	fruits & vegetables
Fresh Pineapple Slices with Rum	1½ ◪	fruits & vegetables
	1 ▲	fats & oils
Hot Apricot Soufflé	2 ◪	fruits & vegetables
Iced Raspberry Mousse	3 ◪	fruits & vegetables
Kiwi Sorbet	3½ ◪	fruits & vegetables
Lemon Roll	1 ▢	starchy;
	2 ◪	fruits & vegetables;
	1 ▲	fats & oils
Peach Crêpes	½ ▢	starchy;
	1 ◪	fruits & vegetables
Oranges in Grand Marnier	4½ ◪	fruits & vegetables
Pineapple-Orange Sorbet	2½ ◪	fruits & vegetables

Recipe	Food Choice Per Serving	
Rhubarb Stewed with Apple	2 ◨	fruits & vegetables
Rhubarb-Strawberry Sorbet	2½ ◨	fruits & vegetables
Streusel Plum Cake	1 ☐	starchy;
	3 ◨	fruits & vegetables;
	2 ▲	fats & oils
Strawberry Meringue Tarts	4½ ◨	fruits & vegetables
Strawberry Mousse	2 ◨	fruits & vegetables
	1 ▲	fats & oils
Winter Fruit Compote	3½ ◨	fruits & vegetables
Whole-Berry Blueberry Sorbet	2½ ◨	fruits & vegetables
Baked Goods		
Applesauce Raisin Squares	1½ ◨	fruits & vegetables;
	½ ▲	fats & oils
Basic Crêpes	½ ☐	starchy
Birdseed Granola Squares	1½ ◨	fruits & vegetables
	1 ▲	fats & oils
Buttermilk Bran and Blueberry Muffins	1 ☐	starchy;
	1 ◨	fruits & vegetables;
	2 ▲	fats & oils
Cranberry Orange Muffins	1 ☐	starchy;
	1 ◨	fruits & vegetables;
	1 ▲	fats & oils
Easy Oat Bran and Date Cookies (2 cookies)	1 ☐	starchy;
	1 ◨	fruits & vegetables;
	2 ▲	fats & oils
Five-Grain Soda Bread	1½ ☐	starchy;
	1 ▲	fats & oils
Flatbread Crackers	1½ ☐	starchy;
	2 ▲	fats & oils
Microwave Oatmeal Squares	½ ☐	starchy;
	1 ▲	fats & oils

Recipe	Food Choice Per Serving
Multigrain Date Bread	1 ▫ starchy
Oat Bran Banana-Raisin Muffins	1 ▫ starchy; 1 ◪ fruits & vegetables; 1 ▲ fats & oils
Oatmeal-Apricot Cookies	1 ◪ fruits & vegetables
Oatmeal-Carrot Muffins	1 ▫ starchy; 1½ ◪ fruits & vegetables; 1 ▲ fats & oils
Whole-Wheat Zucchini Bread	1 ▫ starchy; 1 ◪ fruits & vegetables; 1 ▲ fats & oils
Whole-Wheat Oatmeal Bread	1 ▫ starchy
Lifestyle	
All-Purpose Spaghetti Sauce	2 ◙ protein; 1 ◪ fruits & vegetables; 1 ▲ fats & oils
Frozen Hamburger Patties	3 ◙ protein
Frozen Strawberry Yogurt	1½ ◪ fruits & vegetables
Herb-Breaded Chicken	3 ◙ protein; ½ ◪ fruits & vegetables
Last-Minute Pasta Casserole	1 ◙ protein; 2 ▫ starchy; ½ ◪ fruits & vegetables; 1 ▲ fats & oils
Mexican Beef Tacos	2 ◙ protein; 1 ▫ starchy; ½ ◪ fruits & vegetables; 1 ▲ fats & oils
Middle-Eastern Burgers	3 ◙ protein; 2 ▫ starchy; 1 ◈ milk (2%)

Recipe	Food Choice Per Serving		
Mushroom, Broccoli and Onion Pizza	3	⊘	protein;
	2	☐	starchy;
	1	◪	fruits & vegetables;
	1	▲	fats & oils
Oven-Baked French Fries	2	☐	starchy;
	1	▲	fats & oils
Pita Pizzas	2	⊘	protein;
	2	☐	starchy;
	1	◪	fruits & vegetables
Red and Green Cabbage Slaw	1	++	extra vegetables;
	1	▲	fats & oils
Stir-Fry for One	3	⊘	protein;
	1	◪	fruits & vegetables;
	2	▲	fats & oils
Sole with Tomatoes	3	⊘	protein;
	1	++	extra vegetables
Vegetable Taco Sauce	1	◪	fruits & vegetables

INDEX